AA
Essential

explorer
TURKEY

Diana Darke

AA Publishing

Essential

Written by Diana Darke
Original photography by Paul Kenward

Edited, designed and produced by AA Publishing
Maps © The Automobile Association 1995

Distributed in the United Kingdom by AA Publishing,
Norfolk House, Priestley Road, Basingstoke, Hampshire,
RG24 4NY.

A CIP catalogue record for this book is available from the
British Library. ISBN 0 7495 0935 X

Published by AA Publishing (a trading name of Automobile
Association Developments Limited, whose registered
office is Norfolk House, Priestley Road, Basingstoke,
Hampshire RG24 4NY. Registered number 1878835).

Colour separation by Fotographics Ltd
Printed by LEGO SpA, Vicenza, Italy

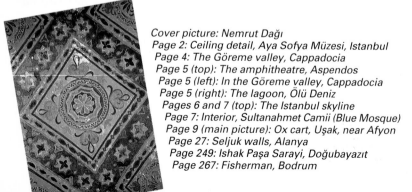

Cover picture: Nemrut Dağı
Page 2: Ceiling detail, Aya Sofya Müzesi, Istanbul
Page 4: The Göreme valley, Cappadocia
Page 5 (top): The amphitheatre, Aspendos
Page 5 (left): In the Göreme valley, Cappadocia
Page 5 (right): The lagoon, Ölü Deniz
Pages 6 and 7 (top): The Istanbul skyline
Page 7: Interior, Sultanahmet Camii (Blue Mosque)
Page 9 (main picture): Ox cart, Uşak, near Afyon
Page 27: Seljuk walls, Alanya
Page 249: Ishak Paşa Sarayi, Doğubayazıt
Page 267: Fisherman, Bodrum

Diana Darke first became interested in the Near East when she read Arabic at Oxford. For the last 16 years she has lived, worked and travelled extensively in Turkey and the Arab world, initially with the Foreign Office, then as an Arabic translator and interpreter.

Her travel-writing career began with the Discovery Guides *Aegean and Mediterranean Turkey* and *Eastern Turkey and the Black Sea Coast* for Michael Haag Limited, now in their third editions. She is also the author of guides to North Cyprus and to Jordan and the Holy Land, as well as *Turkey* in the Thomas Cook Travellers series. She is married with two children.

Afyon, with the citadel visible beyond

How to use this book

This book is divided into five main sections:

❏ **Section 1: *Turkey Is***
discusses aspects of life and living today, from the economy to ethnic minorities

❏ **Section 2: *Turkey Was***
places the country in its historical context and explores those past events whose influences are felt to this day

❏ **Section 3: *A to Z Section***
is broken down into regional chapters, and covers places to visit, including walks and drives. Within this section fall the Focus-on articles, which consider a variety of subjects in greater detail

❏ **Section 4: *Travel Facts***
contains the strictly practical information vital for a successful trip

❏ **Section 5: *Hotels and Restaurants***
lists recommended establishments throughout Turkey, giving a brief résumé of what they offer

How to use the star rating
Most of the places described in this book have been given a separate rating:

▶▶▶ **Do not miss**

▶▶ **Highly recommended**

▶ **Worth seeing**

Not essential viewing

Map references
To make the location of a particular place easier to find every main entry in this book is given a map reference, such as176B3. The first number (176) indicates the page on which the map can be found, the letter (B) and the second number (3) pinpoint the square in which the main entry is located. The maps on the inside front cover and inside back cover are referred to as IFC and IBC respectively.

Contents

Quick reference

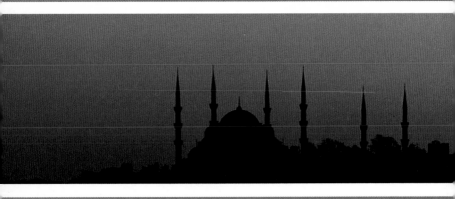

This quick-reference guide high-lights the features of the book you will use most often: the maps; the introductory features; the Focus-on articles; the walks and the drives.

Walks

Drives

Boat trip

Travel Facts

Semra Kulin Tat
Born and raised in Istanbul, Semra Kulin Tat's ancestors include a grand vizier, one of Turkey's first women MPs and, from the 12th century, early rulers of Bosnia. She was one of Turkey's first television producers, a career she was forced to abandon when her second husband's work commitments took her abroad. She is now a famous pastry chef, and divides her time between Istanbul and Bodrum, where her cheesecakes and brownies are in great demand.

My Turkey

by Semra Kulin Tat
Istanbul, the city that never sleeps, has been my family's home for over 400 years. It remains its charming, unpredictable self despite – or perhaps because of – the constant influx of newcomers from every corner of Turkey.

A leisurely day in my historic city might begin by taking a boat from Eminönü all the way up the spectacular Bosphorus to Anadolu Kavağı, an unspoilt fishing village on the Asian side of the entrance to the Black Sea. The distinctive smell of fried mussels, sardines and grilled swordfish greets you if you arrive at lunchtime, perhaps hungry after a walk around the bustling market.

The afternoon takes you back to the European side, visiting the old area of Pera, now known as Beyoğlu. This was inhabited by Levantines during the Ottoman Empire. The fine, tall stone buildings proudly bear the name of their architects, and the date of their construction is engraved above their entrance doors, while elsewhere in Beyoğlu green parks surround more fine mansions. Since Atatürk moved Turkey's capital from here to Ankara these elegant buildings have been relegated from embassies to consulates, though they have lost none of their splendour. Also here is the prestigious Galatasaray College, established in the mid-19th century as a French school where the elite of society was – and still is – educated. Somehow, a past era lives on in this dignified area of Istanbul.

The day ends on an indulgent note further up Beyoğlu, with a chance to devour some of the best profiteroles in Turkey at Inci (Pastanesi, Istiklal Caddesi 124/2, Beyoğlu).

My Turkey

by Mete Taşkiran
Even some of my closest non-Turkish friends seem to doubt my assertions that women in Turkey do indeed enjoy a position of equality with men.

History clearly recounts that Atatürk, the architect of modern Turkey, declared that it was impossible for a nation to progress unless its women were truly emancipated. To this end, he passed laws to prevent discrimination – and in 1934 granted them the right both to elect and be elected as MPs – many years before their sisters in France and Italy achieved universal suffrage. But it was not just the right to vote; Atatürk opened up high offices, of ambassador, university dean, supreme court judge, even the leadership of political parties, so that they could be held by women.

But all is not quite perfect: women's rights are not universally observed in Turkey. There *is* discrimination, and women's representation in parliament has fallen below past levels. Moreover, the rise of Islamic fundamentalism, a potent force waiting threateningly in the wings, poses a serious threat to true equality.

Nevertheless, the outlook is still healthy; the changes engendered over 70 republican years are deep-seated, and Turkey enters the 21st century a stronger nation for its men and women walking hand-in-hand.

Mete Taşkiran
Born in Istanbul in 1936, Mete Taşkiran was awarded a BA in Humanities by Robert College in Istanbul before going on to gain an MA from the University of Lausanne in Switzerland. Fluent in both English and French, Mete Taşkiran has swapped a career in interior design for one of freelance translating and copywriting. He now lives permanently in Istanbul.

TURKEY IS

■ **Although it is variously classed as both a struggling first world economy and a 'developing' nation, Turkey conforms to the conventional model for neither. The modern Turkish state is unique in that – rather than being the product of an imperialist power – against all the odds, it managed to create itself and evolve its own political identity......■**

Image For centuries the Turks were seen through western eyes as the scourge of Christendom and a threat to the European order. In the western countries of medieval Europe the very word 'Turk' came to symbolise everything that was savage or barbaric, and in the popular imagination of the time Turks took their place in the litany of plagues, floods, earthquakes, Tartars and comets used by the Almighty as punishments for the wicked. In the 16th century, for example, Martin Luther prayed for deliverance from 'the world, the flesh, the Turk and the Devil'.

From the Renaissance onwards, the root of this prejudice lay partly in Europe's historic ties with Greece. As far as most western thinkers were concerned, the Greek civilisation stood at the dawn of their own.

Fishing is a tradition that has kept its importance in modern Turkey

From them they inherited so much, and all that was classical was considered noble and pure. As recently as the 19th century, poets such as Byron sang the praises of Greece, its great ideals and romantic traditions. With Turkey, on the other hand, the countries of northern and western Europe have fewer historical and religious ties. When the Greeks and Turks violently disputed Cyprus in the 1950s and 1960s, and when the island was partitioned in 1974, it was perhaps not surprising that many westerners chose to side with the Greek Cypriots, simply because they seemed the more familiar faction. Thus the problem was assumed to be of Turkish Cypriot making, and world opinion apportioned more blame to Turkey than to Greece.

As far as the Ottoman Empire (which lasted from the 14th until the early 20th century) is concerned, in the minds of most westerners it still conjures up images of decadence and harems, and it is left to a few historians to marvel at its extraordinary religious tolerance and at an astonishingly fair system of 'promotion', under which a slave could (and frequently did) rise to be Grand Vizier, the equivalent of prime minister.

Reality In 1949 Turkey became a member of the Council of Europe, and in 1952 it was admitted to NATO, largely because its strategic position controlling the Bosphorus made it a vital ally against the Soviet Union during the Cold War. Military considerations and self-interest therefore lay behind these organisations' readiness to include Turkey among their members, rather than

any sense that Turkey truly belonged to the body of Europe.

Religion has of course played its part in the formation of these attitudes. The Hungarians, the Finns and the Bulgarians all have their origins in the Eurasian steppelands over a thousand years ago, just like the Turks. Unlike the Turks, however, they converted to Christianity – and are now accepted as Europeans.

Geographical position It is hard to over-emphasise the importance of Turkey's strategic position, lying at the geographical meeting point of different forces and ideologies, of Europe and Asia, of Christianity and Islam, and of Arabism, (vestigial) Communism and Hellenism. If Turkey were to leave NATO and ally herself with ex-Soviet or Arab powers, the West would lose control of the vital Bosphorus Straits, as well as relinquishing its ability to carry out air strikes from Turkish NATO bases on Iraq (as it did in the Gulf War), Iran or any ex-Soviet trouble spot. At present, Turkey represents the only

The natural harbour at Antalya, the main port on Turkey's southern coast for the past 2,000 years

area of relative stability in the most unstable and unpredictable part of the world.

❑ At critical points in their history, the Turks have a habit of doing something totally unexpected. In this century alone, after their official defeat in World War I, they fought back to oust the Allies, and went on to achieve recognition as an independent country. In 1945, President Inönü changed a dictatorship into a democracy overnight; and in 1961 the military, who had seized power in a coup 18 months earlier, handed it over in an orderly manner to a parliamentary regime. In each case, the Turks' actions ran contrary to the confident predictions of the experts. ❑

Türkiye Cumhuriyetinin temeli küllürdür. K. Atatürk

■ Modern Turkey is very largely the creation of one man, Mustafa Kemal, later known as Atatürk, Father of the Turks. Atatürk realised that his government could achieve his reforms only by securing the support of the mass of the Turkish people. In 1923, he formed the Republican People's Party, intending that its hundreds of thousands of members should constitute the local leadership in every town and village throughout the country......■

Kemalism According to Kemalist philosophy – that propounded by Atatürk – civilisation assures freedom, and happiness lies in an independent life, that is in life without political, social or religious constraints. It especially abhors religious extremism, blaming it for creating many inequalities among people, for excluding women from playing an active role in society, and for provoking a large number of wars. It is opposed to the class system and scornful of the intellectual elite, believing passionately in the need to educate workers and peasants in order to deliver them from capitalist oppression. By popularising language, literature and music it aims to bring civilisation closer to the ordinary Turk. The final keystone is patriotism, considered essential for the defence of a people's independence. In its application, this remarkable philosophy demonstrated that, through disciplined education, it was possible to achieve in one generation what could easily have taken ten or more.

A guard on duty at Atatürk's mausoleum in Ankara

World War II By the time Atatürk died in 1938, his 15 years of decisive, if dictatorial, leadership had won for Turkey a credible place in the international arena. That the regime he left behind him was able to withstand the stresses and strains of World War II so soon after his death is perhaps the best testimony to his achievement. Turkey managed to stay neutral during the war, despite pressure from the western powers. The war years subjected the country to great economic strain, and the risky position of armed neutrality in a world at war gave rise to a more authoritarian government which imposed martial law.

Struggle for secularism In the years since Atatürk's death, Turkey has been dominated by the struggle between secularism and religion, with the army officers, teachers and

❑ The constitution as laid down by Atatürk states that the Turkish army has a duty imposed by law 'to defend and watch over the Republic of Turkey' – and to intervene when necessary. The army has three times invoked that duty – in 1960, 1971 and 1980. If the words of the constitution are to be interpreted literally, the only way future Turkish governments can safeguard against army intervention is to govern efficiently and in accordance with Atatürk's principles. ❑

bureaucrats who formed the backbone of the Republican People's
Party supporting the former, and
rural people favouring the latter.
After three coups in 20 years, the
election of Tansu Çiller as prime minister in 1993 would seem to make
Turkey's break from its military past
more secure. Çiller's True Path Party
espouses many Kemalist principles,
and she herself, an American-
educated economist in her late
forties, would certainly have had
Atatürk's approval. She not only
understands the economic ambitions
of the lower middle-class Turks who
form the majority of her supporters,
but also embodies the aspirations of
women in an evolving society. Her
election is the more remarkable in
that she only entered politics in 1991,
whereas the current president,

*Atatürk's mausoleum is a powerful
symbol of the personality cult his
memory has inspired*

Süleyman Demirel, is a veteran of
the coup era who was deposed by
the military in 1971 and 1980. Her
election is widely seen as a decisive
step away from the religious politics
of the Middle East (where many
countries are Islamic states), assert-
ing Turkey's westward alignment, as
Atatürk would have wished (see also
pages 42–3 and pages 196–7).

*Election posters – a sign that mili-
tary rule may be a thing of the past*

❏ 'Turkey is a bridge to peace,
a bridge to the independent
countries that have separated
from Russia, a bridge for
western values in the Middle
East.'
Tansu Çiller, Turkish Prime
Minister, echoing the
sentiments of Atatürk. ❏

■ **There is an important distinction to be made between Turkey as a state and the Turks as a people. The Turks are Muslim, but, since Atatürk's reforms, Turkey is not an Islamic state. Orthodox Muslims regard the secularisation of Turkey as an apostasy from Islam, and Atatürk as a heretic......■**

Turkish Islam Mosques in Turkey are unusually welcoming to foreigners, who are allowed to stroll about freely and to linger at will. In the rest of the Islamic world such tolerance of outsiders is rare; and many countries, even some surprising ones such as Morocco and Tunisia, do not permit non-Muslims to enter their mosques at all.

When you cross the border from Greece or Bulgaria into Turkey, it is

❏ The Islamic belief that all things are pre-ordained is behind orthodox Islam's rejection of insurance. How can one insure against dying early or the collapse of a building, when such things are the will of God? Insurance is therefore seen as indicating a lack of trust in the supreme power of God. ❏

The skyline of much of urban Turkey is dominated by minarets – this is Fatih Camii in Istanbul

not the appearance of the people or their dress (almost everybody wears western clothes) which makes the country visibly different, but its mosques and minarets. It is this outward stamp of Islam which makes Turkey instantly appear unlike any western European country, and although religion is not an explicit consideration, it is Islam that will probably always bar Turkey from full membership of the European Union.

Islam is a very visible religion: on hearing the call to prayer, ordinary people everywhere – gardeners in parks, peasants in fields, businessmen in their offices – stop what they are doing and drop to their knees to perform the ritual bows laid down in the Koran. There is no embarrassment during these prayers, which last about 10 minutes, and nothing is allowed to intrude or distract. Even telephones and doorbells are left unanswered.

'Europeanisation' Most of Atatürk's extraordinary reforms of the 1920s and 1930s were concerned with religion, in recognition of the fact that Turkey could not become part of Europe until Islam had been contained as much as possible. He therefore put a stop to religious

14

education in schools and replaced the Arabic alphabet with the Latin one; this was a double blow for Islam, for Arabic is not only the script of the holy Koran but also the sacred calligraphy that adorns all mosques. The effect of the alphabet reform has thus been to alienate the younger generation of Turks almost completely from their Islamic cultural background. Strict Muslims associate the very sight of the Latin alphabet with the infidel; while travellers arriving from Iran or Syria, on seeing signposts using the Latin alphabet, instinctively think of Turkey as the gateway to Europe.

The law No other Muslim country has abolished Koranic law: a remarkable reform, as in many ways the law is the most sacred part of Islam and the very essence of the religion. Atatürk replaced it with European codes of law, an extraordinary affront

The act of prayer five times a day is one of the basic tenets of Islam

to orthodox Muslims. All reference to Islam was erased from the new Turkish constitution, and by becoming a secular republic in 1923, Turkey effectively withdrew from the world of Islam.

After 50 years of Atatürk's secularism, many modern Turkish intellectuals occupying senior positions in government and business are more or less atheists, with manners and appearance which on first acquaintance frequently surprise many of their western counterparts .
Atatürk's aim was not to abolish religion, however, but to free the people from what he believed to be Islam's frequently oppressive and backward-looking influence: a necessary step in order to allow them to look forward, and to make progress towards the elusive goal of modernisation.

■ **Istanbul's intellectual elite would recoil in horror from the very idea of setting foot in an Anatolian village, and most have never done so. Cultural dualism is alive and flourishing in Turkey today, despite Atatürk's attempts to make the peasant 'master of Turkey' and the blurring effect of contemporary peasant migration to the cities......■**

East–West divide The split between the residents of Istanbul and Ankara is illustrated by one of the nationalists' favourite epithets for Istanbul: *kozmopolit*, a word whose disparaging overtones are not conveyed by the English 'cosmopolitan'. A recent Turkish dictionary defines a person described thus as 'having no national or local colour, but assuming the outward form that suits his purpose.' Atatürk himself deliberately did not set foot in the old imperial capital from 1919 to 1927.

The economic imbalance between the east and west of the country con-

The rural poor are flocking to Istanbul in search of prosperity

❑ 'Ankara's one attraction,' runs the wisdom of Istanbul, 'is the road out.' Another contemptuous Istanbuli description refers to Ankara as 'a cloud of dust near the railway line'. ❑

stitutes one of Turkey's major long-term problems. Eastern cities such as Erzurum, Van and Kars have almost no industries, and the cold forbidding climate limits the possibilities for agriculture. Unemployment is endemic, resulting in a constant exodus of people to the big cities in search of a better life and more money. The braver ones have even emigrated beyond Turkey, mostly to Germany or other parts of western Europe; many make the dramatic transition from their Anatolian villages to cities such as Düsseldorf, Münich, Vienna and Paris, without ever before having travelled further than their nearest town.

Different customs A major area of difference between city and village life surrounds marriage and its customs. In the country, girls are generally made to marry by their families at the age of 13 or 14. The ceremony is a religious one, and ignores the Swiss-based civil law according to which marriage is forbidden for girls below the age of 15 and boys below the age of 17. In omitting the civil marriage ceremony altogether, these rural couples technically render their children illegitimate. Polygamy, banned under the civil code, is still practised in the villages (and is the major reason why the divorce rate

there is so low) while in the cities the civil law is obeyed and polygamy is unheard of. Traditionally, village husbands bought their brides with cash, a pre-Islamic custom which still continues in remoter central and eastern regions, though it is now much less common in the Aegean and Black Sea regions. As a girl's virginity greatly enhances her bride price it is in her family's interests to marry her young.

Another tradition peculiar to the villages – especially in the eastern Kurdish and Black Sea areas – is the blood feud. In the Black Sea region, known as Turkey's Texas, it is estimated that blood feuds are responsible for about 500 murders each year. Sometimes continuing for generations and resulting in scores of deaths, blood feuds seem to resist all the governments' attempts to stamp them out.

Ethnic minorities Historically Turks have distanced themselves from the Jews, Armenians and Greeks living in their country, viewing them as minorities which cannot be assimilated. Regarded as 'clever ones', the three ethnic groups are ranked in order by a Turkish proverb:

'One Greek can cheat two Jews
One Armenian can cheat two Greeks.'

Resorts such as Alanya have boosted the economy of Mediterranean Turkey

Significantly, Turkey's record on tolerance of Jews, viewed as the least crafty, has been good, while its treatment of the so-called super-crafty Armenians has been the worst.

Life remains hard in the vast, barren regions of eastern Turkey

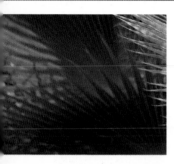

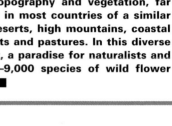

■ Turkey sits at the meeting point of three different climatic zones: the Euro-Siberian, the Mediterranean and the Irano-Turanian. The result is a tremendous variety of topography and vegetation, far greater than in most countries of a similar size, with deserts, high mountains, coastal plains, forests and pastures. In this diverse environment, a paradise for naturalists and botanists, 8–9,000 species of wild flower flourish ......■

18

Climate Of Turkey's three climatic zones, by far the largest is the Irano-Turanian. This is the steppeland of the central Anatolian plateau, very dry in summer and very cold in winter, with temperatures dropping to as low as minus 40°C and snow lying for up to 120 days of the year. The Euro-Siberian zone includes the Istanbul region and the Black Sea coast. Here you will find European-type deciduous forests, with ash, oak and beech trees, and summer temperatures that rarely exceed 28°C. On the Mediterranean coast lies a different world again; the fertile Cilician plain with its cotton-fields, palm trees and orange groves, has more of a Middle Eastern

A spectacular waterfall to the north of Lake Van

climate, with temperatures as high as 43°C in the southeast. Here seasonal variation in temperature – sometimes as much as 50°C – is one of the most extreme to be found anywhere in the world.

❑ In soil erosion and deforestation the Anatolian plateau has undergone two catastrophes. The corn that has been grown on the plateau for centuries has exhausted the soil, and animal dung is burned as fuel instead of being used as fertiliser to enrich the soil. Deforestation is continuing despite attempts to stop it; the forestry service is understaffed and has little authority to enforce the laws. ❑

Gentle, rolling hills typify the hinterland of the Aegean coastline

Geology Turkey's geological structure is extremely complex, with rocks of almost all ages. The country consists largely of several old plateau blocks, against which masses of younger rock series have been squeezed to form fold mountain ranges of varying sizes. These fold mountains run in many different directions with considerable irregularity, as one range unexpectedly gives way to another, or turns equally abruptly to plain or plateau.

The highest mountains are in the east, forming a natural border with Georgia, Armenia and Iran. Mount Ararat, an extinct volcano, is the highest peak in the country at 5,165m, and volcanoes have played an important part in the formation of landscapes in the central and eastern parts of Anatolia. In some places the lava sheets are so recent that soil has yet to form on top; in other areas, particularly Cappadocia, the volcanic tufa has created a wondrous landscape of spectacular rock formations (see pages 172–3).

In the north and west of the country there has been enormous cracking and disturbance of the rocks,

Cappadocia's rock formations were caused by ancient volcanic activity

with earthquakes occurring regularly. Cracks in two different directions, splitting the land so that the lower parts sank beneath the sea, are responsible for the long, indented Aegean coast with its numerous oddly shaped islands and estuaries. Both the Bosphorus and the Dardanelles also owe their origin to this faulting action, and the whole of the Black Sea coast is the result of subsidence along a series of such fissures.

Another remarkable feature of Turkish landscapes is the number of lakes they contain, both saltwater and freshwater: the result of a combination of topography and relatively high rainfall. The largest, Lake Van, covers an area of almost 4,000 sq km, making it seven times as big as Lake Geneva (see pages 234–5).

Turkey is a potentially rich country: its mountains are full of minerals; its climate and land are perfect for a wide range of agricultural produce; the seas all around are full of fish. There is no shortage of manpower. But the country is burdened with huge foreign debts, and the struggle for growth has not been easy......■

The problems The scale of Turkey's recent economic problems is the legacy of the dynamic but extravagant Menderes government (1950–60; see pages 44–5) which incurred debts that will not be paid off until 2014. Another curious hangover from the past is the continuation of Atatürk's policy of exempting agriculture from taxation, a move which he initiated in the 1920s to encourage expansion. At least half the population works in agriculture, which produces 35 per cent of the gross national product (GNP) but less than five per cent of total taxation. Although this is patently absurd, no government now dares to impose taxes on the big farmers and landowners whose support is critical to them. Big landowners, known as *ağas*, seem, moreover, to have no actual title to their lands, but simply to have acquired them, sometimes

❏ Historically, the Turks have not been good businessmen. In Ottoman times most commercial and technical matters were left to the talents of Greeks, Armenians, and Jews. With the expulsion of many members of these minorities at the end of the empire, the Turks had for the first time to run the economy of the country themselves, and their lack of experience and expertise showed. ❏

by taking them over from peasants who have migrated to the cities. In much of central and eastern Anatolia, they 'own' as many as 100 villages and for thousands of peasants their word is law. At election time, the *ağas* are therefore in a position to deliver thousands of votes to whichever party they choose.

Population increase is another problem. The population has more than doubled in the last 25 years, and at

Traditional farming methods survive in eastern regions

At least half the population of Turkey works on the land

three per cent net increase per year has one of the highest rates of growth in the world. Part of the reason for this is the fall in the death rate with the eradication of diseases such as malaria. The birth rate is extremely high, however, and attempts to introduce birth control often encounter substantial opposition. Partly as a result of this, there is enormous pressure on Turkey's resources, unemployment is rising, and the trade gap is widening as agricultural produce that could have been exported is used to feed new mouths. Many children still receive no primary education, and in rural areas a single teacher may face classes of up to 100.

The solutions Land reform, essential for any real economic recovery but never seriously attempted in the past, is now being implemented to a limited extent, together with reforms of the tax system.

Turkey's main raw materials of cotton, wool, mohair, beet-sugar, olive oil and tobacco tend to be produced by state-owned enterprises, and the new prime minister Tansu Çiller has begun a drive to privatise these and other state organisations, in an attempt to raise cash and to make them more profitable. Market forces,

it is believed, will increase the efficiency of the incompetent public sector, which currently sits on 40 per cent of GNP.

Current position Inflation has run at around 70 per cent in recent years, reaching 125 per cent in early 1994, so interest rates continue to discourage investment. Trade and current account deficits are at record levels. Income from tourism has been adversely affected by the Kurdish terrorist campaign, and money has been pouring into the fight against the guerrillas. In spite of all this, shops are full, company profits are buoyant and there are no shortages of commodities. Indeed labour costs are low and confidence high; growth in the value of the Istanbul Stock Exchange was 216 per cent in 1993, the highest figure in the world. Short-term visitors to the country, therefore, may well notice few underlying problems.

❑ There is a long tradition of tax evasion in Turkey, aggravated by inefficient book-keeping and incompetent collection methods. As a result, some of Turkey's richest citizens contribute little or nothing to the exchequer. ❑

■ The Turks have dignity, nobility, honesty, great physical endurance and courage. They are relatively silent, not full of wearisome chatter like some of their neighbours. Neither are they volatile in a typically Mediterranean way, but rather they are like bottled-up volcanoes, erupting from time to time after long periods of quiescence......■

Who are the Turks? This is a vexed question which still puzzles historians. Just how was it that a relatively small number of Turkish invaders from the steppelands of Central Asia (between the Caspian Sea and Mongolia) succeeded, after a comparatively short period of time, in stamping their Turkish identity on Anatolia, rather than being absorbed by the ethnic mix that was already there? There were after all no massacres or mass deportations of the indigenous population. The pre-Turkish Anatolians were a thorough mixture of all the races that had gone before – Hittites, Phrygians, Lydians, Celts, Jews, Greeks, Romans, Armenians, Kurds and Mongols. Yet when a mere handful of Turks

❑ '*Ne mutlu Türküm diyene*' ('How happy is he who can say he is a Turk') was one of Atatürk's great sayings, still to be seen all over Turkey on banners and carved into hillsides. '*Biz bize benzeriz*' ('We resemble ourselves') was another of his slogans designed to endow Turks with sense of pride in their identity. ❑

arrived, they managed to transform a Greek- or Armenian-speaking Christian population into a Turkish-speaking Muslim people, henceforth to be known as Turks.

A Turkish woman in the Aegean region

The Turkish perspective The Turkish view of history, still taught in many schools today, is that the original Turkish homeland – from the Caspian to Mongolia – was the cradle of world civilisation. One group of the people here migrated eastwards in about 7000BC, and founded the Chinese civilisation, another group went to India, and yet others headed to northern Europe (the Celts), south into the Middle East and across to North Africa. As a result some Turks regard the Greek and Roman civilisations as successors to earlier Turkic civilisations, such as the Phrygians, Lydians and Hittites.

Personality The Turkish character is one of extreme contradictions and contrasts. Turks are hard-working, yet realise the futility of hurry and worry;

Young girls in traditional costume

serious yet cherish a comic character as their favourite folklore hero (see pages 106–7). They respect the authority of the state, yet insist on democracy; they are ruthless, yet kind and hospitable. Many are poor, yet they disdain money. Trust and honour are paramount. Theft is regarded as the most shameful of all crimes, and is rare outside the big cities. Murderers form the elite of the prison population, as most such crimes are the result of affairs of honour; thieves, on the other hand, are spat upon as the lowest of the low. Turks despise what they see as a lack of control: it does not pay to lose your temper with a Turk, for it achieves nothing and merely earns you contempt. Loyalty in male friendships is all-important, probably encouraged by the all-male military service. Extremely tough and compulsory for 18 months, it is regarded by most as an important educational experience, teaching the illiterate to read and write and instructing them in a trade.

Turkish officers, drawn from the middle and lower classes, regard themselves as the nation's elite and its social conscience: all reformist movements in modern Turkey have stemmed from the army.

A shepherd from the Kahta Cayi mountains

■ **The Turks love their festivals, which are in no way shows put on for tourists. All their folk culture is concentrated into these annual events which usually last a week or more, each region having its own authentic specialities in terms of dance, music and plays......■**

City festivals Most of the big cities throughout Turkey have an annual fair. The main one, not surprisingly, is in **Istanbul**, held from about 20 June to 30 July and featuring an extra-ordinary range of dance, art and music in a wide range of venues. **Izmir** holds an International Fair from 20 August to 20 September, which includes commercial exhibitions as well as cultural and folklore events. **Samsun** holds a similar fair in July. **Bursa**'s annual festival, from 12 June to 12 July is entirely cultural, and attracts some international singers and musicians.

Cultural festivals in ancient settings Turkey is blessed with numerous magnificent venues for festivals, including Graeco-Roman theatres, Byzantine churches and medieval fortresses. In April and May each year **Ephesus** hosts an excellent **Culture and Art Festival**, with folk dancing in the Graeco-Roman theatre. The Asklepeion theatre is the setting for the plays and dancing of the enter-taining **Pergamum Festival**, which takes place during May/June. In August the **Çanakkale Troy Festival** uses the setting of ancient Troy for rather mediocre folk dances and other musical performances, while the very professional

A dancer at Antalya

❑ Each region in Turkey has its own folk dance and its own costume. The men of the Black Sea region perform the Horon dance, dressed in black with silver trimmings. Bursa's Sword and Shield Dance, representing the Ottoman conquest of the city, is performed by men in early Ottoman battledress. The celebrated Spoon Dance is performed from Konya to Silifke by both men and women, colour-fully dressed and clicking a pair of wooden spoons like castanets in each hand. ❑

Antalya Film and Art Festival, held annually in October, makes creative use of the splendid Roman theatre at **Aspendos** for several of its showings.

Wrestling: men and camels In the months of December and January throughout the province of **Aydın,** and especially in the town of **Germencik,** you can see camel-wrestling, involving two male camels pushing and shoving each other. While quite vicious, it is not usually a blood sport.

Grease-wrestling between two male humans is popular throughout Turkey; the major festival is held each year in the first week of July near **Edirne** on the little island of **Saray Içi.** Up to a thousand contes-tants take part, clad in leather knick-ers and greased all over with olive oil. Gypsies arrive in force to provide entertainments, as well as the drum and single-reed oboe music that accompanies the wrestling warm-up exercises.

A performance in the Culture and Art Festival at Ephesus

Mevlana Festival This is probably Turkey's most internationally famous festival, held each year in **Konya** from 14 to 17 December to commemorate the death of Mevlana, founder of the mystic Whirling Dervish order (see pages 204–5). Temperatures in Konya at this time are perishingly cold and hotel prices double, so many prefer to watch the famous dervish dance (known as *sema*) at the restored *semahane* ('dance room') in **Galatasaray**, Istanbul.

Traditional dress is an important part of Turkish folk culture

❏ During the last week of June a remarkable festival, the Artvin Kafkasör Culture and Art Festival, takes place in Artvin, high in the Georgian mountains inland from the Black Sea coast. Bullfights are staged on the Kafkasör plateau, along with wrestling and folk dancing. ❏

■   Turkey's exceptionally mountainous topography and high rainfall have combined to make it unusually rich in lakes and rivers – most notably the Tigris and the Euphrates, whose sources lie high on the Anatolian plateau. It has been predicted that this essential resource will be the cause of the next war in the region......■

The Southeast Anatolia Project

Known as GAP, this ambitious scheme envisages the transformation of the current wasteland around Şanlıurfa in southeast Turkey into fertile agricultural land, by means of a series of 22 dams on the Upper Euphrates, with the massive Atatürk Dam as the centrepiece. The Tigris, meanwhile, will be used mainly to provide hydroelectric power, and a planned total of 19 generating plants will then guarantee Turkey's self-sufficiency.

Social implications Throughout the Middle East, more than 80 per cent of water is consumed by agriculture. Such water consumption is almost always heavily subsidised by governments, not only because they want to ensure food supplies, but also because

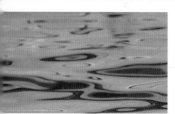

❏ When Turkey suspended the flow of water through the Euphrates in 1990 and 1992, as it filled up the new Atatürk Lake behind the Atatürk Dam, it demonstrated its ability to turn off the taps in both Iraq and Syria. Syria responded by giving support to the PKK, Turkey's Kurdish guerrilla movement. ❏

by supporting the rural economy they hope to stem the drift to the cities. The Turkish government's hope is that the semi-nomadic Kurds currently engaged in sheep-rearing in the Urfa area will be tempted by the hundreds of thousands of new jobs in the cotton and cereal fields, and that social unrest will thus be calmed by economic prosperity.

Water is one of Turkey's most precious natural resources

TURKEY WAS

The Hittite Empire

■ **The most ancient relics found so far in Asia Minor date to the seventh millennium BC. Remains from the early second millennium BC reveal the existence of Assyrian trading colonies in Cappadocia and an important Copper Age culture in Central Anatolia. Later in the second millennium, most of Asia Minor fell under the rule of the Hittites, whose empire flourished from about 1750BC to 1200BC, reaching its peak in the 14th and 13th centuries BC......■**

Mystery of the Hittites Three thousand years ago the ancient Hittites rivalled the Egyptians as the greatest power on earth. Yet until a century ago they remained a mystery race, with the only documentary evidence of their existence appearing in the Old Testament, where they were mentioned as a tribe living in Palestine. When Egyptian hieroglyphs were first deciphered, an

Powerful carvings such as this are among the most evocative relics of the Hittite civilisation

inscription was found relating to a defence treaty between Rameses II and Hattusilis, king of the Hittites. To cement the treaty, Rameses married the Hittite king's daughter.

No further clue as to the mystery of the lost Hittite Empire was found until in 1834 a Frenchman, Charles Texier, discovered the ruins of the Hittite capital, Hattusas, at Boğazkale. In 1906, German excavations on the site uncovered thousands of cuneiform tablets. When these were finally deciphered in the 1940s, the full history of the Hittites was at last revealed, an achievement heralded as one of the greatest archaeological triumphs of the 20th century. As most of the research and decipherment was carried out by German and Czech scholars, Hittite culture remains less well known in the English-speaking world than perhaps it should be.

❏ The elaborately wrought bronze 'sun discs' found in the graves at Alacahöyük are unique to Hittite art. They appear to have been endowed with mystical properties, and their unusual criss-cross pattern was perhaps intended to symbolise the sun and its rays. Sometimes an antlered stag appears at the centre of the design, indicating that they are the work of a mountain people. A sun disc has been chosen as the emblem of the Turkish Ministry of Culture and Tourism. ❏

28

❏ The most memorable relics left by the Hittites are their simple but powerful rock-cut sculptures, to be found on all their sites, depicting their gods and ceremonies. The figures – broad, heavy and squat, with none of the grace and subtlety associated with Egyptian or Babylonian art – indicate a tough, warlike mountain people, used to a harsh climate and conditions. Hittite culture stands in sharp contrast to the valley cultures of Mesopotamia and the Nile, where the inhabitants were able peacefully to pasture their flocks beside the great rivers, and where there was no need for defences or fortifications. ❏

Many of the finest Hittite sculptures are displayed in the Museum of Anatolian Civilisations in Ankara

the sophistication and graces of their Near Eastern neighbours.

Tutankhamun link One of the cuneiform tablets found at Boğazkale indicates a curious link between the Egyptian boy-king Tutankhamun and the Hittites. According to the inscription, the Hittite king Shubbililiuma was encamped by the Euphrates when a messenger arrived from the Egyptian queen, begging him to send her one of his many sons to marry, for her own husband Tutankhamun had died. Shubbililiuma eventually sent one of his sons, who was put to death on his arrival in Egypt on the orders of an ambitious official who went on to marry the queen himself. Scholars, intrigued by the fact that the fall of Troy coincided roughly with the disintegration of the Hittite Empire, have also found evidence recently to suggest a link between ancient Troy and the Hittite kingdom.

Storage amphorae excavated on the site of the Hittite capital

Mountain culture The Hittites were the only ancient civilisation to exist and develop in inhospitable mountainous country. While their military strength, necessary to their survival, was awesome, they were humane in the treatment of conquered enemies (unlike the Assyrians), and in peacetime were governed by statesmen with sound and well-developed policies. A practical and intellectually unpretentious people, they lacked

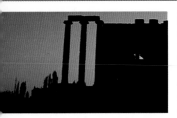

■ After the break-up of the Hittite Empire, Asia Minor disintegrated into a number of dynasties and peoples – Phrygians, Cimmerians, Lydians and others – which remain largely obscure. At this time the Greeks began to invade the Aegean coast, entering upon a long struggle which was to encompass the Trojan War......■

Alexander and Hellenisation When, in the spring of 334BC, this 21-year-old Macedonian crossed the Hellespont into Asia Minor at the head of some 35,000 soldiers, he was heralding the dawn of an era that was to last a thousand years, to be eclipsed only by the rise of Islam. The Greeks and the Persians had battled for decades over the cities of Asia Minor, and Alexander resolved now to drive them out once and for all. Having swept triumphantly through western and southern Anatolia, by 333BC he stood poised at Issus, in the easternmost corner of the Mediterranean, where his army routed a Persian force three times its size. The cultural consequences of these great military exploits were immeasurable, since by opening up a corridor for cultural interaction and fusion between East and West, Alexander was initiating the process that was later to become known as Hellenisation (see pages 144–5).

The Hellenistic age was characterised by independent city-states such as Antioch, with fine public buildings erected at the ruler's expense. Although these states were constantly at war with one another, a solid administrative foundation was nevertheless created by the various Hellenistic kings of Asia Minor, which was later to prove very useful to the Roman Empire.

One of the remarkably preserved streets of the Graeco-Roman city of Ephesus

❏ Alexander's avowed ambition on marching into Asia was to liberate the Greek cities from their Persian rulers under Darius the Great. Alexander had been brought up on the works of Homer, and throughout his campaign against the Persians he kept a copy of the epic poems beside him to remind himself of that earlier Greek war against the east. ❏

Ankara retains many vestiges of its Roman past

The atmospheric ruins of the sanctuary of Zeus at Labranda, near Milas

The Roman age The Romans were at first drawn with reluctance into Asia Minor, crossing the Hellespont in 190BC to crush the ambitious Seleucid king. When in 133BC the king of Pergamum bequeathed his entire kingdom to Rome, the Romans were obliged to organise western Asia Minor into the Roman province of Asia. Problems with troublesome Cilician pirates and the Pontic kingdom of Mithridates in the 1st century BC later drew the Romans eastwards to take over the whole of Anatolia, which enjoyed 200 years of comparative peace and prosperity under Roman rule.

The Romans recognised the cultural achievements of the Greeks who were now subject to them: Roman artists, writers and architects gradually began to imitate all forms of Greek art. All over the eastern empire there sprang up cities inspired by Greek models, with a distinctive Roman provincial city architecture – often including splendid theatres such as that at **Aspendos**. While landowners and the ruling elite lived lives of opulence in these cities, peasants were tied to the land. This period of stability lasted until the late 2nd century AD, when a succession of barbarian invasions caused havoc

❑ The Romans were altogether less refined than their Greek predecessors; their theatres were generally used not for sophisticated perfomances of plays and music, but for bloody fights, with savage beasts tearing each other or early Christians limb from limb. ❑

and weakened the economic structure of the empire.

Even during times of prosperity, Christianity had been troublesome to the Roman emperors, and the Christians were brutally persecuted for their refusal to comply with the cult of the emperor. Gradually opposition to the new religion waned, however, and in 312 the Roman Emperor Constantine was himself converted. The following year he proclaimed Christianity the official religion of the Roman Empire.

A gracefully carved column at Perge, near Antalya

■ **The name Byzantium is derived from Byzantion, a former trading colony of ancient Greece said to have been founded in 657BC by a Greek named Byzas. In AD330 the Roman Emperor Constantine moved the capital of his new eastern Roman Empire here and changed the name to Constantinople......■**

Start of the Empire After the collapse of the rival western empire, the eastern Roman Empire, known henceforth as the Byzantine Empire, acquired great political strength, untold wealth, and a dynamic cultural life. Clear evidence of this last can be seen in the mosaics and miniatures created in its monasteries, and in the impressive architecture of its churches, of which **Aya Sofya** is the most important. The Byzantine civilisation, centred on Constantinople, became by far the most influential of all the eastern Christian cultures, and the Byzantine emperors considered themselves to be the representatives of God's will on earth.

A detail from the Obelisk of Theodosius in the Hippodrome

❏ Justinian the Great's rule (527–65) is considered to have been the climax of the Byzantine Empire. His wife Theodora, a former actress, is reputed to have performed nude shows in which her chief trick was to invite geese to come and eat the grain seeds she had sprinkled in her pubic hair. ❏

Within Constantinople the three key buildings were Aya Sofya, the centre of religious life, the palace (on the site of the later **Topkapı**), the centre of political and administrative life, and the **Hippodrome (At Meydanı)**, which was the focus of public and social life. On the site of the gardens that now lie between the **Blue Mosque** and Aya Sofya was the Forum of Augustus, the public meeting place.

Doctrinal divisions The early years of the Byzantine Empire were racked with divisions over doctrine and many church councils were convened to resolve questions of heresy. The earliest, at Nicaea (Iznik) in 325, was held to discuss what became known as the Arian heresy,

❏ Pondering on the contrast between Turks and Byzantines, Rose Macaulay observed that it was 'difficult to discuss theology with Turks, as one had been used to with Byzantines, who had reasoned themselves in and out of all the heresies in the world'. ❏

Aya Sofya contains some of the finest of all Byzantine mosaics

proposed by Arius of Alexandria, according to which Jesus Christ was not the Son of God. The rejection of this doctrine resulted in the Nicene Creed, still an important part of Christion worship. The Council of Nicaea also declared the emperor head of the church as well as of the state, with five bishops – of Rome, Constantinople, Alexandria, Antioch and Jerusalem – pre-eminent under his rule.

Byzantine art Although it was heir to the cultures of ancient Greece and Rome, Byzantine art rejected the balanced proportions that had been so central to Greek aesthetics. The figures in Byzantine art, which was always essentially religious in subject matter, were deliberately depicted as flat and two-dimensional, using techniques that were apparently less skilled than those to be seen in the murals of ancient Rome and Greece.

The intention, however, was to create the illusion that all the religious figures depicted were in fact observing the spectator, rather than vice versa.

Justinian the Great (527–65) Under Justinian culture and the arts flourished; some of the finest achievements were in the realm of architecture, with the construction of Aya Sofya, Aya Irena and many other churches. Military matters were also in the ascendant as North Africa, Italy and southern Spain were regained by the empire. Such success was not to continue after Justinian's death, however, when the empire suffered a series of setbacks. Persian aggression under the Sassanians was followed by the rise of the Arabs with their new religion Islam. Arab incursions all along Turkey's south coast during the 7th and 8th centuries were to have a gradual weakening effect on the empire.

■ **The event which signalled the beginning of the end of the Byzantine Empire was the Battle of Manzikert in 1071. The Byzantines were defeated by fierce horsemen from Central Asia, known as Turks or Seljuks, who then cut a swathe through the country as far as the Sea of Marmara......■**

Break up of the empire Civil war followed and the empire began to disintegrate. The Seljuk Turks rapidly seized control of most of Asia Minor, leaving only the Aegean regions and the capital under Byzantine rule. Although the beginning of their rule was marked by massacres, enslavements and forcible conversions to Islam, the Seljuk Turks soon established a secure state administered from their new capital Nicaea (Iznik).

Armenia One of the most successful states to break away from the Byzantine Empire was the Cilician kingdom of Armenia which

A 19th-century representation of the fall of Constantinople in 1453

❑ Despite its economic weakness, the Byzantine Empire saw a last tremendous flowering of art and scholarship in the early 14th century. The mosaics and frescoes that can be seen in the Kariye Museum in Istanbul date from this time. ❑

established itself in 1080 and continued until 1375. In its heyday, under Levon the Magnificent (1187–1219), the kingdom introduced advanced systems of justice and taxation as well as many social improvements, and the arts flourished. Many of Armenia's castles, such as **Anamur** and **Silifke**, date from this time.

The Crusades The growing tension between the Byzantine Empire and the Crusader nations led to the greatest blow that Constantinople had yet suffered. At the time of the First Crusade, the Byzantines were willing to support any movement that might help them re-establish their own political control in Asia Minor, whatever its stated aims. In the event, although they did indeed regain a number of cities, their lands suffered considerably from the undisciplined passage of the motley Crusader army. One of the Norman Crusader princes even founded a principality in Antioch, which then renounced its allegiance to the empire.

By the time of the Second Crusade, in 1147–9, the Byzantines were more reluctant to allow the Crusaders free passage, and once again the armies left a trail of rape and pillage in their wake. The German emperor Frederick Barbarossa, impatient with the Byzantines, this time encouraged the Seljuks to march on Constantinople. The armies met near Lake Eğridir in 1176 and the Byzantines were defeated almost as decisively as at Manzikert a century earlier.

The Third Crusade, again led by Barbarossa, began in 1189 with the storming of Adrianople (Edessa) but petered out when Barbarossa drowned in a river near Silifke. The fateful Fourth Crusade gathered at Venice in 1202 with the express aim – prompted by the trading ambitions of the Doge – of taking Constantinople *en route* to the Holy Land. Their greed and lust for conquest satisfied by the siege and sack of

The Crusaders' capture of Constantinople in 1204 was one of the most violent episodes in its history

Constantinople, the Crusaders simply abandoned their march on the Holy Land, and crowned a Flemish prince the first Latin Emperor of Constantinople. Afterwards a handful of small successor states sprang up, and one of these, based at Nicaea, recaptured Constantinople in 1261, retaining it until the Ottoman conquest in 1453. The real death blow to the Byzantine Empire had been dealt in 1204, however, when the Crusaders captured the city.

The city besieged from the sea by Mehmet II in 1453

❏ The historian Steven Runciman noted that 'There was never a greater crime against humanity than the Fourth Crusade. Not only did it cause the destruction or dispersal of all the treasures of the past that Byzantium had devoutly stored, and the mortal wounding of a civilisation that was still active and great; but it was also an act of gigantic folly... It upset the whole defence of Christendom.' ❏

The Seljuks

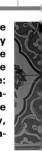

■ **The Seljuk Turks formed the first wave of the Turkic peoples who were eventually to make themselves masters of the Byzantine Empire. With their arrival, the culture of Anatolia saw a dramatic change: many of its Greeks fled westwards, but others remained and their descendants became Turkish-speakers. By the 15th century, almost all of Asia Minor was Turkish-speaking......■**

Origins The Seljuks were originally nomads from the region of Samarkand and Bukhara, who were ultimately descended from the Tu-Kin people of the Mongolian steppes (hence the modern name 'Turk'). In the 11th century, a wave of Seljuks surged out from their homeland and into Persia, Iraq, Syria and Palestine, where they were converted to Islam. When they pushed up from Antioch (modern Antakya) into Anatolia and Konya, under the leadership of Alp

Ishak Paşa Sarayı, at Doğubayazıt, combines elements of the Seljuk, Persian, Georgian, Armenian and Ottoman styles

Arslan in 1067, they brought their new religion with them.

Although the Seljuks were effective fighters and renowned for their physical prowess, once the fighting was over their greatest sultans – notably Alp Arslan, Malik Shah, Keykavus I and Keykubad I (Alaeddin) – were enlightened rulers who laid the foundations for commercial prosperity and the development of education and the arts. Over the two centuries of their rule, the Seljuks evolved a remarkable form of welfare state, in which medical schools were linked with hospitals, orphanages, poor-houses, mental homes, baths and religious schools, all offering free services to the needy.

Art and architecture The 13th century was the high point of Seljuk civilisation in Asia Minor, with a flowering of military and artistic

❏ The network of caravanserais established along trade routes by the Seljuks was a great encouragement to commerce. The services they offered to travelling merchants were remarkable: around the central mosque and ablution fountain were arranged sleeping quarters, baths, cafés, blacksmiths' and leatherworkers' workshops and areas for listening to music. The most remarkable feature of all, was that these services were offered free by the state, which funded the system through taxation. ❏

talent. The elaborately decorated tiles and carvings of Seljuk architecture distantly reflect Persian influence, and the massive power of their castles and minarets displays traces of Syrian Arab influence. But whereas the later Ottomans often converted churches into mosques, Seljuk mosques were without exception built on new foundations. They also developed their own distinctive forms of architecture, such as the cylindrical mausoleum (*türbe*) on a square base with a conical roof (the most famous example being the **Mevlana Tomb** in Konya), which is thought in its shape to recall the pointed tents of the Seljuks' nomadic origins. The double-headed eagle, symbol of the Seljuk state, can be seen on many of their buildings, which were usually plainly constructed in red brick, in contrast with the very elaborate decorations and carving in niches and doorways. The main entrance was always intricately decorated with honeycomb (or stalactite) carving, as can be seen in the surviving caravanserais and *madrasas*. *Madrasas* were generally charitable foundations that were similar to the gymnasiums of the ancient world, teaching theology, the arts and sciences alongside sport. Their layout was similar to the classical model, too, with buildings arranged round a courtyard.

The impressive Seljuk fortifications at Alanya

The Seljuks were also prolific and skilled builders of bridges, many of which, solidly built in stone with a single pointed arch, remain in use today. The Seljuk pointed arch, used to great effect in windows and doorways, was possibly taken back to Europe by the Crusaders as the inspiration for the later Gothic arch.

The Seljuks brought the exquisite art of tilework (unknown to the Greeks and Romans) with them from Persia, developing the Persian style into their own form of tile mosaics in plain colours and geometric designs, so often seen on their mosques, tombs and *madrasas* (see page 61). The other great Seljuk art, recalling their nomadic background, was carpet-weaving (see pages 94–5).

❏ The Seljuks' single most significant contribution to religion was the foundation of the Mevlana order of Whirling Dervishes at Konya, the Seljuk capital. This form of Islamic mysticism continues today, despite Atatürk's dissolution of the order in 1925 as part of his drive to secularise modern Turkey. ❏

TURKEY WAS *The Ottoman Empire*

■ **In the 13th century the Seljuk sultanate of Konya fell into decline, to be succeeded by a number of smaller principalities. One of these, in the northwest, was ruled by a certain Osman Gazi (1288–1326), who gave his name to a small tribe known as the Ottomans or Osmanı Turks......■**

38

Expansion Under Osman, the Ottomans embarked on a great movement of expansion, and by 1400 they ruled most of the Balkan

peninsula and Anatolia. In 1453, after a siege led by Mehmet II, they took Constantinople and established their capital there. Renamed Istanbul by the Turks, the city remained the capital of the Ottoman Empire until 1923.

While maintaining many aspects of the Byzantine administrative system, the Ottomans also made innovations, introducing institutions such as the corps of Janissaries and *vakifs*. The latter were religious trusts, set up on captured land to provide revenues with which baths, hotels and other public amenities were established.

Süleyman the Magnificent The reign of Süleyman the Magnificent (1520–66) was unquestionably the climax of the Ottoman age. A contemporary of Henry VIII of England, the Habsburg emperor Charles V,

Left: Süleyman the Magnificent
Below:The Ottoman Empire in 1676

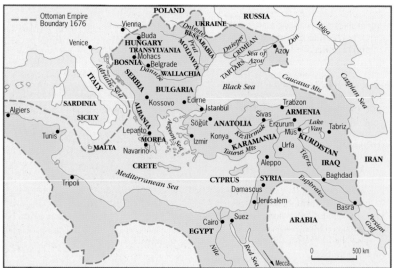

François I of France and Ivan the Terrible, Süleyman was an outstanding leader, legislator and patron of the arts. Under his rule the Ottoman Empire doubled in size. His armies took Belgrade in 1521 and Buda in 1526, and almost captured Vienna in 1529. His navy evicted the Knights of Saint John from Rhodes in 1522, ravaged the French, Spanish and Italian coasts and in 1538 defeated the navies of Europe. These victories were made possible not only by the quality of his troops and generals, but also by their superior weapons, the superb financial organisation of his armies, and above all by their discipline, the envy of European rulers. Meanwhile Süleyman's architects, notably Sinan (see pages 64–5), court architect from 1538, transformed the skylines of the great cities of the empire: Istanbul, Edirne, Damascus, Baghdad, Jerusalem and Mecca.

Ottoman soldiers (1825), before the abolition of the Janissaries

❏ On the death of their father Murat I, Beyazit I had his brother Yakoub murdered, thereby initiating the Ottoman sultans' practice (or frequently their wives') of having all their male relatives killed on the day of their accession, in order to avoid any quarrels over legitimacy. The Koranic verse claiming that 'rebellion is worse than execution' was cited in their justification. ❏

Early 19th-century Ottoman dress

❏ Founded by Murat I (1362–89), the Janissaries for centuries formed the backbone of the Ottoman army. Chosen from Christian families on the basis of physical prowess, they were converted to Islam and trained to exceptionally high standards of discipline in the palace schools. By the 18th century the Janissaries had become something of a law unto themselves, and they were finally abolished in 1826. ❏

■ Süleyman's successors, incapable of emulating his great powers of leadership, found themselves increasingly unable to control his vast and disparate empire. Only five years after his death, in 1571, the once invincible Ottoman navy was destroyed by Venice and her allies at Lepanto, off the Greek coast......■

Harem politics Süleyman's marriage to Hürrem Sultan, known as Roxelana in the West – the first time in two centuries that a sultan had committed himself to a single wife – helped to forge the first link in the chain of events that eventually brought about the downfall of the Ottoman Empire. Also of crucial importance was the fact that the administration of the empire had never been in Turkish hands, but was always entrusted to a huge, mainly Christian slave community, trained in the palace schools.

❑ In her book *Beyond the Sublime Porte* (1931), Professor Miller wrote of Süleyman: 'Between him and his immediate successors, who ceased with surprising suddenness to be either soldiers or statesmen, there was no graduation whatever. Enervated and enfeebled by seclusion and idleness, filled with ennui, they sought pleasure and diversion in every conceivable form of extravagance, self-indulgence and vice.' ❑

LA RÉVOLUTION EN TURQUIE
Sanglant combat autour d'Yildiz-Kiosk. -:- Victoire des Jeunes-Turcs

The seeds of the empire's demise were thus already sown, but it was hastened by the ineffectual rules of a long string of sultans – starting with Roxelana's son Selim 'the Sot' – who were feeble, incompetent or worse. Selim's disastrous rule ended when, in an alcoholic daze on the way to his bath, he fell and cracked his skull. His wife, Nur Bana, shared Roxelana's obsessive ambition for power, and from then on politics and policies were decided from the harem and implemented through murder and intrigue. Thus the empire was left to decay gradually from within.

The Young Turks and World War I The first stirrings of a new spirit among the Turks (prompted by political developments in western Europe) came during the reign of Selim III (1789–1807), and for much of the 19th

In 1909 Le Petit Parisien *reported victory for the Young Turks at Yıldız-Kiosk*

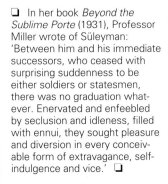

century a series of reforming sultans and ministers worked on a programme of modernisation. This process came to an abrupt end in 1876 with the accession of Abdul Hamid II, who ruthlessly repressed every liberal thought and reform. In 1908 the Young Turks, a liberal opposition group, led a revolution which temporarily overthrew Abdul Hamid in the name of freedom but quickly degenerated into a repellent dictatorship, rent by internal dissension and foreign wars.

In 1914 Turkey entered World War I on the side of Germany, an alliance which was of immense military value to the Central Powers but disastrous for the Turks. Having held out against Allied attacks on the Dardanelles and Mesopotamia, they were finally isolated by British attacks from Egypt and India, and signed an armistice in 1919.

After the débâcle of World War I the victorious Allies drew up their arrangements for the dissolution of the Ottoman Empire, 'the Sick Man of Europe'. Under the terms of the Treaty of Sèvres, described by historians as 'the death warrant of the Ottoman Empire', the empire lost all its lands except Istanbul and part of Anatolia. So harsh were these conditions – harsher by far than those imposed on Germany – that they were to inspire a popular nationalist uprising among the Turks, under their new leader Atatürk.

LE CONCERT EUROPÉEN

A French view of the war between Turkey and Greece in 1897

Sultan Abdul Hamid, overthrown by the Young Turks

❏ German influence, which had grown under Sultan Abdul Hamid II (1876–1909), increased yet further under the Young Turks. German officers reorganised the Turkish army, German businessmen and technicians extended their hold on the country's economy, and German engineers and financiers began construction of the famous Baghdad railway, which was to provide a direct rail link between Germany and the Middle East. ❏

41

■ **The excessively harsh terms of the Treaty of Sèvres were in fact never implemented in full, for while the Allies were busy imposing their conditions on the sultan and his government in Istanbul, in the depths of Anatolia a new Turkish state was rising up, based on a total rejection of the treaty......** ■

War of Independence So complete was Turkey's defeat at the end of World War I, and so abject its humiliation under the Treaty of Sèvres, that the spirit of its people might well have been crushed. The Allied carve-up of Ottoman lands might have continued unhindered, had it not been for the exaggerated territorial ambition of Greece, which set its sights on occupying the whole of the Aegean coast. Opposed by all the Allies except Britain, Greece landed an invasion force at Izmir in May 1919. Pushing deep into the interior, it was routed by forces under the command of Atatürk. This was the catalyst needed by the budding Turkish nationalist movement. The Turkish campaign against the Greek forces (1919–22) became known as the War of Independence, and during these years the nationalist movement, which had started among a small class of intellectuals,

Istanbul's airport is named after Atatürk

❏ Atatürk's words, 'In life the only real guide is science', are inscribed on the faculty buildings of Ankara University, which was founded by him. ❏

mushroomed into a country-wide uprising bent on creating a Turkish state based in Anatolia. Atatürk's efforts were crowned by the terms of the Treaty of Lausanne in 1923, under which Turkish sovereignty was recognised within approximately its present-day borders.

Westernising reforms During the remaining 15 years of his life, Atatürk effectively ruled Turkey as a dictator at the head of a single-party state. The Republican People's Party implemented his radically new policies, founded on a series of far-reaching reforms which sought to westernise Turkey and integrate it into the modern world.

The Turkish war memorial at Gelibolu (Gallipoli), where the Allies were routed by Atatürk's forces

12 Pages

Le Petit Journal
HEBDOMADAIRE
61, rue Lafayette, Paris

illustré

12 Pages

PRIX : 0 fr. 30
24 Septembre 1922

La défaite Grecque en Asie-Mineure

Après les longues années de guerre dont le monde entier a souffert, voici encore une fois le sang qui coule, là-bas, sur la terre d'Asie. Le lamentable défilé de l'armée grecque, vaincue, fuyant devant les troupes turques de Mustapha Kemal pacha, ressuscite un douloureux spectacle que nous pensions aboli.

Having exiled the sultan, Atatürk issued a series of edicts abolishing the Ministry of Religious Affairs, religious orders and religious schools, and sequestrating religious land. He abolished Koranic law, replacing it wholesale with European legal codes, and in 1928 disestablished Islam itself and amended the constitution to make Turkey a secular state. Atatürk was not opposed to religion in itself, and upheld everyone's right to be a devout Muslim in private, but he was convinced that religious concerns should not impinge on public or political life. He abolished the Arabic alphabet, the language of the Koran, giving a body of academics six months (they had asked for six years) to devise a new Latin alphabet for Turkish. Once ready, this alphabet was introduced virtually overnight, resulting in total chaos in the printing world: only one book was published in the whole of 1929.

Concerned to improve the position of women, whom he wanted to see accepted as equals, he encouraged the casting off of the veil, which he called an oppressive device used by men to hold women back; and in 1934 he gave women the vote and the right to stand for parliament. He himself married a woman as modern and emancipated and independent in

In 1922 the Greek army was finally vanquished in what came to be known as the Turkish War of Independence

spirit as he declared all Turkish women should be, but the partnership was soon dissolved.

Although undoubtedly an autocrat, Atatürk was not only an outstanding leader but also a man with a great appetite for life, renowned for his sense of humour, charm and sheer stamina. His early death – at the age of 57, from cirrhosis of the liver – was a tragedy for Turkey (see pages 196–7).

❑ The word 'civilisation' occurs again and again in Atatürk's speeches: 'We shall live as a progressive, civilised nation. We shall follow the road to civilisation and get there. We must prove that we are capable of becoming active members of the society of civilised peoples.' By 'civilisation', he meant the secular civilisation of the West, as opposed to the religious civilisation of Islam. ❑

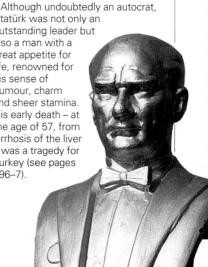

A bust of Atatürk at Gallipoli

■ **Turkey was the only defeated power in World War I which went on to achieve a negotiated settlement with the Allies. As an independent republic, it sought to increase its GNP through industrialisation and more efficient agriculture, and to play a part in world affairs......■**

44

The Reaction When in 1945 President Inönü turned Turkey into a democracy, there was a popular movement away from Kemalism, or the secular ideology of Atatürk (see pages 12–13), which had been widely misunderstood and opposed as an assault on Islam. This movement back towards religion, known in Turkey as the Reaction, became extremely influential, and ruling parties have ever since felt compelled to make concessions to it for the sake of gaining votes. In an unpopular move, for example, Atatürk had changed the call to prayer from Arabic to Turkish; in 1950 Adnan Menderes' Democrat Party changed it back to Arabic in order to gain popular support. Most political parties since then have exploited the power of Islam for the sake of political advantage, with leaders having themselves photographed at prayer,

Türgüt Özal, President of Turkey from 1984 until his death in 1993

❑ Atatürk's belief in the new Turkey never translated itself into a desire to take over other nations' territory. He wished only to keep Turkey for the Turks, and his foreign policy slogan was 'Peace at home, peace in the world'. ❑

promising to build more mosques, and so on. Since 1949 religious education, abolished under Atatürk, has also crept back by popular demand and continues to expand. Increasing numbers of Turks now make the pilgrimage to Mecca and observe Ramadan.

The 1960 coup After 10 years of controversial rule by Adnan Menderes, this near-bloodless coup was the army's attempt to return Turkey to Kemalist principles. Menderes' mishandling of the economy had resulted in massive inflation, huge foreign debts, budget deficits and falling exports. His response to criticism was to muzzle the press and imprison journalists, and he also managed to antagonise the army and alienate Kemalist intellectuals and writers. Tried and hanged by the army, he became

❑ President Inönü, a man of brilliant intellect who was a contemporary of Atatürk, inspired the observation that '40 foxes go round in his head, and the muzzle of one fox never touches the tail of the next'. Active in politics over 60 years, he knew every move in the game. ❑

something of a popular legend.
General elections in 1965 returned
the Justice Party, under Süleyman
Demirel. By the end of Demirel's
term of office, in 1971, Turkey was
slipping into chaos.

The 1980 coup In September 1980
the armed forces, led by General
Evren, seized power in a bloodless
coup, prompted by the government's
failure to deal with a state of economic and political chaos, the ineffective-
ness of the police force and the
sudden resurgence of Islamic fundamentalism. They detained thousands
of 'extremists', establishing law and
order at the expense of human rights.
The West responded by banning
Turkey from the Council of Europe
and suspending EEC aid. Elections
were reintroduced in 1983. Türgüt
Özal and Demirel served as prime
minister before Tansu Çiller's election
in 1993. The country now follows a
nominally democratic path, though it

*Istanbul today: capital of a strug-
gling democracy or of a regime of
political oppression and abuse?*

is still severely criticised – notably by
Amnesty International – for its
atrocious record of human rights
abuses against its Kurdish population.
  Mrs Çiller's government is now
faced with the difficult task of showing the world that Muslims are capable of running a successful
democracy. Turkey today is a country
overwhelmed by unsolved problems,
its frustrated people hungry
for reforms under a political regime that has so
far been unable to
deliver them.

ISTANBUL

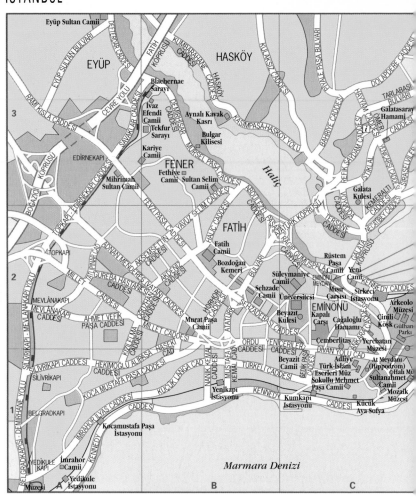

Map labels:

Eyüp Sultan Camii

EYÜP

HASKÖY

EYÜP SULTAN BULVARI

DEFTERDAR CADDESI

FATİH KÖPRÜSÜ

KUMBARAHANE CADDESI

KULAKSIZ CADDESI

PİYALE PAŞA BULVARI

DOLAPDERE CADDESI

TARLABAŞI

ÇEVRE YOLU

Blachernae Sarayı

İvaz Efendi Camii

Tekfur Sarayı

Aynalı Kavak Kasrı

HASKÖY CADDESI

KASIMPAŞA-HASKÖY YOLU

BAHRİYE CADDESI

REFİK SAYDAM CADDESI

Galatasaray Hamamı

İSTİKLAL CADDESI

SIRASELVİLER

RAMİ KISLA CADDESI

SAVAKLAR CADDESI

KÖPRÜSÜ

BOGAZKÖY

KARİYE CAMİİ

DEMİRHİSAR CADDESI

Kariye Camii

Bulgar Kilisesi

Halic

Galata Kulesi

KEMERALTI CADDESI

NECATBEY CADDESI

EDİRNEKAPI

Mihrimah Sultan Camii

FENER

Fethiye Camii

Sultan Selim Camii

MÜRSEL PAŞA CADDESI

ABDÜLEZEL PAŞA CADDESI

ATATÜRK KÖPRÜSÜ

Galata Kulesi

TOPKAPI

TEVFİK PAŞA CADDESI

YAVUZ SELİM CADDESI

FATİH

Fatih Camii

Bozdoğan Kemeri

RAGIP GÜMÜŞPALA CADDESI

Rüstem Paşa Camii

Yeni Camii

TERSANE CADDESI

GALATA KÖPRÜSÜ

TOPKAPI

ADNAN MENDERES CADDESI

VATAN CADDESI

AKSEMSETTİN CADDESI

KÖVENÇ CADDESI

ŞEHZADEBAŞI CADDESI

BÜLVARI

Süleymaniye Camii

Şehzade Camii

Üniversitesi

Mısır Çarşısı

EMİNÖNÜ MEYDANI

Sirkeci İstasyonu

KENNEDY CADDESI

MİLLET CADDESI

GUREBA HASTANESI CADDESI

Beyazıt Kulesi

Kapalı Çarşı

EMİNÖNÜ

Arkeoloji Müzesi

MEVLÂNAKAPI

AHMET VEFİK PAŞA CADDESI

HORHOR CADDESI

ATATÜRK BULVARI

Cağaloğlu Hamamı

Çinili Köşk

Gülhan Parkı

MEVLÂNAKAPI CADDESI

Murat Paşa Camii

Çemberlitaş

Yerebatan Sarayı

SİLİVRİKAPI CADDESI

KOCA MUSTAFA PAŞA CADDESI

NAMIK KEMAL CADDESI

MUSTAFA KEMAL CADDESI

ORDU CADDESI

YENİÇERİLER CADDESI

DİVAN YOLU

At Meydanı (Hippodrom)

Halı Mü

SİLİVRİKAPI

HEKİMOĞLU ALİPAŞA CADDESI

KÜÇÜK LANGA CAD

TÜRKELİ CADDESI

GEDİK PAŞA CADDESI

Beyazıt Camii

Adliye

Türk-İslam Eserleri Müz

Sokullu Mehmet Paşa Camii

Sultanahmet Camii

Mozaik Müzesi

BELGRADKAPI

İMRAHOR İLYAS BEY CADDESI

Kocamustafa Paşa İstasyonu

Yenikapı İstasyonu

KENNEDY

Kumkapı İstasyonu

Küçük Aya Sofya

BELGRADKAPI

DEMİRHANE YOLU

KENNEDY

YEDİKULE KAPI

İmrahor Camii

Yedikule İstasyonu

Müzesi

Marmara Denizi

A   B   C

Sunset over the Yeni Cami, or New Mosque, so-called because it is a mere three centuries old

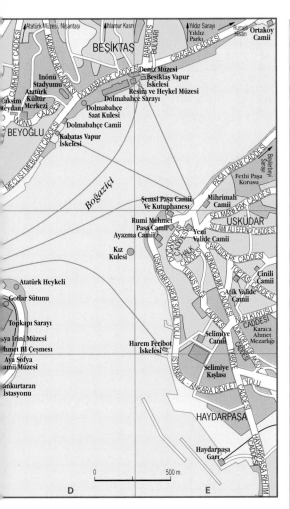

Map labels:

Atatürk Müzesi, Nişantaşı
Ihlamur Kasrı
Yıldız Sarayı
Yıldız Parkı
Rumeli Hisarı
Ortaköy Camii
BEŞIKTAŞ
BARBAROS BULVARI
ÇIRAĞAN CADDESI
Deniz Müzesi
İnönü Stadyumu
Beşiktaş Vapur İskelesi
Atatürk Kültür Merkezi
DOLMABAHÇE CADDESI
Resim ve Heykel Müzesi
Dolmabahçe Sarayı
Taksim Meydanı
KADIRGALAR CADDESI
CUMHURIYET CADDESI
Dolmabahçe Saat Kulesi
Dolmabahçe Camii
MEYDANI
BEYOĞLU
Kabataş Vapur İskelesi
PAŞA LIMANI CADDESI
Beylerbeyi Sarayı
Fethi Paşa Korusu
MECLISI MEBUSAN CADDESI
Boğaziçi
Şemsi Paşa Camii Ve Kutuphanesı
Mihrimah Camii
SELMANI PAK CADDESI
Rumi Mehmet Paşa Camii
ÜSKÜDAR
SELAMI ALI EFFENDI CADDESI
Ayazma Camii
DOĞANCILAR CADDESI
HALK CADDESI
Yeni Valide Camii
ÇAVUŞDERE CADDESI
TOPTAŞI
Kız Kulesi
Çinili Camii
TUNUS BAĞ CADDESI
GÜNDOĞUMU CADDESI
Atatürk Heykeli
Atik Valide Camii
Gotlar Sütunu
NUH KUYUSU CADDESI
Topkapı Sarayı
ÜSKÜDAR-HAREM SAHIL YOLU
Karaca Ahmet Mezarlığı
Aya İrini Müzesi
Ahmet III Çeşmesi
Selimiye Camii
DOKTOR FAHRI ATABEY
TIBBIYE CADDESI
Aya Sofya Camii/Müzesi
Harem Feribot İskelesi
Selimiye Kışlası
NÖBETHANE
Ankurtaran İstasyonu
İSTANBUL - ANKARA DEVLET YOLU
HAYDARPAŞA
Haydarpaşa Garı
HAYDARPAŞA CADDESI
HAYDARPAŞA RIHTIM
0   500 m
D   E

Istanbul

If you want to feel that you have done more than merely scratch the surface of Istanbul you need a full fortnight, though few of us ever have this luxury. One week with a carefully planned itinerary (see panel) will enable you to visit the essentials; if you have less time than this, you may find it helpful to choose days from the suggested itinerary rather than attempting to rush round and see everything in too short a time.

Any first-time visitor to Istanbul immediately becomes aware of the sense of ancient culture, a legacy of the city's distinguished history as capital to three empires, the Roman, the Byzantine and the Ottoman. For nearly a thousand years this was one of the dominant cities of the western and near-eastern worlds.

The setting More than 2,000 years before Christ, the city's position made it a vital link on the trade route from eastern Europe to Asia Minor. Covering the hills on both sides of the estuary of the Bosphorus with the Sea of Marmara, it was the halfway point between the cultures

Freshly barbecued
fish for sale on the
Galata landing stage

Outside Istanbul
University

of Europe and the Orient. Its natural harbour, the inlet of the Golden Horn, provided a safe base for naval and commercial shipping. During the Byzantine period wealth poured into the city from all corners of the world: silk, ivory and spices from China and India, wheat and dried fruits from Anatolia and Egypt, and skins and furs from Russia, transported by river and across the Black Sea. All routes then led to Constantinople and its colossal waterways were busy with the shipping necessary to service the capital of a vast empire.

Life and vibrancy Besides the staggering wealth of its historical monuments, contemporary Istanbul is also memorable for its vibrant atmosphere, alive with movement and bustle. A further element of magic is added by the city's setting astride the Bosphorus straits, so that its humming activity is transferred from land to water and back again, as vehicles cross bridges reflected in the Golden Horn and ferries ply their way to virtually every quarter.

*A tea vendor on
Eminönü Square,
considered the hub of
the city by Istanbulis*

Current status When Atatürk moved political power to Ankara and made it the new capital of Turkey in 1923, Istanbul was deprived of its status as a capital city for the first time in 16 centuries. Yet in the minds of most Istanbulis the city remains Turkey's most important centre, the place where almost all cultured and educated Turks would choose to live. It continues to generate 40 per cent of the country's gross national product (GNP) through its commercial and cultural activities, and its pop-ulation is expected to exceed 12 million by the year 2000, compared with Ankara's projected 4 million.

Population growth has been especially high in recent decades, with the number of inhabitants doubling every 15 years since 1950 as country dwellers have flocked to the city in search of a better lifestyle. Their unsightly shanty towns sprawl out from the suburbs of Istanbul, especially on the Asian side, unseen by most visitors. Even so, the consequences are clearly evident in the overcrowding on the roads and public transport and the pressure on the city's struggling infrastructure. If the dreaded century-long earthquake cycle continues (the last major ones were in 1766 and 1894), it is these shanty towns that will suffer most.

For now, however, in defiance of all its problems, Istanbul is a positive, active, energetic place, with the confidence of a city assured of its dominant role. Yet so much of its rich past remains for the visitor to discover in its astonishing legacy of historic buildings and monu-ments: it is not for nothing that *The Times* correspondent James Wilde recently called it 'the best kept secret in the world'.

One-week itinerary
Day 1 am Topkapı Sarayı.
Day 1 pm Archaeological Museums, Aya Irena, Aya Sofya, Yerebatan Sarayı.
Day 2 am Sultanahmet Mosque, Hippodrome, Ibrahim Paşa Sarayı.
Day 2 pm Grand Bazaar, Turkish Bath.
Day 3 am Dolmabahçe Sarayı ferry from Kabataş to Üsküdar.
Day 3 pm Karaca Ahmet cemetery, Selimiye Barracks, ferry back to Galata Bridge.
Day 4 am Süleymaniye Mosque, Rüstem Paşa Mosque, Spice Bazaar.
Day 4 pm Along the Golden Horn, Kariye Museum, Tekfur Sarayı, Pierre Loti Café for sunset.
Day 5 am and pm Bosphorus cruise up to Anadolu Kavağı and back.
Day 6 am Princes' Islands cruise.
Day 6 pm Yedikule and walk along the Land Walls. Sunset view from Galata Tower.

Orientation

Stamboul
This is the western name for the oldest quarter of the city, the original Constantinople. Aya Sofya, Sultanahmet Camii (the Blue Mosque), the Grand Bazaar, the Topkapı Palace and the Suleymaniye Mosque are all to be found here.

Istanbul is divided into its European and Asian sides by the Bosphorus. The famous monuments lie almost exclusively on the European side, as do the wealthier suburbs. The Asian side was traditionally a place of quiet retreat; more recently it has become overcrowded with migrants seeking a better life in the city, who through their large numbers have contributed to the deterioration of its utilities and rising levels of pollution.

Beyoğlu This huge quarter full of grand 19th-century Italianate buildings lies on the European side; known in Ottoman times as Pera, in contemporary times it was home to all the European embassies before the capital moved to Ankara in the 1920s. It then went into decline, but has recently undergone a revival and now bustles with jazz bars, late-night tavernas, cinemas and esoteric shops such as furniture restorers and antiquarian booksellers. A tramway was reinstalled in 1990, and pedestrianised zones have been created, notably in the main street, **Istiklal Caddesi**. At the upper end of this is **Taksim Square**, the commercial hub of the city, busy with traffic and studded with modern hotels and fast-food restaurants. Famous landmarks in Beyoğlu include the conical **Galata Tower**, built by the Genoese in 1348 (it now houses a restaurant and nightclub), and the elegant but faded **Pera Palas**, built to accommodate travellers on the Orient Express and still a hotel.

Boğaziçi (Bosphorus) The 32-km long straits between the Black Sea and the Mediterranean have largely created Istanbul's character. Two bridges link the European and Asian sides. The first, known as the old **Bosphorus Bridge (Boğaziçi Köprü)**, was built in 1973. The second, **Fatih Sultan Mehmet Köprüsü**, was completed in 1988 and spans the narrowest point, between the famous fortresses of **Rumeli Hisarı** and **Anadolu Hisarı,** where the Persian King Darius built his bridge of boats in 512BC.

The Bosphorus Bridge, linking the Asian and European sides of the straits

Haliç (Golden Horn) This inlet of the Bosphorus, which separates old Stamboul from Beyoğlu, originally formed Constantinople's safe natural harbour. Now it is crossed by three bridges: to the north the Haliç motorway bridge, linking the Bosphorus Bridge to the international airport; in the centre the Atatürk Bridge, running up under the **Aqueduct of Valens**; and to the south the new Galata Bridge, which recently replaced the old Galata Bridge after an explosion in one of its colourful floating restaurants blew a hole in it. The Stamboul shoreline of the Golden Horn makes a very pleasant quiet stroll.

Nişantaşı North of Beyoğlu, further away from the old heart of Istanbul, Nişantaşı is the smartest part of Istanbul, offering chic hotels and restaurants and sophisticated shopping. The main shopping street is **Teşvikiye Caddesi**, turning into **Rumeli Caddesi**.

Eminönü Square
Considered the hub of the city by its inhabitants, this perpetually bustling square lies below the Topkapı on the western shore of the Golden Horn. All the boat stations are to be found here, as well as the European railway station, Sirkeci.

In a crowded city every space is valuable: here a flat roof serves as play area and workshop

Minaret counting
Aya Sofya has four minarets and the Blue Mosque has six, so you can always tell them apart in the Istanbul skyline. The norm for other mosques throughout the city is just one.

Sultanahmet This district takes its name from Sultanahmet Camii, the **Blue Mosque** (see pages 66–7), and is the heart of the old city. The city's major sights are concentrated here, within easy walking distance of each other. The main entrance of the Blue Mosque faces the long thin **At Meydanı (Hippodrome)**, recognisable by the Egyptian obelisk in its centre. The side entrance, the one open to tourists, takes you out on to **Aya Sofya Meydanı**, the pedestrianised landscaped gardens that lie between the Blue Mosque and **Aya Sofya** (see pages 52–3), the domed 6th-century Byzantine basilica which was the largest building in the world for the first thousand years of its existence. It is now a museum. Behind it lie Istanbul's main **archaeological museums** (see pages 70–1), and just behind these again is the entrance to the **Topkapı Sarayı**, former pleasure palace of the Ottoman sultans and now also a museum (see pages 76–7).

Üsküdar This sprawling suburb on the Asian side of the Bosphorus, directly opposite the Sultanahmet district, offers superb views over the Istanbul skyline. It also contains the wild and picturesque **Karaca Ahmet Mezarlığı**, the largest Muslim cemetery in the world.

A jewellery seller in the courtyard of the Blue Mosque

51

Ingenious design

The original architects – the Greeks, Anthemius of Tralles and Isidorus of Miletus – designed a vast platform over 6 metres deep to form the foundations. Their plans were carried out by 10,000 workmen supervised by 100 master masons. Special bricks made at Rhodes were used in the dome, so light that 12 of them weighed the same as a single ordinary brick.

▶▶▶ **Aya Sofya Müzesi
(Haghia Sophia Basilica)** *46C1*

Aya Sofya Meydanı, Sultanahmet

This extraordinary building, a masterpiece of Byzantine architecture, embodies more than any other in Istanbul the different phases of the city's history.

Many incarnations The first church on this site was consecrated by the Emperor Constantine in 360 to Divine Wisdom (Haghia Sophia in Greek) in the fourth century, and was enlarged by his son Constantius to become the episcopal church of the capital. In 404 and 532 this building and the church that succeeded it were burned down during revolts, and it was in February 532 that the Emperor Justinian ordered work to begin on the current structure, then the largest church in Christendom. In 1453, on the very day that Constantinople fell to the Turks, Mehmet the Conqueror entered the basilica and ordered it to be converted to a mosque named Aya Sofya. The building remained a mosque until the early 1930s when, in recognition of its unique and pivotal role in Byzantine and Ottoman history, Atatürk turned it into a museum. It was at this time that the American Byzantine Institute embarked on excavation work and on the restoration of the mosaics, which was to continue for some 30 years.

Earthquakes soon took their toll on the over-ambitious dome which caved in several times over the centuries, to be shored up again on each occasion by increasingly large buttresses. These massive buttresses make it difficult to work out the shape of the original groundplan of the basilica from the outside, and the minarets, added by various sultans along with yet more buttresses, help to disguise the original still further. The outlines of the building today are rather suggestive of an enormous crab, tensely poised.

T.C. KÜLTÜR BAKANLIĞI

FİYATI : 20.000 TL.

№ 110695

AYASOFYA MÜZESİ GİRİŞ BİLETİ

The distinctive outlines of Aya Sofya, a masterpiece of Byzantine architecture

The interior The internal architecture of Aya Sofya remains as stupendous today as it must have been in the early days. You enter the precinct through an attractive courtyard garden, in which are scattered various tombs of Ottoman sultans to your right, and the old kitchens and ablutions fountain to your left. There is quite a high entry fee and the ticket office is open daily except Mondays, from 9:30–5.

As you enter the vestibule, look out for the 9th-century bronze-covered doors into the narthex, and for the 10th-century mosaic showing the Virgin Mary holding the baby Jesus, with Constantine I offering her the city on one side and Justinian giving her a model of the basilica on the other. Another notable mosaic is to be found above the main door to the basilica itself. Dating from the late 9th century, it depicts Christ enthroned and holding out his right hand in blessing, while an inscription in his left hand proclaims: 'Peace be unto you. I am the light of the world.'

Inside, the stonework of the nave is awesome; the gigantic green and purple columns supporting the dome, the walls sheathed in marbles of all colours, and above all the sheer scale of the interior space all combine to take your breath away.

The gigantic alabaster urns either side of the entrance were donated by Sultan Murat III, and were once used as ablutions fountains, while Süleyman the Magnificent gave the two candelabra on either side of the *mihrab* (the prayer niche facing towards Mecca). The great chandelier hanging from the centre of the dome was given by Sultan Ahmet III. The tops of the columns are dominated by huge discs bearing the names – in Arabic script – of Allah and Muhammad, along with those of Abu Bakr, Hussein, Hassan, Ali and Umar, the key figures of early Islamic history.

On the left-hand side of the nave as you enter is the stairway to the cobbled ramp which zigzags up to the galleries just below the dome. The south gallery contains the celebrated Gates of Heaven and Hell, false doors of marble decorated with elaborate reliefs from which they take their name. It is in the galleries that the most magnificent of the basilica's mosaics are concentrated, inadvertently preserved in the 18th century by the Ottomans, who covered them with a thick layer of whitewash. The most famous of all is the 13th-century *Deësis*, or *Prayer*, mosaic, considered to be one of the finest of the period. Against a gold background, the figure of Christ is flanked by an expressive Virgin and an agonised John the Baptist.

The greatest internal damage the basilica has sustained throughout its long history was in 1204, when the Catholic armies of the Fourth Crusade stormed it, stripping it bare and hacking the altar to pieces.

Ancient pilfering
To make the new basilica the most magnificent in existence, precious materials, fine marbles and sculptures were plundered from the most celebrated temples of the ancient world. The eight green breccia columns were taken from the Temple of Artemis at Ephesus, and further columns were pillaged from temples in Baalbek (Lebanon), Athens and Delos.

The 13th-century Deësis *mosaic, considered the finest of Aya Sofya's mosaics*

The Sweating Column
Near the entrance to the gallery stairway stands a porous column known as the Sweating Column of Saint Gregory; for centuries the moisture exuded by this column has been said to cure eye diseases and infertility.

■ **Islam originated in the early 7th century in Mecca in the Arabian peninsula with the charismatic figure of Muhammad. It spread to Turkey in the 11th century with the arrival of the Seljuks from Persia, and remained the state religion until 1923, when Atatürk officially secularised the Turkish republic......■**

Cleanliness next to godliness
'He who performs the ablution thoroughly will extract all sin from his body, even though it may be lurking under his fingernails.'
The Prophet Muhammad

Muslim prayer beads

A selection of editions of the Koran on a stall in Istanbul's book market

Allah is One
'"The great stumbling block to Moslems," said Father Chantry-Pigg, "is the Blessed Trinity. To a people who hear the One God proclaimed so many times a day, and so loudly, the Triune God raises all kinds of difficulties in the mind."'
Rose Macaulay, 1956

Later called the Prophet, Muhammad proclaimed himself the mouthpiece of Allah: in no way divine himself, he was simply the medium through which Allah had chosen to reveal his word. Muhammad was illiterate, but the Koran (literally 'Recitation') was revealed to him in bursts over a period of 22 years ending in 632, the year of his death at the age of 62. The entire text of the Koran consists of God speaking to man, offering divine instruction and guidance in the Arabic language; because of this, Muslims all over the world, whatever their own nationality or language, pray and recite the Koran in Arabic, having learnt it by heart even though they may not understand its meaning. One consequence of this phenomenon is that classical Arabic has altered less over the last 1,300 years than any other language.

Islam, meaning 'submission to the will of God', spread rapidly from the Arabian peninsula as a result of the exhortation to *jihad* (holy war), imposing an obligation on all believers to spread the word to unbelievers. Within 10 years Arab armies had conquered Syria, Egypt, Mesopotamia and the Persian Sassanid Empire. The tolerance shown by Muslims to Christians and Jews was frequently in stark contrast to the persecution they had suffered previously, and many of these converted to Islam voluntarily.

Relationship with Christianity and Judaism Christians and Jews are referred to in the Koran as 'People of the Book' (that is, of the Bible), a separate category from straightforward unbelievers. This is because Islam regards Allah as being the same god as the one worshipped by Christians and Jews. Its main point of conflict

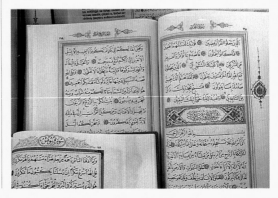

with Christianity lies with the Christian doctrine of the Trinity and the belief that Jesus was the Son of God, rather than merely a prophet like Muhammad. The Koran affirms the righteousness of previous prophets and revelations: 'Surely, We sent down the Torah full of guidance and light', and 'We caused Jesus son of Mary to follow in their footsteps...and We gave him the Gospel'. Muhammad is claimed to be the 'seal' of the prophets, however, the last one with the final word.

The Five Pillars The five basic tenets of faith as laid down by the Koran are known as the Five Pillars. The first is the declaration of faith that 'there is no God but God and Muhammad is the Messenger of God' (proclaimed in the calls to prayer from mosque minarets). The second is the act of prayer, made five times a day – at dawn, noon, mid-afternoon, sunset and before bed. Ritual ablution of hands, feet and face is compulsory before prayer. The third is *zakat*, or alms tax, a yearly charitable donation. The fourth is fasting during Ramadan, the month in which the first revelation of the Koran was given. The 30-day fast during daylight hours applies to food, drink and smoking; the old, the sick and children of up to about eight are exempt. The fifth is the pilgrimage (*hajj*) to the Kaaba, the House of Allah at Mecca, to be undertaken at least once in a lifetime by any Muslim who can afford it.

Islamic culture During the period when it was at its peak, between the 7th and 13th centuries, Islamic culture was responsible for many great intellectual and scientific discoveries, some of which were later borrowed by the western world. Arabic numerals, geometry and algebra were all introduced to western Europe through contact with the Islamic traders of Spain and North Africa. In the field of medicine, meanwhile, many important advances were made by philosopher-scientists such as the 11th-century physician Avicenna.

Midday prayers: every Muslim must stop work for prayers five times a day

Women and Islam
Muslim men are allowed to take up to four wives, but it is rare for them to do so nowadays, especially in Turkey, and most have only one. Traditionally a man may divorce a woman, but not vice versa, though the law has now been reformed in many countries including Turkey. The Koran exhorts women to cover all parts of the body that might be a temptation to men, but again this is very loosely interpreted: most Turkish women, especially in the cities, now wear normal western style of dress.

[Map of the Grand Bazaar area with the following labels:]

Beyazıt Kulesi · MERCAN CADDESI · ÇAKMAKCILAR YOKUSU · SURURİ · ÇARKCILAR SOKAĞI · MAHMUT PAŞA YOKUSU · TARAKCI CAFER SOKAĞI · FUAT PAŞA CADDESI · TIĞCILAR SOKAĞI · TAYA HATUN · TARAKCILAR CADDESI · SULTAN MEKTEBI SOKAĞI · İstanbul Üniversitesi Merkez · Yolgeçen Han · Pastırmacı Han · Mahmut Paşa Hamamı · YAĞLIKCILAR CADDESI · Astarcı Han · Çukur Han · İmameli Han · Kalcılar Han · BEZCİLER SOKAĞI · Sarnıçlı Han · İç Cebeci Han · Zincirli Han · MAHMUT PAŞA SOKAĞI · BAKIRCILAR CADDESI · AYNACILAR · SOKAĞI · Cnhacılar Hanı · CADDESI · Havuzlu · HALICILAR ÇARSISI CADDESI · İç Bedesten · KUYUMCULAR CADDESI · Nuru Osmaniye Camii · BEYAZIT MEYDANI · YORGANCILAR CADDESI · Ali Paşa Hanı · PTT · FERACECILER SOKAĞI · KESECILER CADDESI · Sandal Bedesteni · NURU OSMANIYE SOKAĞI · VEZIRHANI CADDESI · Beyazıt Camii · Sahaflar Çarsısı · Bodrum Han · FESCILER CADDESI · CADDESI · Rabia Hanı · Yağcı Hanı · Nuru Osmaniye · BEYAZIT · KALPAKCILAR · OKCULARBASI CADDESI · BALMUMCULAR SOKAĞI · ÇARSIKAPI SOKAĞI · BILEYCILER SOKAĞI · TAVUK PAZARI SOKAĞI · Vezir Hanı · YENICERILER CADDESI · Çemberlitaş · TIYATRO CADDESI · Atik Ali Paşa Camii · YENICERILER CADDESI · Çemberlitaş Hamamı

0 · 100 m

A · B · C

3 · 2 · 1

𝒲𝒶𝓁𝓀 The Grand Bazaar

Beginning at Istanbul University, this walk wanders through the Grand Bazaar – the world's largest bazaar, and an essential expedition for all visitors to Istanbul – and ends with a well-deserved Turkish bath. The walk described will take about 2 hours; the Bazaar is open 8:30–7, except Sundays.

Colourful traditional slippers

Start by taking a taxi to Beyazıt Meydanı. At the back of this busy square, up a few steps, is a large gateway in Moorish style which opens on to the grounds of Istanbul University, on the site of the palace of Mehmet the Conqueror. The only building of any age is now the **Beyazıt Tower** (1823), straight ahead. From the upper gallery there are fine views.

Return to the Beyazıt Meydanı and walk through the attractive marble-paved courtyard of the **Beyazıt Camii**. Descend the steps at the back to reach some pavement cafés. From here an alleyway leads to the right into the **Sahaflar Çarşısı**, Istanbul's premier book market.

Leave by the far end and cross the busy **Çadırcılar Caddesi**, Street of the Tentmakers, to enter the Grand Bazaar at the **Fesçiler Caddesi** (Fez makers' Street) which, with the demise of the fez, now sells denim and canvas bags. In accordance with oriental tradition, all trades in the

A glittering array of brass ware

Bazaar are grouped together in order to ensure the keenest competition between merchants. The Grand Bazaar (Turkish Kapalı Çarşısı, meaning 'Covered Market'), has occupied the same site since the 15th century in many incarnations, burning down at regular intervals – most recently in 1954. As you walk through, look up at the tilework high on the walls and pillars. The streets are reckoned to total 8km in length, with 4,000 shops.

Bear left for refreshment at **Havuzlu Restaurant**, considered the best in the Bazaar. From here head right into **Halıcılar Çarşısı Caddesi**, the Carpet sellers' Street, until you reach the little fork right into the **İç Bedestan**, the heart of the Bazaar and the oldest part.

Leave by the opposite exit and walk in a straight line (never easy here) to reach **Kalpakçılar Caddesi**, Fur cap makers' Street, the main thoroughfare. Turn left and, after a short detour into **Sandal Bedestan**, a 16th-century hall where carpet auctions used to be held, leave the Bazaar by the attractive Nuruosmaniye Gate. Turn right along **Tavukpazarı Sokağı**

to reach the Column of Constantine (AD330), its dark porphyry drums reinforced with metal bands. Beside this is **Vezir Hanı**, once Istanbul's principal slave market, next door to which stands the **Çemberlitaş** Bath, a fitting reward for dusty travellers.

Bargaining is expected

Churches

Part of the painted decoration in Mehmet the Conqueror's Fatih Camii

New roles
Most churches in Istanbul were converted into mosques in the 15th century by the conquering Ottomans, who added minarets externally, and *mihrabs* (prayer niches) and *minbars* (pulpits) internally. Others served as warehouses, arsenals or grainstores.

A detail of one of the superb 14th-century mosaics in Kariye Camii, which mark a turning point in Byzantine art

▶ **Aya Irini Müzesi (Haghia Eirene Museum)** 46C2

Between Aya Sofya and the Topkapı Palace, Sultanahmet
Tucked away in a corner of the Court of the Janissaries as you approach the Topkapı Palace, the large and beautiful basilica of Haghia Eirene (Divine Peace) was one of the first Christian sanctuaries of Byzantium. The present building is virtually contemporary with Haghia Sophia. In Ottoman times it served as the Janissaries' arsenal, and now it is used as an exhibition hall or venue for concerts during the Istanbul Festival. It is closed and under repair at present (1994).

▶ **Bulgar Kilisesi (Saint Stephen of the Bulgars)** 46B3

Mürsel Paşa Caddesi, Fener
This extraordinary church, made entirely of cast iron, was prefabricated in Vienna in 1871 and shipped down the Danube and across the Black Sea to be assembled here on the shoreline of the Golden Horn. It is generally kept locked, but a guardian who is often to be found in the garden can be persuaded to open it for a small consideration. Istanbul's tiny Bulgarian community continues to worship here regularly.

▶▶ **Fethiye Camii (Church of the Theotokos Pammakaristos)** 46B3

Fethiyekapası Sokak
This large red and white stone church standing on a terrace overlooking the Golden Horn was the seat of the Greek Orthodox Patriarchate until 1568, when it was converted into a mosque. Following restoration work by the Byzantine Institute, the mosque area has been divided off, allowing part of the church to be turned into a museum exhibiting the 14th-century mosaics that survive in the dome and the side chapel. It is open only with special permission from the authorities at Aya Sofya.

▶▶ **Imrahor Camii (Saint John the Baptist of Studius)** 46A1

Imam Asır Sokak, off Imrahor Ilyas Bey Caddesi, near Yedikule
There is no entry fee to see this impressive, heavily ruined church, built in 463 and for many years the focus of the Byzantine monastic movement. An important centre of intellectual life, it became home to the University of Constantinople in the early 15th century. Later that

century it was turned into a mosque by Beyazit II, and in 1894 it was abandoned after a severe earthquake which brought down part of the minaret. Among the remains are some fine columns and a lovely mosaic pavement.

The breathtakingly colourful mosaics of Kariye Camii

▶▶▶ Kariye Camii (Saint Saviour in Chora)   46A3

Kariye Meydanı, near Edirnekapı

The early 14th-century frescoes and mosaics in this church are the finest in Istanbul and indeed the world. They reveal a new style of Byzantine art, anticipating the Renaissance in its profound spirituality and vitality, with a striking use of colour and a tremendous sense of passion. Restored by the American Byzantine Institute between 1948 and 1958, they cover the walls in images of astonishing variety, including scenes from the lives of Christ and the Virgin Mary, Christ's miracles, portraits of the Saints and the Last Judgement. Perhaps the most celebrated of all is the fresco of the Harrowing of Hell, between the apse and the dome, in which Christ is shown forcibly wresting Adam and Eve from their tombs.

The Byzantine name Saint Saviour in Chora means 'in the country', as the church stood outside the original city walls. Now a museum, it is set in a pretty cobbled courtyard, away from the traffic of central Istanbul. It is open daily except Tuesdays 9–4:30.

Wood only
After the Ottoman conquest, Christians in Istanbul were not allowed to build churches with domes or masonry roofs, lest their silhouettes should detract from the new mosques. From the 15th century, all Christian churches in the city were therefore built as small basilicas with timbered roofs; a good example is the Greek Orthodox Patriarchate church of Saint George (1720).

▶ Küçük Aya Sofya
(Saints Sergius and Bacchus)   46C1

Küçük Aya Sofya Caddesi, Sultanahmet

One of the most beautiful Byzantine churches to survive in the city today, Küçük Aya Sofya was built by Justinian in 527, before the great basilica of the same name, which it is said to anticipate in miniature. The interior decorations repay detailed inspection, and the garden courtyard, heavily overgrown, has an almost rural feel. The church was converted to a mosque in about 1500 and is still in use as such today. It is approached through a picturesque quarter of old wooden Ottoman houses with characteristic overhanging balconies.

Mosaic masterpieces
The 14th-century mosaics and frescoes of the Kariye Camii are held to be the finest examples of Byzantine mosaic art in the world, splendidly preserved thanks to the whitewash with which the Ottomans painted the walls during the centuries when the building was used as a mosque.

FOCUS ON *Turkish music*

■ **Turks love music, and in Istanbul you will be struck by the number of tape cassette shops offering a bewildering variety of styles. 'Arab-esque' or taverna music is frequently to be heard in shops, teahouses and even on coaches, and live music is often played in restaurants, especially in the evenings......■**

Jazz renaissance
Istanbul has recently become a flourishing jazz centre, featuring performers of international stature as well as home-grown talent. An interesting new dimension is provided by Süleyman Erguner, who plays the *ney*, the traditional Ottoman reed flute, as part of his jazz set.

Folk music in an Istanbul restaurant

'Erotic whine'
Turkish music on the radio was described by Rose Macaulay as 'the eternal Turkish erotic whine'. 'The Turkish radio seems to love and cuddle and yearn without a break,' she continued, 'Turks being an excessively loving people...'

A traditional reed flute, or ney

Turkish folk music Apart from the special folkloric evenings held for tourists in cities, Turkish folk music is also still performed in its natural setting, at village weddings or festivals, as an accompaniment to dancing by segregated groups of men and women. More specialised is *ozan*, the music of the folk poets or *aşıks* ('those in love') of Anatolia, who accompany themselves on the *saz*, a kind of lute with three sets of strings. *Aşıks* still wander the towns and villages of central Anatolia, and many of them – notably the blind Aşık Veysel, who died in 1973 – have recorded their music on cassette.

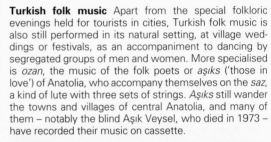

Kurdish folk music differs markedly from Turkish folk music: its *dengbeis* (bards), the best-known of whom are Sivan, Perwer and Temo, sing of Kurdish myths and legends and the Kurdish struggle for freedom, to the accompaniment of haunting wind instruments. In the cities you may hear *özgün*, the protest music of Turkey, sophisticated and quite addictive. The most impressive of *özgün* musicians is Livaneli, whose cassettes – some of them recorded with the famous Greek musician Theodorakis – are widely available.

Turkish Ottoman and religious music The classical music of the Ottoman court can be heard on the radio or in concert, performed by ensembles of over 30 on traditional Turkish instruments such as the *ney* (a reed flute), the *tambur* (a long-necked lute) and the *kemençe* (a three-stringed fiddle from the Black Sea villages, held vertically). The dominant religious music of Turkey is that composed by the Mevlevi order of dervishes. This mystical soothing music performed on the *ney* and the *kudum* (small kettle-drums) can be heard live in Istanbul or at the annual Mevlana Festival in Konya (see pages 24–5 and 204–5).

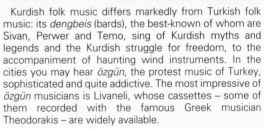

Turkish tiles

■ The development of tile and ceramic art began in Turkey in the 11th century, when the Seljuks moved westwards from their newly established capital in Persia. When in 1097 they made Konya their western capital, the town soon became one of their leading tile and ceramic production centres......■

Konya ware The Seljuk polychrome technique brought from Persia was known as *minai* (from *mina*, meaning 'enamel' in Persian). The ceramic slabs were first painted in pale blues, greens or turquoise, covered in a transparent glaze and fired. Then they were decorated in black and vitrifiable colours such as red, yellow, blue and brown and fired again. The tiles were generally star-shaped, and the motifs used were a blend of Persian styles and images such as hunting dogs and horses, inspired by the steppelands of central Asia. Examples can be seen in early Seljuk palaces such as that of Alaeddin Keykubad I (1220–35) beside Lake Beyşehir.

Iznik ware In the 15th century, under the Ottomans, the centre of tile production moved to Iznik – a traditional centre of Byzantine earthenware – in response to a sudden and unprecedented need for fine tiles and ceramics to decorate the palaces and mosques springing up in the new capital, Istanbul. During the 16th century styles gradually became more refined, with delicate 'blue and white' decoration used to imitate Chinese motifs such as wave scrolls and lotus flowers. Turquoise, green and red (produced from a thick clay rich in iron found only near Erzurum in eastern Turkey, and especially characteristic of the period 1560–1600) were subsequently added to the range of colours, flower motifs became popular, and the Iznik production remained highly successful until the 17th century.

Kütahya ware From the early 17th to the mid-18th century tiles of a lower quality were produced in great numbers in Kütahya. In the 20th century, the industry has undergone a revival, producing many good quality tiles.

The best display
The best place to see a full range of ceramics and tiles is the Çinili Köşk, the Tile Museum in Istanbul. It shares the courtyard, entrance fee and opening hours of the Archaeological Museum (see page 70).

61

A section of Iznik tiles from the Eyüp mosque complex, showing the exceptional beauty attained in both their colours and their motifs

Panels of Iznik tiles decorate the walls of the shrine to Eyüp, one of the holiest places in the Muslim world

Istanbul mosques

Ablutions fountains at the Eyüp mosque complex, which houses the sacred tomb of the Prophet Muhammad's friend and standard bearer

The baroque türbe of Mehmet the Conqueror, rebuilt after an earthquake in 1766

► ►　**Atik Valide Camii**　　47E2
Kartal Baba Caddesi, Üsküdar
Built in 1583 by the famous architect Şinan (see page 65), this mosque complex dominates the Üsküdar skyline. It is considered to be his finest building in Istanbul after the Süleymaniye (see pages 66–7), and one of the city's best examples of Ottoman architecture. Its fine decorative features now stand in contrast to the poverty – even squalor – of its present-day surroundings.

► ► ►　**Aya Sofya Camii**　　46C1
See pages 52–3.

►　　**Çinili Camii (Tiled Mosque)**　　47E2
Çavus Dere Caddesi, Üsküdar
This small sanctuary built in 1640 is an excellent example of a highly decorated Ottoman mosque, covered with magnificent Iznik tiles, predominantly blue in colour. From here there are superb views over Istanbul and its skyline.

► ►　**Eyüp Sultan Camii**　　46A3
Cami Kebir Caddesi, Eyüp
The most sacred shrine in Istanbul is built around the tomb of Eyüp, friend and standard bearer of the Prophet Muhammad, who is reputed to have been killed here in 670, during the Arab siege of Constantinople. The current mosque complex was built in 1800, earlier structures having been destroyed by earthquakes. The tomb itself lies

off the courtyard, in a curiously shaped room whose walls are covered with Iznik tiles of exceptional beauty.

▶ Fatih Camii (Mosque of the Conqueror) 46B2

Tophane Sokağı Fatih

This vast complex, built for Mehmet the Conqueror from 1463–70, was the largest and most elaborate in the entire Ottoman Empire at that time. Mehmet's express intention was to outdo Aya Sofya, the symbol of Christian Byzantium, and according to tradition he cut off the architect's hands in rage on discovering that the dome of his mosque was slightly smaller than that of its rival. The 'Kulliye' or theological college also boasted eight *madrasas* (schools), a hospital, a caravanserai, public baths, a hospice, a soup kitchen and a graveyard.

An earthquake destroyed most of the complex in 1766, and it was immediately rebuilt to a different plan. The exterior features of the mosque are of most interest today. The attractive courtyard has cypress trees surrounding the central *şadırvan* (ablution fountain), and contains fragments of antique marble columns which are thought to be the remains of the earlier Church of the Holy Apostles, the ruins of which served as a convenient quarry for the new mosque.

A Muslim at prayer

▶▶ Fethiye Camii 46B3
See page 58.

▶▶▶ Kariye Camii 46A3
See page 59.

▶ Küçük Aya Sofya 46C1
See page 59.

▶▶ Imrahor Camii 46A1
See page 58.

▶ Mihrimah Sultan Camii 46A3

Edirnekapısı

One of the most prominent landmarks on the Istanbul skyline, this mosque stands on a raised terrace just inside the Edirne Gate, on the summit of the sixth of Istanbul's seven hills and the highest point in the old city. Built by Sinan for Princess Mihrimah, favourite daughter of Süleyman the Magnificent, the mosque has a delicate – almost feminine – feel. Notice especially the marble and granite porch columns as you enter, and the exquisite white carved marble of the *minbar* (pulpit).

▶▶ Rüstem Paşa Camii 46C2

Kutucular Caddesi, Eminönü

Built in 1561, this is one of Sinan's most beautiful and unusual mosques, hidden away in a narrow street inland from the Spice Bazaar and Eminönü Square. It stands above a row of vaulted shops and is reached by internal flights of steps which lead up into an open courtyard apparently among the rooftops, the only one of its kind in the city. The most famous feature, however, is its extensive and beautiful tilework, all from the most distinguished Iznik period (1555–1620).

63

Terrace with a view
From the Eyüp Mosque complex, take the path up through the famous Ottoman cemetery for 10 minutes to reach the Pierre Loti Café, a simple place with a wonderful rustic terrace giving fine views over the Golden Horn, especially at sunset.

Minaret technology
Mosques are always recognisable by their minarets, the tall thin towers from which the call to prayer is made. The *muezzin* used to climb the stairs to the top to summon the faithful, but nowadays his voice is broadcast by tape recorder and loudspeaker.

FOCUS ON *Ottoman architecture and art*

■ After the Turkish conquest of Constantinople in 1453 there developed the distinctive style of art and architecture which we now think of as typically Ottoman. It reached its peak in the reign of Süleyman the Magnificent (1520–66), and the buildings now considered to be most typical of the Ottoman style are the grand imperial mosques such as the Fatih (see pages 62–3), the Süleymaniye and the Sultanahmet (Blue Mosque) (see pages 66–7)......■

Exotic drinking water
The fountain house of Ahmet III, built in 1728 at the entrance to the Topkapı Palace, is Istanbul's most magnificent, a perfect example of Turkish rococo architecture, every surface elaborately decorated in rich golds, greens and reds.

Public fountains were a precious source of free, pure water in Ottoman times

Ottoman institutions These mosques lay at the centre of huge religious, educational and philanthropic foundations called *külliyes*, consisting of *madrasas* (theological schools), *mekteps* (primary schools), a *darüşşifa* (hospital), a *han* (caravanserai), and *imaret* (public kitchen), where travellers were given free food and lodging for three days after their arrival in the city, and which also distributed food to the poor of the district. The *hans*, built round a courtyard like most Ottoman buildings, provided all the services necessary to travelling merchants, even blacksmiths, and they were the key to Istanbul's thriving commerce during Ottoman times. Recently, some of these remarkably advanced Ottoman institutions have been restored, to serve again as libraries, student halls of residence and clinics.

Two other notable Ottoman foundations were the *hamam* or public baths, over 100 of which still function today, and the *çeşme* or public fountains, more than 700 of which are still standing. In Ottoman times attendants would stand at these fountains handing out cups of clean drinking water free of charge to passers-by.

The typical Ottoman mosque has a large central dome with cascades of smaller domes clustered around it, offset by the tall thin minarets. The basilica of **Haghia Sophia** (see pages 52–3) is thought to have provided the inspiration for the dome, but the other elements are original to the Ottoman style.

Süleyman's patronage The arts flourished under Süleyman the Magnificent, and the hallmark of this period was its scrupulous attention to and delight in detail. This is clearly evident in superbly illustrated and decorated copies of the Koran, as well as in ceramics, textiles and paintings. Ottoman rulers such as Süleyman were not only connoisseurs and patrons of bookbinding, calligraphy and illumination, but were also themselves prolific authors, especially of poetry. The art of calligraphy was highly esteemed, and its techniques were applied both to books and to the design of monumental inscriptions for mosques in Istanbul. Calligraphy even appeared on garments, such as the talismanic shirts, decorated with victorious verses

64

Sinan, the greatest and most prolific of all Ottoman architects, built an astonishing 81 large mosques, 50 smaller ones, 55 *madrasas*, 19 mausoleums, 15 public kitchens, 3 hospitals, 6 aqueducts, 32 palaces, 22 public baths and 2 bridges. No fewer than 84 of his buildings remain standing in Istanbul. His achievement is all the more remarkable in view of the fact that he did not build his first mosque until he was 50; he completed his masterpiece, the Selimiye Mosque at Edirne, at the age of 85.

65

Sultanahmet Camii, or the Blue Mosque, built in the early 17th century for Sultan Ahmet I and one of the most beautiful of Istanbul's imperial mosques

The courtyard of Sokullu Mehmet Paşa Camii, built by Sinan for one of the greatest Grand Viziers

from the Koran, which were worn for protection on the battlefield. All court costumes were elaborately decorated with leaf and flower patterns, with such lavish use of gold and silver thread and costly materials and jewels (Süleyman's parade helmet and mace were encrusted with turquoises, rubies and gold) that the Habsburg ambassador to the Sultan's court was spellbound: '...everywhere the brilliance of gold, silver, purple, and satin... No mere words could give an adequate idea of the novelty of the sight.'

Sinan The name of a single architect, Sinan, is virtually synonymous with the architecture of the Ottoman era. A protégé of Süleyman, he was born to Christian parents in Kayseri, Cappadocia, and was recruited into the Sultan's service at the age of 20. Having served in the Janissaries as a military engineer, he was promoted in his late forties to the position of Chief of the Imperial Architects. By the time of his death in 1588, at the age of 100, he had changed the skyline of Istanbul forever. This contemporary of Michelangelo and Leonardo da Vinci remains little-known in the West, perhaps because of western difficulty in appreciating non-figurative art.

Istanbul mosques

The sumptuous Süleymaniye Camii, built by the great architect Sinan as a tribute to his patron Süleyman the Magnificent

Ottoman climax
The Süleymaniye is the most important building in Istanbul. Tucked into the walled garden behind the Süleymaniye are the impressive octagonal *türbes* (tombs) of Süleyman and his wife Roxelana ('the Russian'), decorated inside with extremely fine Iznik tiles, in far greater numbers than in the whole vast space of the mosque itself. Sinan's own *türbe* stands a short distance to the northeast of the complex, just past the caravanserai.

▶▶ **Sokullu Mehmet Paşa Camii**   46C1
Sehit Mehmet Paşa Yokusu, Sultanahmet
This lovely mosque lies down a steep hill below the Blue Mosque, on the way to Küçük Aya Sofya. A minor masterpiece, it was built by Sinan for Sokullu Mehmet, one of the greatest Grand Viziers of the Ottoman Empire. The exterior courtyard, with its little domed roofs round the sides, is particularly charming; it still houses a Koranic school. Inside, there are some splendid tile panels, especially round the prayer niche. The square of black stone set above the entrance is from the Kaaba in Mecca (see pages 54–5).

▶▶▶ **Süleymaniye Camii**   46C2
Hesapçeşme Caddesi, Beyazit
Universally considered the finest and most sumptuous of Istanbul's imperial mosques, the Süleymaniye was built by the great architect Sinan (see page 65) as a tribute to his patron master, Sultan Süleyman the Magnificent. Second in size only to the **Fatih** complex (see page 63), it is the largest of Sinan's many mosques in Istanbul, and took only seven years to complete, from 1550 to 1557. One of the distinctive features of the exterior is Sinan's method of disguising the enormous buttresses needed to support the four central piers of the dome: incorporating them into the walls as far as possible, he camouflaged the remaining projections by building double galleries with arcades of columns between them.

As you enter the vast walled outer courtyard, you cannot fail to be impressed by its sheer scale and power. The terrace to the north has a fine view over the rooftops to the Golden Horn. The inner courtyard is ringed by a porticoed colonnade with columns of porphyry, marble and granite, while a minaret stands at each of the four corners.

The scale of the interior is overwhelming. There are no galleries or aisles, and colossal porphyry columns support the arches and dome. The powerful austerity of the vast space is relieved by splashes of colour from the stained-glass windows, and from a few panels of Iznik tiles patterned with leaf and flower motifs in turquoise, dark blue and red, the earliest known examples of their type (see page 61).

▶▶ Sultanahmet Camii (Blue Mosque)　　46C1

Mimar Mehmet Ağa Caddesi, Sultanahmet
Popularly known as the Blue Mosque from the predominant colour of its interior decoration, Istanbul's chief mosque competes with the Süleymaniye for the title of the most beautiful imperial mosque in the city. Built for Sultan Ahmet I by the architect Mehmet Ağa between 1609 and 1616, it is the only mosque in Istanbul to have six minarets. Its position close to the Topkapı Palace ensured that it was used by sultans for the following 250 years, with splendid imperial processions from the palace to the mosque.

Tourists enter through the side door facing Aya Sofya and are restricted to the back half of the mosque. The finest feature of the interior is the tilework on the lower walls and galleries: over 20,000 tiles in all, of the best Iznik workmanship, decorated with rose, tulip, lily and carnation motifs, mainly in blues and greens. Light floods in through the 260 windows with their reproduction stained glass.

▨ Yeni Cami (New Mosque)　　46C2

Eminönü Meydanı
Dubbed 'new' because it is a mere 300 years old, this Ottoman mosque is notable mainly for its prominent setting looking out over the Golden Horn. The courtyard has a lovely ablution fountain (*şadirvan*). The interior walls are decorated with 17th-century tiles in shades of blue, but the overall effect is rather sombre, not least because of the accumulated filth on the windows from exhaust fumes and smoke.

Egyptian Spice Bazaar
When you visit Yeni Cami and Rüstem Paşa Camii, take a little time to stroll through the single covered passageway of the Mısır Çarşısı, the Egyptian Spice Bazaar. This is a delicious hubbub of crowds and aromas, where herbs, nuts and spices are on sale, as well as Turkish delight in all shapes and sizes. The courtyard beside it is a market selling animals, from monkeys to parrots, as well as garden and house plants. Look out for the tiled staircase at the bazaar entrance; this leads up to the famous Greek Pandeli restaurant in the vaulted rooms above the gateway, a good place to stop for lunch.

67

The tranquil interior of Sokullu Mehmet Paşa Camii, one of Sinan's minor masterpieces

Walk Around the Aqueduct of Valens

Starting at the imposing Aqueduct of Valens, this walk leads through narrow streets with ramshackle wooden Ottoman houses and early churches turned mosques, to end with a stroll along the shoreline of the Golden Horn (see Central Istanbul map on pages 46–7). Covering a total distance of 2.5km, the basic walk will take at least 2 hours. It can easily be expanded by an hour or more by continuing northwards along the shoreline of the Golden Horn, past the church of St Stephen of the Bulgars to the Eyüp Mosque complex; if you still have the energy you could carry on through the Eyüp cemetery to reach Pierre Loti's Café, with its panoramic views back over the Golden Horn and the Istanbul skyline. This would make an 8km walk, ending with a steep 20-minute ascent through the graveyard.

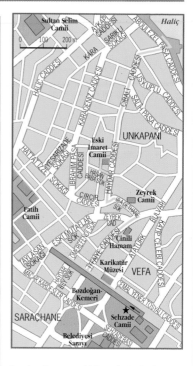

Take a taxi to the **Aqueduct of Valens** (Turkish Bozdoğan-Kemeri), the colossal two-tier structure linking Istanbul's third and fourth hills, which still runs for over 650m of its original one-kilometre length. Its highest point today straddles **Atatürk Bulvarı**.

Stairs at either end climb to the top, where there is no parapet. Begun by Constantine the Great and completed

The colossal arches of the Roman aqueduct dwarf modern traffic

by the Emperor Valens in 378, the aqueduct channelled water to the Byzantine palace. Restored by both the Byzantines and the Ottomans, it remained in use until the late 19th century, when it was replaced by the present water system.

At the foot of the aqueduct, housed in a 16th-century *medrasa* (theological college) with a pretty courtyard garden, is the **Karikatür Muzesi** (open daily, 9–6), with a display of cartoons that changes weekly and gives an intriguing insight into the Turkish sense of humour.

Now walk along the foot of the aqueduct to **Itfaiye Caddesi**. Turn down this street to investigate the **Çinili Hamam** (Tiled Baths), built by Sinan in 1545 and probably the prettiest and most intimate of the Turkish baths that welcome foreigners.

Continuing downhill, turn left to **Zeyrek Camii**, originally the 12th-century Byzantine Church of the Pantocrator, which is kept locked except at prayer times. Two of the last three Byzantine emperors are buried here.

Carry on through the steep cobbled streets of **Zeyrek**, a little-explored district of Istanbul whose charm lies principally in its dilapidated wooden houses, which give an idea of what the city would have looked like in Ottoman times.

Head now towards **Haydar Caddesi**, forking left into **Hasan Baba Sokağı**, then right into **Küçük Mektep Sokağı**, at the end of which stands **Eski Imaret Camii**, its 12-sided dome belying its origins as a 12th-century church. It has one of the most important and interesting exteriors of any Byzantine church in the city, with brickwork designs including rose medallions, swastikas and Greek keys.

From the little square in front of the church there is a fine view across to the Golden Horn. Head down to the shoreline, turning left into the recently landscaped parkland that now runs the whole length of this western side of the Golden Horn.

Masonry built to last

Istanbul museums

▶▶ Arkeoloji Müzesi (Archaeological Museum)   *46C2*

Sultanahmet

The entrance to this complex of museums – it also houses the **Eski Şark Eserleri Müzesi** (Museum of the Ancient Orient) – lies just past Haghia Eirene. The portal of the Museum of the Ancient Orient is flanked by a pair of Hittite lions. Inside are fascinating relics of the ancient Egyptian, Sumerian, Babylonian, Hittite, Urartian and Assyrian cultures. Among the most memorable are a series of Babylonian blue and yellow tile panels of lions, and a number of colossal Hittite sculptures in black basalt. Out in the courtyard in front of the Archaeological Museum are the staggering purple porphyry sarcophagi of various Byzantine emperors. Inside, this museum is bewilderingly huge, and a full visit would take many hours. If pressed for time concentrate on the ground floor, where an astonishing display of Roman and Greek sculpture includes the head of Alexander the Great and the famous Alexander Sarcophagus. The museums are open daily except Mondays 9:30–5.

▶▶▶ Aya Sofya Müzesi   *46C1*

See pages 52–3.

▶ Halı Müzesi (Turkish Carpet Museum)   *46C1*

Sultanahmet

The museum is housed in huge vaulted rooms that once served as storerooms and elephant stables, in the northeast corner of the Blue Mosque. It is open daily except Sundays and Mondays 9–4.

▶▶▶ Kariye Müzesi   *46A3*

See pages 58–9.

▶ Mosaik Müzesi (Mosaic Museum)   *46C1*

Sultanahmet

Tucked between the Blue Mosque and the new Arasta Bazaar, this small museum shelters the remains of the Great Palace of the Byzantine Emperors, consisting largely of 6th-century mosaics of great vivacity. It is open daily except Tuesdays 9:30–5.

▶ Sadberk Hanım Müzesi   *80B5*

Piyasa Caddesi, Büyükdere

Housed in a late 19th-century *yalı* (summer house) on the European shore between Büyükdere and Sarıyer, this museum boasts a fine collection of Turkish and foreign antiquities. It is open daily except Wednesdays 10–5.

▶▶▶ Topkapı Müzesi   *47D2*

See pages 76–7.

▶▶ Türk-Islam Eserleri Müzesi (Museum of Turkish and Islamic Art)   *46C1*

At Meydanı, Sultanahmet

Formerly housed in the Süleymaniye, this museum has now moved to the 16th-century palace of Ibrahim Paşa,

A statue from the Arkeoloji Müzesi

Fishy reservoir
In the century that followed the Ottoman conquest, the whereabouts of the city's largest underground water cistern, built in the mid 6th century and now known as Yerebetan Müzesi, were unaccountably forgotten. It was the detective work of an enterprising French 16th-century archaeologist, who discovered that people in the neighbourhood were drawing water from holes in their basement floors, and sometimes even catching fish, that brought it to light again.

A traditional rug displayed in the Türk-Islam Eserleri Müzesi

the splendid building which occupies most of the Hippodrome frontage, directly opposite the Blue Mosque. This magnificent palace, the largest private residence ever built in the Ottoman Empire, makes an excellent setting for a fine collection of carpets, illuminated copies of the Koran, wood-carvings, ceramics and glassware. There is also an impressive display of the tents and furniture used by the Yürük people, who are Anatolian nomads. It is open daily except Mondays 10–5.

A reclining figure from the Arkeoloji Müzesi

▶▶ **Yerebatan Müzesi**
(Underground Museum) 46C1
Yerebatan Caddesi, Sultanahmet
This remarkable underground cistern, by far the largest of all those left by the Byzantines, is guaranteed to take your breath away. Built by the Emperor Justinian in the mid 6th century and known as the Basilica Cistern, it was used throughout the Byzantine period to supply water to the palace, its gardens and all surrounding buildings. The insignificant entrance at ground level gives no clue to the splendour that lies below. Steps lead down to slippery walkways and operatic music complements the drama of the setting. With a total of 336 columns, the cistern is the same width as Aya Sofya.
It is open daily 9–5.

Istanbul palaces

The sumptuous interior of Beylerbeyi Sarayı

▶ Aynalı Kavak Kasrı (Pavilion of the Mirroring Poplars)   *46B3*

Kasımpaşa-Hasköy Yolu, Hasköy
A lovely example of late Ottoman architecture, noted for its stained glass windows, this small mid-19th-century palace is currently closed for repairs (1994).

▶▶ Beylerbeyi Sarayı (Beylerbey Palace)   *80B2*

Asian Bosphorus
Set in beautiful gardens next to the old Bosphorus Bridge, Beylerbey (meaning 'Lord of lords'), is the biggest and most impressive palace on the Asian Bosphorus. The present 19th-century building is divided into the *selamlık* (male reception areas) and the harem, the former being magnificently decorated with treasures from all over the world. It is open to the public daily except Mondays and Thursdays 9:30–4. The best way to reach it is to take a ferry to Üsküdar, then taxi.

▶▶▶ Dolmabahçe Sarayı   *47D3*

Dolmabahçe Caddesi, Beşiktaş
This immensely impressive and beautiful building, with its 600m-long white marble façade overlooking the Bosphorus near the Beşiktaş landing stage, became the residence of the sultans on its completion in 1853, replacing the hilltop Topkapı Palace.

Visits are by guided tour only and there is a daily limit of 1,500 visitors, after which the palace closes. Normal hours are 9–3 except Mondays and Thursdays. Some two-thirds of the enormous interior is taken up by the harem; the lavish furnishings, the most fabulous of any palace in Turkey, are reminiscent of Versailles. In the attractive gardens are a café, souvenir shop and bird pavilion, and near by stands a matching white marble waterfront mosque for the private use of the palace.

▶▶ **Ibrahim Paşa Sarayı**   46C1
See page 71.

▶ ░░░ **Ihlamur Kasrı (Linden Pavilion)**   80A2
Ihlamur Teşvikiye Yolu, Teşvikiye
This attractive 19th-century palace in the hills above
Beşiktaş consists of two pavilions, the **Maiyet Köşkü** (for
the sultan's harem) and the **Merasim Köşkü** (for his
guests). Excellently restored, it is now open daily except
Mondays and Thursdays 9–4.

▶ ░░░ **Küçüksü Kasrı (Little Waters Pavilion)**   80C3
Küçüksü Caddesi, Göksu
This tiny but exquisite rococo palace, (1856), stands on
the Asian Bosphorus at the estuary of two rivers known
as the **Sweet Waters of Asia**. It was used as a holiday
retreat by the Ottoman sultans, and is still popular today.
It is open daily except Mondays and Thursdays 9–4.

▶ ░░░ **Tekfur Sarayı**
(Palace of the Porphyrogenitus)   46A3
Şişhane Caddesi, Avçı Bey
Virtually all that remains of this 10th-century palace built
by Constantine Porphyrogenitus, one of the few to survive from the Byzantine era, is the façade, in three-storey
arches of red brick and multicoloured marble. There is no
ticket kiosk, but the owner of the nearby hut will expect a
small gratuity.

▶▶▶ **Topkapı Sarayı**   47D2
See pages 76–7.

▶ ░░░ **Yıldız Sarayı**   80B2
Yıldız Caddesi, Yıldız
Set in Istanbul's loveliest park, the pavilions and mosque
of **Yıldız Palace** enjoy superb panoramas over the
Bosphorus. The lavishly decorated main pavilion, the **Şale
Köşk**, has some 50 rooms, and was used by visiting roy-
alty. It is open to the public daily except Mondays and
Thursdays 9:30–4. Others are now cafés.

*The white marble
façade of
Dolmabahçe Sarayı,
residence of the sul-
tans from the mid-
19th century, viewed
from the waters of
the Bosphorus*

*The Şale Köşk is the
largest and grandest
of the pavilions of
Yildiz Sarayı, with
some 50 magnificently
decorated rooms*

The Turkish bath

■ No visit to Turkey is complete without the experience of a Turkish bath. Set aside all notions of prudery and take the plunge, and you will remember this as one of the highpoints of your visit, savouring that feeling of supreme cleanliness and relaxation that is so different from the experience of a western bath or shower. Indeed, western baths are regarded as most unhygienic by Muslims, who cannot understand why we should want to sit and wash in our own dirt (hence the absence of plugs in washbasins; it is always considered best to wash under running water)......■

74

Ever popular
There are still over 100 functioning *hamams* in Istanbul. These baths were founded by the Ottomans as a public utility, with their revenues used to support other foundations, such as schools and hospitals. Because of water shortages, the *hamams* remain as popular among Istanbul's poor as they were in Ottoman times.

Sybaritic pleasures in the hot steam room

The best time to visit a Turkish bath is at the end of a long and dusty day's sightseeing or shopping, and the best place to visit one is Istanbul. Here there are several baths (see side panel) geared to the requirements of foreigners, where English is spoken, and where you will probably be reassured by the presence of other foreign bathers.

The layout The interior design of a Turkish bath is roughly the same as an ancient Roman bath, with three distinct areas: the *camekan* (Roman *apoditarium*) is the reception and changing room, where you undress and leave your clothes and sip tea afterwards; the *soğukluk* (Roman *tepidarium*) is like a passageway between the *camekan* and the steam room, and it is where the lavatories are generally sited; and the *hararet* (Roman *calidarium*) is the hot steam room, where the massaging and actual washing

take place. The *hararet* is usually the most elaborate and beautiful chamber of all, with marble-clad walls and marble basins with brass taps round the sides. In the centre is a large marble slab, heated by a wood fire below in the furnace room. This is the so-called belly-stone, where you lie to sweat, relax and be massaged, all the while gazing up at the shafts of patterned light that pour through the domed ceiling.

Prices for a *kese* massage (during which you are rubbed with a camel-hair glove), face massage and foot massage are displayed in the *camekan*. If you are only going to make one visit have the lot, as the total cost still amounts to very little.

The ritual Mixed bathing is not permitted except in the *hamams* of tourist hotels; indeed, the penalty for a man discovered entering the women's baths used to be death. On undressing, both sexes are given wooden clogs in which to clip-clop along into the *hararet*, and a towel for drying off later. In men's baths, where modesty is strictly observed, a cotton sarong called a *peştamal* is issued for wrapping tightly round the waist, an impediment which makes thorough washing a bit tricky.

Women's baths are altogether more relaxed, with nakedness or knickers adopted according to choice, and children scampering about too. The masseuses are homely and jolly, full of songs and gossip, bosoms flying wildly as they scrape off the layers of grime and lather you all over into a soapy bubbling heap like a baby. You will emerge feeling you have shed 10 years' worth of ingrained dirt. Allow at least an hour for the whole thing.

The Turkish bath: the perfect marriage of the need for cleanliness (required by Koranic law) and the desire for sensual indulgence

Best for foreigners
The best *hamams* for foreign visitors to try in Istanbul are the Cağaloğlu and the Çemberlitaş, both near the Grand Bazaar, or the smaller Çinili Hamam, near the Aqueduct of Valens. They offer separate facilities for men and women, and function between 8am and 8pm daily. Internally, all three are of architectural interest, and they retain their original marble basins. Their prices, though very low by western standards, are too high for most Turks.

Harem etiquette

The harem system had its origins in a practice adopted by soldiers who were to be away from home for long periods, who had their women locked up and guarded by eunuchs. From this beginning, a whole complex hierarchy evolved, governed by strict rules. Each night, for example, the lucky lady selected by the sultan as his companion in the imperial bedchamber was expected to kiss the imperial bedclothes at the foot of the bed, before wriggling her way under them to encounter the waiting sultan. No Turkish woman is ever thought to have been thus favoured – only thousands of foreigners.

The Baghdad Köşk in the Fourth Court, built by Murat IV in 1638 in honour of his capture of that city

Acropolis setting

Built on the site of the acropolis, or citadel, of ancient Byzantium by Mehmet the Conqueror in about 1460, the Topkapı was laid out on the highest ground and surrounded by gardens stretching down to the seashore. Despite the ravages of fires and earthquakes, the three inner courtyards remain largely as they were in the 15th and 16th centuries.

► ► ► **Topkapı Sarayı (Topkapı Palace)**   *47D2*
Sultanahmet

If you have time to see only one thing in Istanbul, it should be the Topkapı. Ideally you should spend the whole day here, breaking for lunch at the excellent restaurant in the furthest court, with its stunning views over the Bosphorus towards Üsküdar. The Topkapı has an amazing capacity to absorb swarms of people, and its setting on the headland of old Stamboul, in the city centre but away from all the noise and traffic, makes it a relaxing place to visit. It is open to the public daily except Tuesdays 9:30–5.

The buildings This vast palace was the residence of the Ottoman sultans from the 15th to the 19th centuries; it has been a museum since 1924, displaying a breathtaking collection of porcelain, jewels, calligraphy, weapons and other valuables belonging to the Ottoman Court. The Topkapı was also the seat of government, housing institutions such as the judicial council, known as the *divan*, in its different courtyards. The First Court (sometimes called the Court of the Janissaries) was the palace service area, containing dormitories for guards and servants, storage areas, the state mint, an arsenal, a bakery and a hospital. It now contains the ticket kiosk. The Second Court housed the *divan*, flanked by kitchens and stables. The Third Court was devoted to the palace school, where young men (often Christians) from all over the empire were trained for the civil service and for the Janissaries. Finally, the Fourth Court, with its gardens and pavilions, was reserved for members of the sultan's household. The main residential quarters, including the harem, occupied the whole of one side of the first three courts.

The harem The harem was officially disbanded in 1909, and some of its rooms were opened to visitors in 1960. It has a separate ticket kiosk in the Second Court, and may only be visited in guided tours of up to 60 people, on a first-come, first-served basis. Queues can be long in high season. Only some 20 rooms out of the total labyrinth of about 300 are on public view, and many of these are surprisingly small. Life in the harem was presided over by the Valide Sultan, the sultan's mother, whose apartments lay in the centre, well placed for her customary domination and manipulation. The harem was guarded by the Black Eunuchs, who had their quarters alongside. The White Eunuchs, mainly Caucasians, were not allowed in the harem but served in the men's reception area, while a third group of special servants, the Halberdiers-with-Tresses, acted as guards and porters. Once a month they were permitted to enter the harem carrying firewood, their gaze restricted by their extraordinarily high collars flanked by wool tresses.

The exhibits The museum proper begins in the Second Court, which contains collections of porcelain – including one of the world's richest collections of Chinese porcelain – clocks and arms and armour. In the Third Court is the world-famous Treasury, which along with the Harem is the most popular – and therefore the most crowded – part of the palace. Here the most celebrated exhibits are the Topkapı dagger, with three colossal emeralds, the Spoonmaker's diamond, the fifth largest in the world, and jewel-encrusted thrones. At the entrance to the Fourth Court, do not miss the ever-changing collection of Turkish and Persian miniatures.

A fine example of the calligrapher's art

The gardens are a haven of peace, with panoramic views

Istanbul parks and City Walls

A bizarre part-Byzantine and part-Turkish construction, Yedikule has seven towers, four of which are built into the 5th-century walls

The gardens of the imperial Dolmabahçe Palace offer restful views over the Bosphorus

►► City Walls   46A1–B3

These imposing walls, built by the Emperor Theodosius in the 5th century, when they were held to be the strongest in Christendom, run from the Sea of Marmara over the hills to the Golden Horn, enclosing the city of Byzantium. For added protection there was a deep moat, 20m wide, which was flooded at times of attack. The original structure comprised an inner and outer wall; what remains today is mostly the inner wall and its towers.

The walls begin at the Sea of Marmara with the 13m high Marble Tower – once a prison – standing on a little promontory. Further inland, some 600m distant, stands Yedikule, the Castle of Seven Towers.

Yedikule►► This curious structure built on to the inside of the wall by the **Golden Gate**, is a hotchpotch of Byzantine and Turkish styles, with four of its towers set in the Theodosian wall itself, and three extra towers built inside by Mehmet the Conqueror. It is open today as a museum (9:30–4:30 except Mondays). In Ottoman times it served as a prison, and instruments of torture feature large among the exhibits. The Golden Gate itself was originally a free-standing Roman triumphal arch, later bricked up when the arch was incorporated into the walls.

It is possible to walk along the top of the walls from Yedikule to **Belgrad Kapısı**, passing 11 towers, and on to **Silivri Kapısı**, past another 13 towers. After this the walls deteriorate until you reach **Edirne Kapısı**, the highest point in the old city, just beside the **Mihrimah Sultan Camii** (see page 63). From here you can walk inside the walls to the impressive façade of the **Tekfur Sarayı** (see page 73), and on down the hill past the **Ivaz Effendi Mosque** into the area that was once the **Palace of Blachernae**. Now largely reconstructed, this final section before the Golden Horn has no moat, but is much thicker, and shelters clusters of picturesque if slightly squalid houses.

► **Emirgan Parkı**   *80B4*

12.5km north of the city centre on the European side
Famous for its tulip gardens, this lovely park overlooking the Bosphorus has three delightful café pavilions, all restored by the Turkish Automobile and Touring Club. The gardens are at their best during the annual Tulip Festival in April.

Gülhane Parkı   *46C2*

Sultanahmet
This is a pleasant place to stroll after a visit to the Topkapı and the Archaeological Museums, with fine views over the headland of Saray Burnu. Istanbul's modest zoo is based here; the aquarium is worth visiting for its setting in a Roman cistern.

► **Haliç (Golden Horn)**   *46B3*

The European shoreline of the Golden Horn, recently transformed under Mayor Bedrettin Dalan into pleasant parkland with lots of children's playgrounds, makes a very enjoyable stroll away from the busy streets of central Istanbul, especially at sunset.

►► **Yıldız Parkı**   *47E3*

Yıldız
Set on the European shoreline of the Bosphorus just north of the new luxury Çirağan Kempinski Hotel, this park is regarded by most connoisseurs as the most beautiful park in Istanbul. Within it lie the imperial kiosks – in the old Ottoman style – and gardens of the **Yıldız Palace** (see page 73).

UNESCO protection
There were 10 gates in the original 5th-century walls, and although parts of the walls have been knocked down to make way for railways and new highways, nearly all the ancient gates are still in use. UNESCO has designated the land walls and the area they enclose as one of the cultural heritage sites of the world.

Rampart walk
The Byzantine walls that protected the city for over a thousand years make an interesting walk. As they are over 6km long, the walk takes three to four hours in all. If you are short of time, the stretches on which to concentrate are around Yedikule and the Tekfur Sarayı.

ISTANBUL

Belgrat Ormanı

Bahçeköy
Kısırmandıra

ALTIN KUM

RUMELİ
KAVAĞI

Anadolu
Kavağı
Kalesi

ANADOLU
KAVAĞI

SARIYER

KEMERBUGAZ

Sadberk
Hanım
Müzesi

BÜYÜKDERE

ORTAÇEŞME

Boğaziçi

KİREÇBURNU

YALIKÖY

Seyhan

TARABYA

BEYKOZ

Fatih
Ormanı

YENİKÖY

PAŞABAHÇE

İSTİNYE

Çubuklu   Deresi

Maslak
Kasırları

Emirgân
Parkı

EMİRGAN

ÇUBUKLU

Hadiv Kasrı
Sarayı

AYAZAĞA

MASLAK

KANLICA

BALTA LİMANI

FATIH SULTAN
MEHMET KÖPRÜSÜ

FATİH SULTAN MEHMET KÖPRÜSÜ ÇEVRE YOLU

Kağıthane Deresi

SEYRANTEPE

Rumeli
Hisarı

Anadolu
Hisarı

Boğaziçi
Üniversitesi

Göksu Deresi

Aşiyan
Müzesi

Küçüksu
Kasrı

BEBEK

KÜÇÜKSU

KANDİLLİ

Küçüksu   Deresi

KAĞITHANE

ARNAVUTKÖY

Kırmızı
Yalı

KURUÇEŞME

VANİKÖY

BOĞAZİÇİ KÖPRÜSÜ ÇEVRE YOLU

ŞİŞLİ

ORTAKÖY

KULELİ

Yıldız Sarayı
Şale Köşkü

Yıldız
Parkı

BOĞAZİÇİ
KÖPRÜSÜ

CENGELKÖY

İhlamur
Kasrı

Ortaköy
Camii

BEYLERBEYİ

Barbaros
Hayreddin
Vapur İskelesi

★ BEŞİKTAŞ

Beşiktaş
Vapur İskelesi

Beylerbeyi
Sarayı

BOĞAZİÇİ KÖPRÜSÜ ÇEVRE YOLU

Büyük
Çamlıca
Tepesi

UMRANİYE

TAKSİM

Dolmabahçe
Sarayı

KUZGUNÇUK

Kabataş
Vapur
İskelesi

Boğaziçi

Mihrimah
Camii

ANADOLU OTO
YOLU

BEYOĞLU

Haliç

ÜSKÜDAR

Kız
Kulesi

Karaca
Ahmet
Mezarlığı

★ GALATA
KÖPRÜSÜ

HAREM

EMİNÖNÜ

ISTANBUL

Topkapı
Sarayı

Selimiye
Kışlası

HAYDARPAŞA

Kurbağalı   Dere

Marmara Denizi

KADIKÖY

Kadıköy Vapur
İskelesi

0   1   2   3 km

A   B   C

6

5

4

3

2

1

Drive and cruise

Along the Asian Bosphorus and Üsküdar

This 5–6 hour, 65km excursion follows the Asian shore of the Bosphorus, visiting the splendid waterfront palaces on the way to the northernmost point at Anadolu Kavağı. The return journey is by ferry, stopping to explore the Asian district of Üsküdar. Organised Bosphorus cruise boats are so speedy that they are only a good idea if you are very short of time. Either way, be sure to take a pair of binoculars, the better to appreciate the magnificent buildings lining the shore.

Boats crowd the shore at Anadolu Kavaği

Take a taxi out through Beyoğlu on the Ankara road, then across the elegant old Bosphorus suspension bridge. The first stop is the **Beylerbeyi Palace**, just beside the Bosphorus bridge, built in 1865 by Sultan Abdulaziz (see pages 72–3). It is open 9:30–4, except Mondays and Thursdays, by guided tour only. You can take tea in the gardens.

Continuing north through Cengelköy, the next stop is at **Kırmızı Yalı**, the best preserved of all the seaside mansions, built of wood and painted the traditional ox blood colour. The interior cannot be visited.

Carry on north to **Küçüksu Kasrı** (open 9–4 except Mondays and Thursdays), another charming imperial pleasure palace (see pages 72–3). A short walk above it is the ruined castle of **Anadolu Hisarı**. From here boats can be hired, (with owner), to explore the Bosphorus at your leisure.

The drive north leads on through **Kanlıca**, famous for its yogurt, before reaching **Anadolu Kavağı**, an attractive town with typical wooden balconied houses lining the shore and a huge selection of fish restaurants. To build up your appetite, climb up to the Genoese castle for views of the **Clashing Rocks** that Jason and the Argonauts had to navigate in their quest for the Golden Fleece.

After lunch, catch a ferry down the length of the Bosphorus, disembarking at Üsküdar (formerly Scutari).

Stroll round the harbour to visit the little **Mihrimah Camii** built by Sinan in 1547 (see pages 64–5), then take a taxi to the **Selimiye Barracks**, housing the colossal building which was Florence Nightingale's hospital, now a school. Continue by taxi to the **Karaca Ahmet Mezarlığı**, the largest Muslim cemetery in the world and a wonderfully wild, overgrown place. From here, you could take the taxi up to the pleasant café and tea house on **Büyük Çamlıca**, the highest point in the area, from where there are unforgettable views over the Stamboul skyline.

Finally, catch the ferry back from Üsküdar to Eminönü, passing close to **Kız Kulesi**, the Maiden's Tower, a 12th-century custom house overlooking the harbour.

Traditional houses line the Bosphorus seafront

Capital of the Ottoman Empire in the 14th century, Bursa has much of historic interest to offer, as well as its famous spa waters

Old-fashioned transport
One of the principal charms of Büyükada and Heybeliada lies in the absence of cars. Apart from a few bicycles, the chief form of local transport is the phaeton, a horse-drawn carriage. Large numbers of colourful phaetons wait in a special parking area close to the ferry terminus, and set rates are offered for long and short tours of the islands. Equipped with roofs that fold back during fine weather, they also boast large cellophane side flaps that flop down during showers. Tinkling bells and clip-clopping hooves make a welcome change from the blare of horns and revving of engines.

►► **Bursa** *86C1*

Much of this ancient spa's popular prestige derives from the fact that it became the first Ottoman capital in 1326. In recent years Bursa has developed as a significant centre for the manufacture of silk and cotton. Now swallowed up among the dusty modern developments of the city some three hours' drive from Istanbul, including the car ferry crossing to Yalova, it makes a very long day trip from Istanbul. If you want to enjoy the spa waters you should spend a night here, as the better hotels all have private thermal baths. Tour agencies offer organised tours of the main sights, which are scattered over quite a long distance.

Bedesten► This maze of little streets right in the city centre, beside the squat brick minarets of the **Ulu Cami** (Great Mosque), is Bursa's covered market, where you can find local cotton goods. Look out too for **Koza Hanı,** the silk cocoon caravanserai, with shops selling beautiful silks and brocades.

Cekirge► The spas and best hotels are concentrated in this pleasant suburb, which still has two public baths (14th-century and 16th-century), open to male visitors.

Muradiye complex ► Built in the reign of Murat II (1421–51), this grouping of mosque, *medrasa* (theological school), *imaret* (soup kitchen) and a very attractive cemetery lies west of the city centre.

Tophane Park► The citadel area above Ulu Cami still has fragments of the Byzantine and Ottoman city walls, as well as the tombs of Osman Ghazi, founder of the Ottoman dynasty, and his son. There are good views from the café at the summit.

Uludağ► The ancient Mount Olympos of Mysia, Uludağ rises 2,543m above Bursa, 36km away, and is Turkey's premier ski resort. It can be reached by road (one hour), or cable car (30 minutes). Snow covers the summit from December to May; in summer it is a popular spot for picnics and walks.

Yeşil Cami and Yeşil Türbe▶▶ Bursa's two principal monuments face each other across a square on a hillside to the east of the city. The mosque, Yeşil Cami, is considered to be one of the finest examples of early Ottoman architecture. Opposite it is Yeşil Türbe, the tomb of Sultan Mehmet I (died 1421). Bursa's loveliest building, it is covered inside with spectacular tilework.

▶ **Büyükadalar (Princes' Islands)**   86C1

These nine islands, of which only the main five are now inhabited, are popular today as a place of retreat from the noise and bustle of Istanbul. From Byzantine times onwards, the islands' convents and monasteries also served as places of exile for out-of-favour royals.

Büyükada, the main island and the most developed, is quite hilly with pine forests. A monastery still stands on each of its two principal hills. The island's old-fashioned charm is emphasised by its extraordinary variety of holiday homes built over the years by Istanbul's wealthy, each more imaginative than the last. The older ones are quite delightful, with elaborately carved balconies and ornate façades.

Heybeliada, the second largest island, is equally charming, but more intimate in feeling. In summer its beaches are crowded with holidaymakers.

Yassiada, one of the smallest islands, was bought by the British ambassador in 1857. The castle he built later became a prison for political detainees. Turkish Prime Minister Adnan Menderes was hanged here in 1961.

The islands are about 25km from Kabataş and the Galata Bridge. Ferries (several times daily) take about one hour each way; in summer, air-conditioned hovercrafts take just 30 minutes. There are also ferries between the four main islands – always be sure to check times at the terminus on the day.

Çanakkale (Dardanelles)   86A1

A frequent car ferry crosses these straits separating Europe from Asia. The town has quite a pretty seafront, with busy hotels and fish restaurants. The Archaeological Museum, open daily except Mondays 8:30–12:30 and 1:30–5, has fine displays including exquisite gold and jewellery from tumuli in the area.

Bursa lifestyle
'There are also no fewer than ninety-seven Buza-houses, which are not to be equalled in the world... In summer the Buza is cooled with ice like sherbet; the principal men of the town are not ashamed to enter these Buza houses, although an abundance of youths, dancers and singers, girt with Brussa girdles, here entice their lovers to ruin.'
Evliya Çelebi, 17th-century traveller.

A display of coffee pots in Bursa

83

A phaeton on car-free Büyükada

Swimming the Hellespont
After emulating Leander and swimming the Hellespont in 1810, Lord Byron observed: '... the immediate distance is not above a mile but the current renders it hazardous, so much so, that I doubt whether Leander's conjugal powers must not have been exhausted in his passage to Paradise.'

Drive **Belgrade Forest and the European Bosphorus**

Waterfront houses at Sarıyer

See map on page 80.

This 5-hour, 70km drive starts by heading straight out to the Belgrade Forest, 20km to the north of the city, before returning slowly along the European shore of the Bosphorus, taking in the splendid fortress of Rumeli Hisarı, to end with tea at the Yıldız Park.

Sarıyer's delightful quayside

Take the road from Besiktaş north to **Büyükdere**, then across to **Bahçeköy**, on the eastern edge of the forest. Originally the hunting ground of the Ottomans, this is the largest woodland near Istanbul and is very popular, especially at weekends. Its name derives from the Belgrade people settled here by Süleyman after his conquest of the city in 1521. Their job was to look after the reservoirs that supplied the city, and the remains of dams, water towers and aqueducts can still be seen here. The finest surviving aqueduct, past Pirgöz on the way to Kısırmandıra, is the **Uzun** or **Long Aqueduct**, 716m long and built by Sinan in 1564.

Now head for **Sarıyer**, a pretty town with a charming waterfront, a lively fish market and a few fish restaurants. A little further south is the **Sadberk Hanım Müzesi** (10–5 except Wednesdays), a 19th-century *yalı* on the Bosphorus with exceptional archaeological and ethnographic displays (see pages 70–1).

Follow the coast road south through **Tarabya**, a wealthy district famous for its fish restaurants and the Büyük Tarabya, reputed to be the best hotel

The Rumeli Hisarı fortifications

on the Bosphorus. Many of the mansions that line the shore here are summer residences for foreign embassies.

The next stop is the highlight of the European shoreline, **Rumeli Hisarı**, the fabulous fortress (open 9:30–5 except Mondays) which dominates the narrowest part of the Bosphorus, here just 500m wide. Built by Mehmet II in preparation for the siege of Constantinople, it was completed within an astonishing four months in 1452. From here there is a good view of the **Fatih Sultan Mehmet** bridge, built in 1988 and the third longest suspension bridge in the world.

Continuing south the road enters the sweeping bay of **Bebek**, once a pretty village, now a wealthy suburb with many magnificent mansions on the shore. On a hilltop above is the superb new **Bosphorus University**, the most prestigious in Turkey. The road continues through **Arnavutköy** and **Ortaköy**, suburbs on either side of the old Bosphorus bridge (1973) with lively street markets which have now become fashionable.

A fitting climax to this tour of the European shore would be a stroll round **Yıldız Park** (open 8:30–sunset), Istanbul's largest and loveliest park, taking tea at one of its beautifully restored kiosks or conservatories.

Exceptionally pretty Sarıyer

Istanbul environs

▶ **Edirne (Adrianople)** 86A2

For those approaching Turkey by road, an overnight stop in Edirne makes a very interesting introduction to the country: a typical Turkish town with a lively bazaar quarter and some superb mosques.

Selimiye Camii▶▶▶ Already 80 years old when he started work here, the great architect Sinan (see pages 52–3) was able to bring together his vast experience in Ottoman architecture to construct this colossal yet surprisingly graceful mosque, completed in 1575. He regarded it as his masterpiece. Its four minarets are the tallest in the world after those in Mecca, and the dome is bigger even than that of Aya Sofya in Istanbul (see pages 52–3). The mihrab and minbar have extremely elaborate geometric stonework, and the imperial lodge in the southwest corner is the finest in all Turkey.

Other mosques worth visiting are the **Muradiye Camii** (1435) and the **Üç Şerefeli Cami** (1447).

▶ **Gelibolu (Gallipoli)** 86A1

This slim peninsula on the northern side of the Dardanelles has now been designated a National Park. In 1915, Allied warships tried to force their way through the straits with a view to opening a supply line to Russia via the Black Sea. They were ill-prepared, however, for the strength and skill of the Turkish resistance, led by Lt Colonel Mustafa Kemal, later to become known as Atatürk. They were also exceptionally badly led by their own commanders. Half a million soldiers are estimated to have lost their lives in the Gallipoli campaign; ANZAC (Australia and New Zealand Army Corps) casualties were especially high. The various war memorials sit rather incongruously in this attractive landscape of green hills, pine forests and pretty beaches. Unless you have your

Unexciting Thrace
This rather flat nondescript area comprises the 3 per cent of Turkey that lies geographically within Europe, having borders with Greece and Bulgaria. Much of it was a military area until the late 1960s, but access is now freely permitted. The only major point of interest to visitors is the town of Edirne.

Istanbul environs

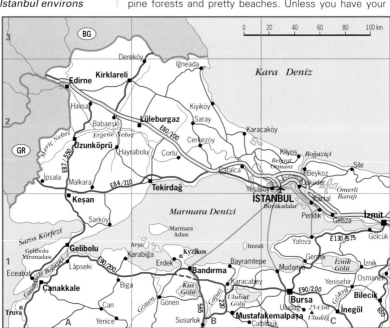

own transport, it is best to take an organised tour. Most last about four hours, starting from either Gelibolu or Çanakkale, on the other side of the straits.

► **Iznik (Nicaea)**   *86C1*

Once a great city, Iznik is today a mere shadow of its former self, shrunk within the mighty Byzantine double walls which defended it against many invading armies, and which are still remarkably well preserved. Iznik became the tile and ceramics centre of Turkey in the 16th century, when Selim the Grim sent 500 Persian potters and their families to settle here. The **Aya Sofya Museum** in the centre (open 9–12 and 1–5 daily), is all that remains of the famous Byzantine church where two important ecumenical councils took place, whose deliberations were central to the development of early Christianity.

► **Kilyos**   *86C2*

Sixteen kilometres north of Sarıyer, a Bosphorus suburb of Istanbul, Kilyos is the best and closest beach to Istanbul on the European shore of the Black Sea, with good hotels and restaurants.

► **Marmara Denizi (Sea of Marmara)**   *86B1*

This region offers pleasant if unexciting scenery; on the northern shore the only resort to consider is **Sarköy**, while on the southern shore the most attractive section is from the Erdek peninsula westwards. From **Erdek** itself, with its pretty cobbled esplanade, you can visit a small group of islands. **Avşa** is the best to visit, with good beaches and clear water. The largest, **Marmara**, has very few beaches and is a little bleak. East of Erdek the coastal developments are unsightly and the water polluted.

► **Şile**   *86C2*

A pretty beach resort on the Black Sea only hours from Üsküdar, Şile tends to be crowded at weekends and holidays. At other times it is a delightful place, with cliffs and white sandy beaches, a tiny island with a ruined Genoese castle, a striped lighthouse and a good range of hotels and restaurants.

The ruined Genoese castle at Şile

ANZAC Memorial
'Those heroes that shed their blood
And lost their lives...
You are now lying in the soil of a friendly country,
Therefore rest in peace.
There is no difference between the Johnnies
And the Mehmets to us where they lie side by side,
Here in this country of ours.
You, the mothers,
Who sent your sons from faraway countries
Wipe away your tears.
Your sons are now lying in our bosom
And are in peace.
After having lost their lives on this land they have
Become our sons as well.'
Kemal Atatürk, 1934

The Victory Beach Memorial, Gallipoli

Accommodation

Height of Luxury
The Çırağan-Palace Hotel: Kempinski is probably Istanbul's most luxurious, with prices to match. Gutted by fire in 1910, it remained a ruin until its recent conversion by the Forte group. The restored palace now houses a conference centre and restaurants, while accommodation is in a new building. The location – on the Bosphorus between Beşiktaş and Ortaköy and below Yıldız Park – is hard to equal.

Like other special licence and Touring Club hotels, the Yeşil Ev offers rooms furnished in Ottoman style

In the past, the majority of comfortable hotels in Istanbul were to be found in the Beyoğlu district, so that sightseeing always involved a taxi ride across the Galata Bridge to the old city of Stamboul. The recent policy of renovating old Ottoman houses and converting them into hotels means that you now also have the attractive option of staying in Stamboul, within walking distance of the major sights. If you are keen to stay in a particular hotel always book a few weeks ahead, as popular ones fill up quickly. Prices are displayed by law in the reception area, often in US dollars.

Deluxe and five star These uniformly large hotels (260–500 rooms), mostly operated by chains such as **Hilton** and **Sheraton**, tend to be located in the business and commercial parts of Istanbul. Many boast panoramic rooftop restaurants, and all have beauty salons, health clubs, shopping arcades, swimming pools, restaurants and bars.

Special licence and Touring Club hotels These smaller hotels (14–58 rooms) are housed in historic buildings, almost invariably restored by the Turkish Automobile and Touring Club. They offer comfortable if rather small rooms furnished in Ottoman style. Some, such as the **Kariye** and the **Yeşil Ev**, have also acquired a good reputation for traditional yet imaginative Turkish cuisine. A few have Turkish baths, and most have mini-bars and TV in the rooms. Prices range from US$80 per double room at the top of the range (for instance Yeşil Ev) to US$50 per double in simpler *pansiyons*, such as the **Turkoman Hotel** and the **Sümengen**.

Famous Pera Palas
The Pera Palas was built in the 19th century as the terminus hotel for passengers on the Orient Express. The rooms are expensive, at around US$150 for a double, but are large and stylish with 19th-century furnishings. If you just want a peek, the bar and café are open to the public.

Middle range hotels Usually rated three and four star, these hotels tend to be in unprepossessing modern buildings in unexciting parts of town. The best known are the **Pullman Etap Istanbul**, the **President** and the **Kalyon**, which enjoys an unusually good location on the Sea of Marmara waterfront, below Sultanahmet. The **Pierre Loti Hotel** is attractive and centrally located on Divan Yolu,

within easy walking distance of the Grand Bazaar and Aya Sofya. Prices range from US$80 to US$140 per double room.

Cheaper hotels Most of the pleasantest cheap hotels and *pansiyons* are located in Sultanahmet, the tourist heart of Istanbul, especially around the Hippodrome. Other reasonable hotels are to be found in the Taksim commercial area, which provides a good base both for nightlife and for access to the Bosphorus. The **Büyük Londra**, a 19th-century Italianate building close to the Pera Palas with a good restaurant and well-furnished rooms, is probably the best of the lot at around US$50 per double room.

Campsites Istanbul's campsites – serviceable but rather noisy because of the proximity of the road and airport – are all positioned along the Sea of Marmara, beside the main road that runs from Atatürk International airport to the city centre. All have restaurants and most have swimming pools.

The 'Atatürk' room in the Pera Palas Hotel, built to accommodate passengers on the Orient Express

The Yeşil Ev serves imaginative Turkish cuisine in traditional surroundings

Food and drink

Pandeli makes a good lunchtime stop in the Egyptian Spice Bazaar

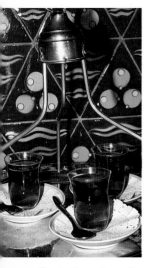

Istanbul is the culinary highpoint of any visit to Turkey. Residents take their food very seriously, as can be seen from the colossal range and variety of restaurants. Ranked with French and Chinese as one of the three great cuisines of the world, Turkish cooking prides itself on the quality and freshness of its ingredients, all of which are traditionally home-produced.

Turkish specialities To the average westerner, the most novel aspect of Turkish meals is the *meze*, an apparently endless succession of delicious appetisers. Some are cold, such as aubergine purée or yogurt and cucumber, and others, such as vine leaves stuffed with meat, and *börek* (tiny fine pastry cases filled with cheese, spinach or meat), are hot. By the time the main course of meat or fish arrives, usually quite simply grilled with rice and a salad, the uninitiated have often eaten themselves to a standstill. The key is to learn how to pace yourself. In places where the food is displayed, always choose from the display rather than the menu; in the simpler *lokantas*, where there may well be no menu anyway, it is accepted custom to go to the kitchen and choose.

Turkish cooking makes generous use of olive oil: an excellent antidote to this is the Turkish national drink, *rakı*, an aniseed-flavoured spirit drunk with ice and water. Turkish wine is surprisingly good and always cheap, the best reds being Yakut and Buzbağ, the best whites being Çankaya and Kavak. The non-alcoholic national drink is *ayran*, a thin rather sour yogurt drink, served chilled and hence very refreshing. Turkish puddings and sweetmeats are described in detail on page 185.

Tea is the universal drink in Turkey

Types of eating place These range from the *kahve*, serving only Turkish coffee and tea, to the *restoran*, a formal restaurant serving Turkish and international food with alcoholic drinks. In between are the *lokanta*, an informal restaurant with home-cooked Turkish meals and no alcohol; the *içkili lokanta*, similar to the *lokanta* but licensed for alcohol; the *gazino*, the same as the latter plus entertainment; the *kebapçı*, serving grilled meats and kebabs; and the *pideci*, a Turkish pizza parlour.

Which district? For the best and cheapest fish, which is available in abundance and variety, head for the Kumkapı district, just inland from the Sea of Marmara, where scores of fish restaurants compete with each other in lively narrow streets. The more expensive fish restaurants are on the Bosphorus shores, and include the **Ali Baba** in Kireçburnu and **Abdullah Effendi** at Emirgan. In the main Sultanahmet area you can eat interesting if expensive Turkish dishes of all kinds at the **Sarnıç**, a converted Roman underground cistern, and at the **Yeşil Ev**, in a pretty courtyard between the Blue Mosque and the Aya Sofya. Excellent value is also to be had at the **Sultanahmet Köftecisi**, on a corner close to the Yerebatan Müzesi, invariably full of locals eating tasty *köfte* meatballs, which can also be taken away. In the Grand Bazaar, the best *lokanta* is the **Havuzlu**; and if you find yourself at the Egyptian Spice Bazaar, climb the stairs to **Pandeli**, an excellent lunchtime stop. In the north of the city, good traditional Ottoman cuisine is provided by the **Aşitane**, the restaurant of the Kariye Hotel, set in a pretty courtyard garden beside the Kariye Müzesi. When visiting the Süleymaniye mosque, look out for the **Darüzzyafe**, housed within the mosque complex, serving authentic Ottoman cuisine.

Traditional Turkish meals start with a selection of mezes

91

Turkish fast food
Istiklal Caddesi, the main street in Beyoğlu, is the fast-food paradise of Istanbul, with office-workers and shoppers alike stopping off at its many kiosks to savour such delights as meatballs stuffed with walnuts (*içli köfte*), kebabs and salad in pitta bread, and sausage sandwiches (*zümküfül*). The best places to try these and other dishes are Şampiyon Kökoreç, Expres and Konak. There is also a Wimpy for the faint-hearted.

Kebabs are available in mouthwatering variety

Vegetarian's delight
Turkish food is highly suitable for vegetarians, as so many dishes are based on aubergines, tomatoes, onions, rice and pine nuts. Dishes to look out for are *imam bayıldı* (literally, the imam fainted – with delight, naturally), a cold aubergine starter, and stewed okra (ladies' fingers).

ISTANBUL

Istanbul shopping

A shop in the book market beside the Grand Bazaar

92

Flea markets
Istanbul is rich in flea markets (*bit pazarları*), which are really rather like streets full of junk shops. The Sunday arts and crafts market in the trendy suburb of Ortaköy is an enjoyable place to browse.

Smart clothes shops line Istiklal Caddesi

In Istanbul everything can be bought somewhere, as long as you know where to look. Prices vary enormously: except in clothes boutiques and bookshops, bargaining is the norm, and you should aim to get at least a third off the initial asking price. Normal shopping hours are 9–1 and 2–7 except Sundays, and the Grand Bazaar is open 8:30–7 except Sundays.

Carpets, kilims and souvenirs Carpet shops abound all over the city, but the biggest concentrations are to be found on **Takkeciler Caddesi** in the Grand Bazaar, and in the secondhand shops off **Istiklal Caddesi** around Altıpatler Sokak.

There is a good selection of carpets and souvenirs at the **Arasta Bazaar**, the renovated Ottoman street market behind the Blue Mosque, and beside the Mosaic Museum. Prices here are a little more expensive than in the Grand Bazaar, but the quality is good and the pace gentler.

The best place for antiques is the **Iç Bedestan** in the centre of the Grand Bazaar, which also sells old silver jewellery and copperware. Gold jewellery is to be found all over the Bazaar, but especially on **Kalpakçılar Caddesi**.

Less expensive and very suitable as gifts or souvenirs are Turkish ceramics, brassware, onyx ware and meerschaum and camel-bone boxes, intricately hand-painted. Look in the **Sandal Bedestan** for these. Look out too for the multicoloured ethnic thick wool socks and gloves knitted by nomads from Erzurum, notably from shops in **Yağlıkçılar Caddesi** in the Bazaar, and the excellent hats in Russian and Turkish wool in the **Emin Gömez** shop in the same street.

Clothes and leather Since the rise to fame of Rifat Özbek, Turkish fashion has been taken more seriously. Clothing manufacturers also have the advantage of home-

Turkish fashion
The exclusive VAKKO clothing shop held its first fashion show in the 1950s, and opened its store on Istiklal Caddesi in 1962. Famous for shoes and accessories as well as clothing, the store also contains an art gallery and elegant tea room.

Amazing fish
The Balık Pazarı (fish market) just off Istiklal Caddesi in Beyoğlu is a good place to stroll without buying, to acquaint yourself with the sheer range and variety of fish on offer in Istanbul.

The Grand Bazaar is a good hunting ground for reasonably priced gifts and souvenirs

produced materials such as Bursa silk, angora (Ankara) wool and fine leather. Apart from the casual leather clothing and denim available in the **Grand Bazaar**, most of Istanbul's classier clothes boutiques are located in **Nişantaşı**, **Şişli** and **Istiklal Caddesi** in Beyoğlu. The easiest clothes shopping is probably at the **Galleria** complex, a new shopping centre at Ataköy, near the airport, where shops are grouped by genre in Turkish bazaar style. The complex also contains fast-food cafés and even an ice rink. Bursa towels, considered among the best in the world, can be bought here at the **Özdilek** shop.

Street vendors are everywhere in Istanbul, offering a variety of tempting snacks

Food Turkish delight, sweetmeats and fresh spices all make good presents. The easiest place to buy them is the **Egyptian Spice Market**, just beside Yeni Cami in Eminönü Square. This crowded covered pedestrian street is lined with shops bursting with Turkish sweetmeats, which they will package in any combination or quantity you desire. It is easy to get carried away, so remember they are very heavy, and a few packets will weigh your suitcase down unmercifully. The aroma of spices, on the other hand, may penetrate everything in your case, but at least they weigh almost nothing.

Books The **Sahaflar Çarşısı**, beside the Grand Bazaar at the Beyazıt Cami end, is an excellent place to browse for new and old books in both English and Turkish. Also to be found here are a few places offering Turkish miniatures and old prints at fairly reasonable prices. Otherwise, the best bookshop for English guides and art books is **Haşet Kitabevi** on Istiklal Caddesi.

■ **Turkish carpets are world famous, and their patterns and designs are so complex that it takes many years to build up a sufficient body of knowledge to enable you to identify their origin at a glance......■**

Bargaining technique
The best way to get a real bargain is to convince the dealer that you really do not like the rug in question. If there are two of you, you can stage-manage this quite well by pretending that one likes it and the other does not. Ask lots of questions about several rugs, so that he cannot tell which is your favourite.

Nowhere offers carpets in greater variety than the Grand Bazaar

Colours can be a useful clue to a carpet's age: the pinks and oranges in this design indicate that the rug was made after about 1850

Kilims Most Turkish carpets are of the 'kilim' variety; *kilim* means 'flat-woven', and these rug-sized carpets are characterised by their almost total lack of pile. Kilims were traditionally made by women for use in their own homes; the patterns and colours were therefore never dictated by commercial motives, but instead reflected the weaver's character and origins. The craft of weaving these intricately patterned carpets was introduced to Turkey in the 11th century by the nomadic Seljuk people, for whom carpets were an essential piece of tent furniture. The material used is normally sheep's wool, but they are sometimes also made of cotton and goat hair. In the Hakkari and Malatya regions of eastern Turkey, silver and even gold lurex thread are sometimes incorporated, as they are thought to ward off the devil or the evil eye. Useful not only as floor coverings, the ubiquitous kilims also served as wall hangings, door curtains, tent dividers and prayer rugs. They were even made into large bags to be used as cushions or saddlebags, or smaller bags to hold salt, bread, grain or clothes.

Natural and chemical dyes Traditionally, natural dyes were used to colour the wool, cotton or silk. These were derived – often by lengthy and laborious processes – from roots, bark, berries, vegetables and minerals. In the

second half of the 19th century aniline chemical dyes became available, and these have gradually replaced most of the old vegetable dyes. Watch out for pink and orange in rugs claiming to be older than this, as these are colours which could never be produced from natural dyes. The quality of chemical dyes has now improved considerably, and they can be quite deceptive: if you want to be convinced that colours are natural, look out for mid-weave colour changes, because with natural dyes there are always slight variations of colour between batches.

A traditional carpet-making workshop in Anatolia

Buying a carpet Always be prepared to spend time talking with carpet dealers, asking over a cup of tea or coffee about the symbols used and their meanings. This will not only give you a feel for the expertise of the dealer, but will also add to your own knowledge and increase the carpet's interest and sentimental value should you decide to buy it and take it home.

As older kilims have become rarer and therefore more valuable, dealers have not been slow to develop techniques for fading newly woven rugs. Leaving them out in sunlight is the commonest method – it can often produce quite effective and pleasing results with mellower colours, but it adds nothing to the rug's value. To detect a sun-faded rug, part the surface and compare the colours at the very bottom of the weave with those at the top. Comparison with the colours on the underside can also be an indication. Some rugs are artificially aged by washing them in bleach, a process which rots the fibres and reduces the life of the kilim. A quick sniff usually reveals whether bleach has or has not been used. Dirt and deliberate scorch marks are other common ageing tricks.

Smaller kilims sell more quickly than larger ones, so sometimes larger ones are cut into pieces and sold as original. Watch out for the newer ends added to make them complete. If colours have been touched up to hide repairs or fading, the felt-tip colouring or shoe polish used may be disclosed by rubbing a damp handkerchief, or sometimes just your hand, over the surface. Look too at the closeness of the weave: the closer the weave and the smaller the knots, the better the quality and durability of the carpet.

Prayer rugs
All prayer rugs have a solid, arch-shaped block of colour to represent the mihrab, or prayer niche, of a mosque wall. These rugs were used exclusively for prayer, and the symbols commonly found on them include the hands of prayer, the mosque lamp, the tree of life, the water jug, the jewel of Muhammad and the star of Abraham.

Where to buy
Istanbul's Grand Bazaar offers the greatest selection anywhere, as its dealers scour the country in search of rugs to bring back and sell. The other noted centres for carpets are Konya and Kayseri, both in Central Anatolia, where the prices are a little cheaper. Coastal resorts such as Bodrum and Kuşadası also have a reasonable selection, though prices are generally higher than in Istanbul.

Nightlife

Traditional dancing in stylish setting

Oasis on the Bosphorus
For an evening of sophisticated disco music, good food and dancing, do not miss the sybaritic Club 29, in its beautiful setting right on the Asian Bosphorus. The décor was inspired by Hadrian's villa in Rome. Open 9pm–4am, it is reached by a 10-minute boat ride from Istinye, on the European side.

Folk dancing is an important part of most cabaret shows

Illuminations
Many of Istanbul's most prominent monuments are illuminated at night. Do not miss the opportunity to see them – especially the Aya Sofya and the Blue Mosque – in this new and spectacular light.

For most Istanbulis, nightlife tends to mean an evening spent in a bar listening to a live group or jazz pianist. Pulsating belly dancers are nowadays only to be found in expensive cabaret nightclubs visited almost exclusively by tourists. More intellectual entertainment, including concerts, ballets and exhibitions, is available at the Atatürk Cultural Centre, especially during the annual Istanbul Arts and Cultural Festival.

Bars, cafés and discos Although these are scattered all over the city, they are concentrated especially in the Taksim/Harbiye district, where they are popular places in which to meet after work. Try **Taksim Sanat Evi** in Taksim (with jazz music; open until 2am). The suburbs of the European Bosphorus also offer lively bars and clubs, such as the **Ziya Bar** in Ortaköy, with its attractive garden and outdoor bar (open until 1am).

If you want disco music and dancing, **Club 29** (see panel) is easily the most exciting venue in Istanbul, frequented by the Turkish and foreign jet set. In winter it

moves from the waterfront at Çubuklu to Nispetiye Caddesi, Etiler, where the teasingly brothel-like décor has leopard-skin seats, and the food is excellent. Istanbul's other famous disco is **Andromeda**, with a young clientele arriving around midnight and dancing into the small hours, often eventually jumping into the pool fully clothed to cool off. Its futuristic laser show and 'video wall' make it one of the leading discos in the world as far as technical equipment is concerned. In summer months the disco has a capacity of 2,000.

Opera and ballet The Istanbul State Opera and Ballet starts its season in October and presents a range of performances, from classics such as Mozart's *Don Giovanni* to experimental modern ballet. Telephone the ticket office (0251 1023 5600) for programmes.

Art and Culture Festival The International Art and Culture Festival is held each year in June and July, with internationally famous visiting performers. Most performances are given in the Atatürk Cultural Centre, though the Open Air Theatre, the Haghia Eirene basilica and the Rumeli Hisarı, as well as several newly opened cultural centres and foreign cultural institutes are also used as venues for films and exhibitions. See pages 120–1 for more details on Turkish cinema.

Belly dancing tends to be found in tourist spots

Night clubs and cabarets The nightclubs frequented by tour groups are the expensive **Kervansaray** and **Orient House**, where the shows begin around 8pm. You are not likely to spot a Turk here, and both the food and the show are distinctly mediocre. Besides belly dancing, there is usually some folk dancing in traditional costumes. It is all over by midnight. The Orient House also goes in for audience participation, soliciting female spectators to come up on stage and have a go at belly dancing.

For a different style of cabaret you could try Eski **Yeşil** in Taksim where you will find a Turkish clientele, often from the media and film worlds, and where the floor show offers such delights as cabaret scripts from the 1920s or spoofs of Ottoman life, with all parts performed by men. The action starts at midnight.

The men's folk dances can be as spectacular as the women's

Galata Tower
The nightclub on the top floor of this 14th-century Genoese tower enjoys fabulous views over Istanbul. The after-dinner floor show begins with belly dancing. It is open 10am–6pm, and again from 8pm onwards.

Practical points

Renovated trams
The tramway along Beyoğlu's Istiklal Caddesi was re-established in 1990; the old trams have been renovated and brought back into use, and the road is now closed to traffic. The very first horse-drawn trams came to Istanbul in 1868, to be replaced by electrified trams in 1914. The last of these stopped running in 1961, until this new revival. There is also a new metro tramway, but its route is designed for commuters from the suburbs rather than for tourists.

To drive in Istanbul is to be faced with the constant headache of navigation and parking problems. By far the best way to get around the city is to walk, or for longer distances to take taxis or ferries. Buses are cheaper but slower, less flexible and impossibly crowded.

From the airport Between 7am and 9pm Turkish Airlines (THY) run a half-hourly bus service from Atatürk International Airport to the THY office at Şişhane, near the top of the Tünel. If your hotel is central you could use this and then catch a taxi. Otherwise, most people take a taxi straight from the airport for the sake of speed and convenience: the journey to the centre takes about 30–40 minutes.

Dolmuş, or shared taxis, can be stylish as well as practical

Taxis Conspicuous by their yellow colour and black taxi signs on the roof, Istanbul taxis are prolific and very reasonably priced by western standards. They all have meters, and it is always worth checking that you are being clocked up at the appropriate rate: the nighttime rate (after midnight and before 6am) is double the daytime rate. No tip is expected, but the fare is normally rounded up to the nearest TL1000. Taxi drivers usually speak a little English and are glad of a chat.

Dolmuş (literally 'stuffed') are shared taxis, taking up to eight people and running along set routes. The main *dolmuş* stations are at Eminönü, Taksim, Sirkeci, Beşiktaş, Aksaray, Üsküdar and Kadiköy. As well as the more mundane minibuses, *dolmuş* are occasionally 1950s Cadillacs,

Old-fashioned trams serve the shopping street of Istiklal Caddesi

Chevrolets and Plymouths shipped over from the US after World War II.

Buses Istanbul buses are cheap, slow, erratic, perpetually packed and not generally recommended for any but the most masochistic of visitors. Tickets are bought in advance in at designated kiosks at the *otogar* (bus station) or newspaper and cigarette booths. On the European side the main bus stations are at Taksim Square, Eminönü and Beyazıt near the Grand Bazaar. On the Asian side they are at Üsküdar and Kadıköy.

Ferries These passenger-only boats run constantly up and down the Golden Horn and across the Bosphorus. The three main landing stages (*iskeles*) are at Eminönü near the Galata Bridge and are clearly labelled with the various destinations. To board, you need a brass jeton bought at the appropriate *iskele*. The boats are very crowded with commuters from 8–9am and from 5:30–8pm, so aim to use them outside these times. The boats are shabby and dilapidated, but have their own faded charm. Wear clothes you do not mind getting a bit grubby. Tea is brought round on a tray by a vendor.

Trains These are not of interest for travel in the city, only for longer distances beyond. On the European side the railway station is at Sirkeci (near the Galata Bridge) and trains run out to the suburbs of Ataköy and Florya (the campsite); on the Asian side the terminus is at Haydarpaşa, serving Ankara and all routes east.

Opening hours Banks are open 9–12 or 12:30 and 1 or 1:30–5 Monday to Friday except at the airport, where they are open 24 hours. Better rates are offered by the ubiquitous money changers at the Grand Bazaar and at the numerous exchange offices, open evenings and weekends, but you should always make a point of first checking the official daily rate.

Typical restaurant hours are 12–3 for lunch and 6:30–10 for dinner, though most smaller informal restaurants are open all day. Shops open 9–1 and 2–7 and shut on Sundays, and the Grand Bazaar is open 8:30–7 daily except Sundays. Note that most museums are shut on Mondays, and palaces on Mondays and Thursdays, so plan your itinerary accordingly. The notable exception is the Topkapı, which shuts on Tuesdays.

Ferries are frequent and characterful, if rather dilapidated

99

Time-saving funicular
The Tünel is the world's shortest funicular railway, running from Karaköy (the other side of the Galata Bridge from Eminönü Square) up to the start of Istiklal Caddesi. It takes just two minutes, instead of an exhausting half-hour climb on foot.

THE AEGEAN

Kara Deniz

Corlu
İpsala
Tekirdağ
E80/100
İSTANBUL
Boğaziçi
İzmit
E84/110
E87/550
Keşan
Sarköy
Marmara
Denizi
Büyükadalar
GR
Samothráki
Marmara
Adası
Erdek
Yalova
İznik
E130/575
Gelibolu
Bandırma
Mudanya
Gemlik
İznik
Gölü
Bilecik
Gökçeada
Eceabat
Lâpseki
Biga
Karacabey
Bursa
Límnos
Çanakkale
Kuşcenneti
Milliparkı
Kuş
Gölü
Mustafakemalpaşa
İnegöl
Çanakkale
Bogaziçi
Truva
(Troja)
Yenice
Gönen
Uluabat
Gölü
2543m
Uludağ
Bozcaada
Susurluk
Ayvacık
Altınoluk
Edremit
Balıkesir
Dursunbey
Tavşanlı
Behramkale
Küçükkuyu
Ören
230
Alaçam Dağları
Kütahya
Baba Burun
Assos
240
Aezanı
Ayvalık
Akrapol
Lésvos
Pergamum
Asklepiyon
Bergama
Sındırgı
Sımav
Gediz
Dikili
Akhisar
Demirci
Çandarlı
Demirköprü
Barajı
Ege
Foça
Yenifoça
Gediz
565
Marmara
Gölü
E96/300
Uşak
Karaburun
İzmir Körfezi
Manisa
Psará
Turgutlu
İldir
İnciraltı
Salihli
Kula
Khíos
Ilıca
Erythraı
İZMİR
Sart
Adıgüzel
Barajı
Çeşme
Sığacık
Urla
Alaşehir
Teos
Boz Dağları
Denizi
Gümüldür
Ödemiş
Buldan
Hierapolis
Pamukkale
Ak Han
Sámos
Efes
Selçuk
Aydın
Tire
Nazilli
E87/320
Büyük
Denizli
Laodikeia
Kuşadası
Meryemana
Karacasu
Ikaría
Güzelçamlı
Söke
Cine
Afrodisias
Acıgöl
Dilek
Milliparkı
Priene
Bafa
Gölü
Alinda
Kemer
Barajı
Solda
Gölü
Mikonos
Milet
Herakleıa
Gerga
Kale
Acıpayam
Didyma
525
Labranda
Pátmos
Altınkum
Euromos
Yatağan
Büyük
Gölgeli Dağları
Dalaman
E87/350
Gülluk
Milas
550
Muğla
Léros
Ortakent
Torba
Náxos
Kálimnos
Turgutreis
Bodrum
Köyceğiz
Dbodbekánisos
Gökova Körfezi
Caunus
Dalyan
Amorgós
Kos
Marmaris
400
Dalaman
Knidos
İçmeler
Fethiye Körfezi
Onoanda
Astipálaia
Datça
Fethiye
Anáfi
Símı
Olü Deniz
Telmessos
Thíra
Tílos
Xanthos
400
Patara
Ródhos
Ak Deniz
Kaş
Kekova
Adası

0   50   100 km

A   B   C

Kuşadası, or Bird
Island

Wicker drying in
bunches near Usak

The Aegean Çanakkale marks the northern edge of the Turkish Aegean, a region which runs southwards through Troy and Pergamum to Izmir, then continues through the heavily developed tourist centres of Kuşadası, Bodrum and Marmaris, as far as the airport of Dalaman at the southern extremity.

Landscape The countryside is for the most part one of gently rolling hills and fertile valleys covered in olive groves, vineyards, cypresses and pine trees. Farming and fishing provide the livelihood for the bulk of the population. The region falls into two distinct sections, of which

THE AEGEAN

The impressive Greek ruins at Didyma

the northern part, from Çanakkale to Izmir, is much the less visited. The sea temperature there is lower (average 20°C in summer) and many of the beaches are rather rocky. The most beautiful stretch of coastline, and also the most developed, lies to the south of Izmir. In ancient times a great flowering of culture took place here, well in advance of that on the Greek mainland, and the ancient cities of Ephesus and Miletos produced a string of remarkable scientists, historians and poets. As well as these great cities, the area is dotted with the remains of literally hundreds of others, the legacy of the waves of Greek settlers who arrived here in the wake of the fall of Troy in about 1200BC. Some of these ancient ruins have been excavated, while many others still lie overgrown with scrub and wilderness. Only a handful, alas, can be mentioned in a book of this size.

Basket weavers on their way to market near Türgütlü

Resorts The largest Aegean resort north of Izmir is Ayvalık, on an indented coastline covered in pine forests. Just to the north are scattered the 23 islands of the Gulf of Edremit, and opposite is the island of Lesbos (Turkish Midilli). Sometimes known as the Olive Riviera because of its extensive olive groves, the Edremit area also has some smaller resorts, such as Çanlık and Sarmişaklı, with its golden sandy beaches, as well as the holiday towns of Ören, Akçay, Altınoluk and Küçükkuyu. The small resort of Behramkale, just north of Lesbos, is probably the best base for a tour of the northern Aegean, as it is within easy reach of both Troy and Pergamum. If you have a chance, stop off at Çandarlı, where there is one of the best-preserved Genoese forts in Turkey.

South of Izmir and directly opposite the island of Chios (Turkish Sakız) is the headland of Çeşme, popular with Turks for its fine sandy beaches. Further south are the small resorts of Sığacık and Gümüldür. Then comes Kuşadası, the major resort of the Aegean, opposite the island of Samos (Turkish Sisam), with the great showpiece site of Ephesus just inland. The pretty resort of Altınkum has grown up south of Kuşadası, near the sites of Didyma and Miletos, offering a quieter base that is still very well placed. Further south are the two charming peninsula resorts of Bodrum and Marmaris, with clusters of smaller

DİDYMA, AYDIN·TURKIYE

offshoot resorts around them; neither of these is suitable as a touring base because of the long drive up the peninsula. At the southernmost point, very close to the airport of Dalaman, is the relatively recent resort of Dalyan in its unusual estuary setting.

The two airports serving Turkey's Aegean coast are the Adnan Menderes International Airport at Izmir (for the north and Kuşadası) and the Dalaman International Airport (for the south, Bodrum and Marmaris).

Endless indentations
Turkey's Aegean shore is endlessly indented with bays and inlets, the result of earth movements over the millennia. This makes the coastline tremendously long, and means that, although a few pockets are now heavily developed, you need never go very far to find empty beaches and unspoilt fishing villages.

Timings
If you are touring in this area, using either Izmir or Kuşadası as a base, a circuit of the places described would take roughly a fortnight.

The Yali Mosque, Izmir

Ionian climate
Herodotus, the famous historian and native of Asia Minor, claimed that the region known as ancient Ionia (from Izmir to Altınkum) had the best climate in the world, with a constant gentle breeze in summer to temper the heat.

The Graeco-Roman stadium at Afrodisias, seating 30,000, is one of the best preserved in the world

Residents of Assos
Aristotle lived at Assos from 347 to 344BC, studying zoology, botany and biology under the patronage of the eunuch ruler, Hermeias. Saint Paul also stayed here in AD56, during his third apostolic voyage.

The Graeco-Roman style attained a peak of perfection in the city of Aphrodite

▶▶▶ Afrodisias (Aphrodisias)   100C2

The relatively isolated ruined city of Aphrodite lies some two and a half hours' drive inland from Kuşadası, on flat fertile ground ringed by distant mountains. It owes its outstanding reputation today to Professor Kenan Erim, a Turkish national attached to New York University, who in 1961 began excavations on the site – abandoned since the 14th century – and devoted the remaining 30 years of his life to the site.

The tour starts from the site museum, which should be left until last (open daily except Mondays 8–12 and 1–5). The path leads first out towards the perfectly preserved theatre, originally Greek, then converted by the Romans for gladiatorial spectacles. Near by are an *agora* (market place) and the theatre baths. Beyond the man-made hill into which the theatre is set lie the impressive Baths of Hadrian, with a handsome exercise ground in black and white marble. From here the path leads to the little *odeon* (theatre) with nine rows of perfectly preserved seats, the most charming of the remains at Aphrodisias. Next to it is the so-called Bishop's Palace, recognisable by its lovely columns in the blue marble from the local quarries. Beyond there looms the gigantic Temple of Aphrodite itself, with 14 of its columns re-erected from the confusing jumble left by the earthquakes and by the building's conversion into a basilica (law court) in the 5th century. To the north is the extraordinary stadium, one of the best preserved in the Graeco-Roman world, with seating for 30,000. The path then loops back towards the museum, passing the recently excavated *sebasteion*: two grandiose porticoes enclosing a processional way where many statues were found.

► **Ayvalık** *100A3*

The major resort of the north Aegean, Ayvalık boasts a picturesque marina, an attractive traditional town centre, and good sandy beaches. Five kilometres from the centre is the island/peninsula of **Alibey**, famous for its fish restaurants and Aegean white wines. The frescoes in the church of Saint Nicholas are also worth a visit. Ayvalık's Greek Orthodox churches, notably **Taksiyarhis Kilesi**, now serve as mosques. The little islands in the **Gulf of Edremit** also bear the remains of monasteries. In summer there are daily departures to the Greek island of **Lesbos** (2 hours by car ferry). The best beaches are to be found 6km south of Ayvalık at **Sarmısaklı** (Garlic Beach), where the tourist hotels are clustered. The site of **Pergamum** is less than an hour's drive away.

► ► **Behramkale (Assos)** *100A3*

Considered by many to be the prettiest small harbour in the northern Aegean, Behramkale offers the unusual combination of the ruins of a Greek city set on the clifftop above, and an attractive little fishing port below, lined with busy small hotels, restaurants and cafés.

As you approach Assos from Ayvacık, passing a 14th-century Ottoman bridge on the way, there are fine views of the headland site with the village clinging to the ridge beside it. The Hellenistic and Byzantine fortifications are still impressive, and at the summit stands the Temple of Athena (530BC), the oldest Doric temple to have survived in Asia Minor. The view from here towards Lesbos and the Gulf of Edremit is quite spectacular.

Expressive sculpture
One of the ancient world's most famous schools of sculpture was housed at Aphrodisias, and it is the quality and quantity of these sculptures, carved from the local marble and displayed in the on-site museum, that make a visit here memorable. Notice especially the expressive faces of the gods and goddesses – and of the Roman officials.

105

Ayvalık is a busy, picturesque little port which is also the major resort of the north Aegean

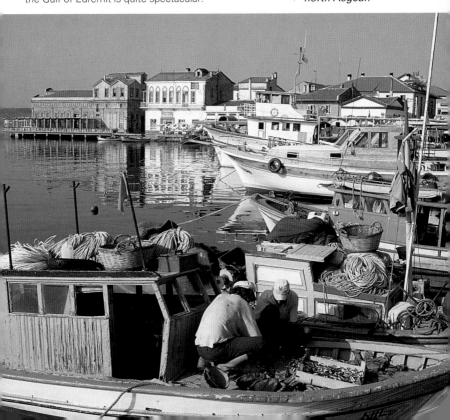

FOCUS ON *Turkish jokes and proverbs*

■ **The importance of humour to the Turk is easily overlooked by outsiders, who may well see only a rather dour exterior. In fact humour, and especially satire, forms a key part of the Turkish character. Turks display a keen taste for political mockery and a finely developed sense of the absurd......■**

Weeping for ugliness
Many stories involve the folk hero Nasreddin and the Mongol conqueror Tamerlane. In one, Tamerlane weeps for two hours because he has glimpsed his face in a mirror and is appalled by its ugliness. Nasreddin carries on weeping, and when Tamerlane asks why he replies: 'If His Majesty weeps for two hours after only catching a glimpse of his face, then surely I, who see him all the time, should weep much longer.'

A sense of humour helps when bartering

Nasreddin Hoca Innumerable tales covering most aspects of life are attributed to this great legendary sage, said to have lived in Akşehir in the 13th century. Here are a few of them.

A neighbour comes to borrow Hoca's rope. 'I'm sorry,' says Nasreddin, 'I can't lend you my rope, my wife's spreading flour on it.' 'What do you mean?' asks the baffled neighbour, 'That doesn't make sense.' 'I'm perfectly serious,' says Hoca. 'If I don't want to lend somebody my rope, flour can very easily be spread on it.' Spreading flour on a rope has passed into idiomatic Turkish as a metaphor for not doing something you don't want to do.

A young man comes to Hoca in despair, having lost all his money. 'What will become of me,' he wails, 'without my money and my friends?' 'Don't worry,' says Hoca, 'you'll soon be all right.' The young man perks up. 'You mean I'll get rich again and get back my friends?' 'No,' says Hoca, 'but you'll get used to being poor and friendless.'

Hoca had lost his donkey. While looking for it, he prayed and thanked God. 'Why are you so grateful, when you have lost your precious donkey?' he was asked. 'I'm happy because I was not riding the animal at the time. Otherwise I would have been lost too!'

106

Turkish jokes and proverbs

Arriving at a banquet in scruffy clothes, Hoca was ignored and not shown to a table. He went home, changed into his fur coat and came back again. This time he was shown to the best table. On sitting down he dipped his fur coat into the soup, saying, 'Eat, eat, my fur coat, for it is you to whom this meal was proffered, not me.'

Proverbs Here is a selection of authentically Turkish proverbs (as opposed to Arabic or Persian), highly revealing of the national character:

The thicker the veil, the less it is worth lifting.
The only worry-free head is a scarecrow's.
Hard work means a long life but short days.
Even if a woman's candlestick is cast in gold, it is the man who must supply the candle.
On a winter's day, the fireside is a bed of tulips.
Distant drums, sweet music.
Where the Turk rides grass will not grow.
Success depends on a man's reputation, not on his soul.
If you dig a grave for your neighbour, measure it for yourself.

Political jokes Akbulut, prime minister from 1989 to 1993 under Türgüt Özal, and notorious for his stupidity, was the butt of many jokes. In a typical example a taxi driver asks his passenger: 'Have you heard the latest Akbulut joke?' 'I am Akbulut!' cries the outraged passenger. 'Don't worry,' replies the taxi driver, 'I'll tell it very slowly.'

Turkey also has a long tradition of satirical newspapers, with cartoons playing a prominent role. Some examples can be seen in changing displays at the **Karikatur Müzesi** (Cartoon Museum) in Istanbul (see pages 68-9).

Karagöz shadow plays These were for centuries a popular form of humour, now alas almost extinct and superseded by press, radio and cinema. The two main characters were Karagöz, the 'common man', and Hadjivat, the pompous intellectual, and many of the skits ended with Hadjivat being kicked off stage. Towards the decadent end of the Ottoman Empire, these shadow plays developed a strong tendency towards political satire. A young man would ask Karagöz, for example: 'What should I do to further myself in my job?' And Karagöz would reply: 'As you are completely ignorant, I advise you to become Chief Admiral.' At this time the Sultan's son-in-law was Chief Admiral and a known incompetent.

Typical invective
'A horse, an ox and a donkey lived up in the hills. One day the Devil whispered to them: "Why not go to town and see what the humans are like?" So they did. A few years later they met to compare stories.

The horse and the ox both related how they were caught and forced to carry heavy loads and pull carts. The donkey laughed, and told how he had arrived in town at election time, and joined in the shouting, shouting louder than everyone else, until he was elected to rule. "But didn't they notice you were a donkey?" asked the incredulous horse and ox. "They did in the end, but by that time four years had gone by and it was time for the next election."'
From a left-wing satirical paper.

107

Wonder of the World

Bodrum in Turkish means 'dungeon' or 'subterranean vault', thought to be a reference to the Mausoleum, the tomb built for King Mausolus by his wife Artemesia, which was one of the Seven Wonders of the Ancient World. Of this structure, originally 55m tall, only the foundations and a few carved fragments remain: some of its distinctive green granite blocks can be seen reused in the castle, however.

▶▶▶ Bodrum (Halicarnassus)   *100B1*

Known as the most upmarket and bohemian of Turkish resorts, Bodrum, with its pretty whitewashed houses and abundant flowers, has always attracted a sophisticated crowd. Despite the invasion of mass tourism in recent years, it has managed to retain its special atmosphere, bustling with people and colourful activity. With its wonderful harbour and marina, full of expensive international yachts and elegant wooden Turkish caiques, available for charter or daily hire, it is also the yachting centre of the Aegean. If you are touring, two nights are enough to sample the nightlife and restaurants and visit the castle. Bodrum is not a suitable base for visiting inland, as each outing involves the hour-long winding drive up the peninsula to join the main coast road.

The Castle▶▶▶ This Crusader castle, built to dominate the harbour by the Knights Hospitaller of St John in 1402, is one of the last and finest examples of Crusader architecture in the east. The knights occupied it until 1523, when Süleyman the Magnificent's conquest of their base at Rhodes forced them to withdraw to Malta. A leisurely

The superb Crusader castle at Bodrum

Building ban

A five-year building ban has now been imposed to halt further development in Bodrum, and to ensure the preservation of its unique townscape of low-rise whitewashed buildings, with their blue shutters and tumbling bougainvillea.

tour takes 2–3 hours and the castle (entry fee) is open daily except Mondays 9–7.

As you enter the castle, through an impressive series of seven gates plus a moat, look out for fragments of reliefs from the Mausoleum set in to the walls and over the gates. Inside are a lower and upper courtyard, attractively laid out as part of an **open-air museum** of ancient stonecarvings and pottery, with a café area alongside. An imaginative **Museum of Underwater Archaeology** charts the techniques used by an American team to excavate the wreck of a ship that sank 32 centuries ago and was found sitting in water 30m deep.

From the fine towers and sentry walkway along the escarpment walls there are dramatic views over the bay and harbour.

Shopping in Bodrum

> **Diving outings**
> Diving has recently become a popular way of exploring the nearby reefs, with their caves and unusual rock formations. Day outings with transport and a picnic can be arranged through Era Turizm or Motif on the west harbour front. A popular spot is the 'Akvaryum' in the Ada Boğazı (Island Strait), with unusually clear water and abundant fish.

Shopping and nightlife Strolling around Bodrum at any time of day or night is always a great pleasure. The main bazaar area lies in the pedestrian precinct, at the foot of the castle, but little shops of all sorts abound in all the narrow streets. Local specialities include natural sponges, soft cotton clothes and lapis lazuli beads to ward off the evil eye, along with the usual endless selection of carpets, jewellery, copper, ceramics, leather and embroidery.

Bodrum is justly renowned for its nightlife, with scores of bars, restaurants and nightclubs, as well as some of the best discos in Europe – notably the **Halicarnassus**, with a laser show focused on the castle. Another form of evening entertainment is the promenade along the waterfront, where you can enjoy the spectacle of locals, hippies and jetsetters all gawping at each other.

Beaches Swimming at the small town beach is not to be recommended, so boats and *dolmuş* (shared taxis) run regularly to the nearby beaches on the peninsula. On the southern side there are good sandy beaches at **Bardakçı**, **Gümbet**, **Bitez**, **Ortakent Yalısı**, **Karaincir**, **Bağla** and **Akyarlar**, which has fine, powdery sand. Ortakent has the longest stretch of undeveloped sand, while Karaincir, with its small village, is one of the most beautiful on the whole peninsula. On the western tip are **Turgutreis**, **Gümüşlük** and **Yalıkavak**, ideal for swimming and watersports, all with friendly villages. On the northern side of the peninsula are the tiny fishing villages of **Gölköy** and **Türkbükü** with their handful of *lokantas* (informal restaurants), and the modern resort of **Torba** with its marina and holiday village.

A herb and spice stall in the bazaar

Boat trips

■ **One of the greatest pleasures of holi-
daying in Turkey is the ease and speed with
which you can hop on a boat to visit one of
many offshore islands with the minimum of
formalities – even when that island is
actually part of Greece......■**

To the Greek islands
Many Greek islands –
Lesbos, Chios, Samos, Cos
and Rhodes are the major
ones – lie just off the
Turkish coast and can be
reached by regular ferries.
No visas are required and
tickets can simply be
bought on the Turkish port
waterfront.

Aegean outings Most boat trips are concentrated in the
southern Aegean region, mainly from **Marmaris** and
Bodrum. The only northern excursion of note is from
Ayvalık marina to the **Ayvalık islands**, all uninhabited
and with lovely beaches and ruined monasteries. There is
also a car ferry service from Ayvalık to **Midilli**, the Greek
island of Lesbos, taking two hours each way (daily in summer, weekly in winter).

Chios (Turkish Sakız) is an easy hop from the Turkish
resort of **Çeşme**, and in season boats run twice daily from
Kuşadası to **Samos** (Turkish Sisam). From **Bodrum** you
can take a boat trip to **Karaada** (Black Island), 30 minutes
away, where you can improve your skin by bathing in a
grotto filled by warm mineral springs. You can also hire a
boat or take a yacht tour lasting two, three or seven days
round the **Gulf of Gökova,** with its thickly wooded coastline and clear turquoise waters. Most boats are hired from
the western harbour. Ferries also run to **Cos** (Turkish
Istanköy).

From **Marmaris** ferries run daily except on Sundays to
Rhodes. As the trip takes two and a half hours, most
people spend at least one night there, exploring the
walled Crusader town. July and August are best avoided,
as the narrow streets on the island can become excessively crowded.

*A gulet under
construction at
Kemer*

Boat trips

Gulet cruising Holidays on *gulets*, traditional motor yachts built from the red pine that grows in profusion all along Turkey's southern shore, are becoming increasingly popular. These extremely attractive boats, with pointed bow and stern, come complete with cook and crew to ensure your total relaxation.

Marmaris, **Bodrum**, **Fethiye**, **Kalkan** and **Kaş** are the main *gulet* centres, and in a 14-day cruise it is possible to explore the coastline all the way from Bodrum to Fethiye. Boats sleep 8 – 12, and most of the cabins are equipped with private shower and toilet. Hot water is provided by an on-board generator, and most boats also have a cassette player for you to play your own tapes. A windsurfing board or two is usually provided. As on all boats space is at a premium, so pack sparingly. There is always a shaded area on deck, and the captain will consult with the passengers to see whether they would like to drop anchor for a swim here or explore an ancient Greek ruined city there. The cook will also consult about menu preferences for breakfast and lunch. The evening meal is usually taken at a restaurant at that night's mooring. Children under 12 are accepted only if the whole boat has been booked by a single party, though most *gulet* cruises are booked by childless couples aged around 30.

Holidays of this type can be booked through specialist tour operators (your local Turkish Tourist Office will give you a list). Out of season (May, April and October) you can arrange them on the spot, though bear in mind that hefty deposits are required. In high season (June to September) prices jump considerably.

A boat trip from Dalyan, where boats are moored along the riverbanks ready to take tourists to local beaches, spas and Greek ruins

Sortie to Turkish Cyprus
If you have more time you could catch a boat at Alanya or Taşucu and find yourself in Kyrenia (Turkish Girne), on the northern coast of Cyprus (5 or 2 hours respectively). Fares are cheap, no visa is required for EEC and US citizens and no advance booking is necessary. The currency here is the Turkish *lira*, and the cost of living is even lower than in Turkey: with car hire rates at only a third of those in Turkey, this is an ideal way to explore the Crusader castles, classical sites and Greek monasteries in the area.

THE AEGEAN

Aegean showpiece
The British archaeologist
H V Morton wrote in 1936:
'Ephesus stands dignified
and alone in its death with
no sign of life but a
goatherd leaning on a
broken sarcophagus or a
lonely peasant outlined
against a mournful sunset.
Few people ever visit it.
Ephesus has a weird
haunted look.' Today,
transformed by
excavations into the showpiece of the Aegean,
Ephesus is visited daily by
thousands.

►► **Dalyan (Caunus)** *100C1*

A 20-minute drive from Dalaman airport, Dalyan makes an excellent base for holidays in the lower Aegean: it is an easy hop from here to the **Marmaris** and **Bodrum peninsulas**, and it is also on the doorstep of **Lycia**, the beautiful mountainous coastline that begins at Fethiye and runs round eastwards to Antalya.

Charmingly set on the riverbanks at the mouth of the freshwater **Lake Köyceğiz**, Dalyan has been spared the worst excesses of tourist development, and offers a small but growing selection of tasteful hotels and restaurants. The local speciality is the fish bred in the estuary, mainly mullet and bass.

In the town, boats are moored along the riverbanks ready to take you to **Istuzu beach**, or 10 minutes upriver to the hot thermal baths at **Ilica**, where you can wallow in mud that reaches a temperature of about 40°C. The third destination on offer is **Caunus**, the ruined Greek city that lies downriver in the marshes, and of which the astonish-

112

*A remarkable series
of ancient tombs is
hewn out of the solid
rock opposite Dalyan*

ing rock tombs which are set in the cliffs opposite Dalyan are but a foretaste.

The boat ride takes about 15 minutes, and there is a further 10-minute walk to reach the site. The first buildings you see are a Byzantine basilica and a huge Roman bath to your left. The well-preserved theatre is set into the acropolis hill, which is crowned in turn by a 4th-century BC fort. Notice too the impressive city walls built by King Mausolus, which also date from the 4th century BC. Excavations began in 1967 and are still continuing, using labour from the prison in Dalaman. Originally on the sea, Caunus now lies 3km inland, owing to the silting up of the river over the centuries. From the top seats of the theatre it is possible to make out the location of the original port.

Wallowing in the thermal springs at Ilıca, accessible by boat from Dalyan. Some tourists take their mud baths, which can reach a temperature of 40°C, to extremes

▶▶▶ Efes (Ephesus)   100B2

Famous throughout history for its Temple of Artemis, one of the Seven Wonders of the Ancient World, this great and sacred city lay in ruins and largely forgotten until the early 20th century. Now it is one of the most extensive archaeological sites in the world, falling into three distinct areas: the **Artemision** (site of the Temple of Artemis); the area around the town of **Selçuk**, with the **site museum** and the **Basilica of Saint John**; and finally the city of **Ephesus** itself, some 3km west of Selçuk along the road to Kuşadası. If you are short of time, concentrate on this last.

The Artemision▶ Signs direct you from the town of Selçuk to the site, set in a hollow and ringed by trees. All that remains is a single column rising out of a muddy pool, and you will need to muster all your imaginative powers to visualise the original 127 columns, each one nearly 20m high and altogether covering an area four times greater than that of the Parthenon. Throughout Asia Minor, Ionic temples tended to be sited on low ground, the better to show off their tall slender columns; broader, squatter Doric columns, on the other hand, needed a higher position (as with the Parthenon) to be seen to their best advantage.

Artemis of the Ephesians was a Greek adaptation of Cybele, the Anatolian earth-mother goddess whose outstanding quality was her fertility. On her annual feast day great orgies took place here. When the Romans arrived they identified her with Diana, their own fertility goddess, and the cult continued for more than a thousand years, conferring great wealth on the city as devotees flocked to it from all over the world. The downfall of the goddess came with the advent of Christianity.

113

Turtle sanctuary
Since the wildlife campaign led by British conservationist David Bellamy, Dalyan has been famous for its loggerhead turtles (*Caretta caretta*), which hatch on the local Istuzu beach between May and October. The beach is now protected by wardens, though it remains open to the public for swimming and sunbathing, and all building projects have been banned. Mosquitoes also thrive in this marshy environment, so go armed with repellent.

A small part of the remains at Ephesus – much of the site is yet to be excavated

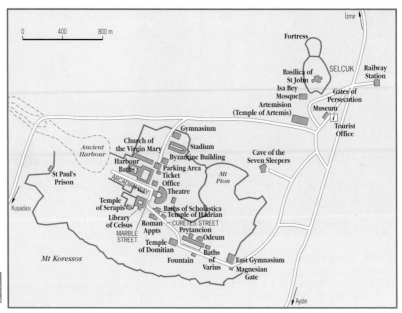

Ephesus

*The Library of Celsus
at Ephesus, built in
AD110*

Selçuk and the Museum▶▶ Many of the beautiful marble blocks of the Artemision can today be seen in the
Basilica of Saint John and the **Isa Bey Mosque,** some
600m away at the foot of the acropolis hill. The 14th-
century mosque, built by the Seljuks who gave the town
its present name, is now itself a picturesque ruin.

A climb of 200m up the road leads to the precinct of the
crenellated fortress, originally Byzantine but rebuilt by the
Seljuks, within which lies the Basilica of Saint John, a vast
early 6th-century building retaining a few floor mosaics
and frescoes.

By the Tourist Office is the little **site museum,** open
daily except Mondays 8:30–12:30 and 1:30–5:30, visited
primarily for its two marble statues of Artemis Ephesia.

The Ephesus Site▶▶▶ The Artemision originally stood
on a natural sheltered harbour, but the river mouth silted
up, and soon after Alexander's death in 323BC the city
was moved to this new site further west. The silting process continued even so, despite the efforts of Nero and
Hadrian, and the ancient port of Ephesus is now over 5km
from the sea.

The approach road today takes you past the ruins of a
vast **Roman gymnasium** and **stadium.** The ticket office
is open from 8 until sunset daily.

Head straight on to the junction of the marble road and
the Arcadian Way, where you can climb the steps of the
theatre to gain a view of the site. The grandiose ruins date
almost exclusively to the Roman imperial age, and their
sheer extent and completeness (thanks to the efforts of
the Austrian excavators) help to give a feel of what life in
an ancient Graeco-Roman city must have been like. The
Hellenistic **theatre** with Roman additions has recently
been renovated to accommodate even more people during the Seljuk Ephesus Festival of Culture and Art, held
each May. The white marble **Arcadian Way** used to lead

straight down to the harbour and was lined with shops and porticoes; it even had street lighting as early as 400BC. It was here that Cleopatra made her triumphal entry into Ephesus when she visited Mark Antony.

Next, explore the enormous **Harbour Baths** and the curiously long and thin **Church of the Virgin Mary,** the setting for the violent Third Ecumenical Council in AD431, at which Nestorius denied the doctrines of the Virgin Birth and the divinity of Jesus.

Walk next along the **Marble Street,** noting the ruts made by chariot wheels, to reach the imposing two-storey façade of the **Library of Celsus,** the best-preserved structure of its kind in the world. Behind the library stands the massive **Temple of Serapis,** still with traces of the original blue and red paint on its columns.

From the library, the impressive **Curetes Street** snakes over the hill to the **Magnesian Gate,** lined to the right with villas of the wealthy and to the left with various public buildings. Among these, do not miss the **Baths of Scholastica,** with their communal latrines in white marble. The 1st to 6th-century villas, some with well-preserved murals and mosaic floors, give a vivid picture of the luxurious lifestyle of these rich citizens.

If you wish, you can leave the site by the Magnesian Gate and visit the **Cave of the Seven Sleepers,** the site of an impressive Byzantine necropolis at the foot of Mount Pion.

115

One of the two marble statues of Artemis Ephesia

The beautifully decorated façade of the Temple of Hadrian

Tomb of the Virgin Mary
In the hills 8km from Ephesus lies the little house/chapel known as Meryemana, where the Virgin Mary is said to have lived her last days. The house was 'discovered' in the 19th century after an invalid German lady, for years confined to her bed, and who had never set foot in Turkey, let alone Ephesus, described its exact location as revealed to her in a vision. A priest from Izmir read her description and in 1891 led a search party to find the house. It is now a place of pilgrimage from all over the world, and received a papal visit in 1967.

Walk Alinda

The impressive hilltop ruins of Alinda, an ancient Greek city where Alexander the Great once stayed, are an easy day trip from Bodrum, Marmaris, Kuşadası or even Izmir, with a chance to see some beautiful inland scenery.

The modern town at the foot of the ruins is Karpuzlu, 25km off the main Aydın to Muğla highway. The total distance from Bodrum or Kuşadası is about 110km (taking about an hour and a half). The walk up to the ruins is quite steep, and also takes about 90 minutes, but you can drive to the summit if you prefer.

The ruins of Alinda, unquestionably among the finest in the area, are only rarely visited as they lie rather off the beaten track. In Karpuzlu, follow the busy market street lined with booths and stalls; at the end, a small blue sign marked 'Alinda' points up a wind-

The neglected but beautiful Greek theatre at Alinda

ing track to the right. Follow this and park at the side of the road on the edge of the town, looking out for a small path on the right that zigzags up past the final group of houses.

This brings you after a few minutes to an open *agora* (market place) at the end of which is a vast and impressive building, the best-preserved of its kind in all Asia Minor: a three-storey **market hall** still standing over 16m high, which evokes the experience of ancient Greek shopping more vividly than any other surviving structure.

From here a steep and slippery path climbs after some 15 minutes to a hollow in the hillside where the heavily overgrown **Greek theatre** looks out over the town below. Characteristic vaulted entrance passages added by the Romans have survived intact, as has much of the stage building. From all around there are excellent views of the superb defensive walls with their towers and battlements.

An energetic half-hour scramble brings you to the **Hellenistic tower** on the summit. Alternatively, you can return to the car and drive up the

T.C.
VALİLİĞİ

RENYERİ
LETİ

10663

TL.

ALİNDA, AYDIN-TÜRKİYE

track until you reach the well-preserved arches of an **aqueduct**, which makes a good picnic spot with fine views. Beyond, a small path climbs up on to the the main acropolis of Alinda. Here can be seen the foundations of what were probably the royal apartments of Queen Ada, exiled to Alinda in a power struggle with her own family. When Alexander the Great swept through Asia Minor in 333BC, she offered to help him plot the siege of Halicarnassus (modern Bodrum), where her younger brother was ruler. Alexander accepted and together, probably on this very hilltop, they prepared for the attack. After the success of their campaign, Alexander brought Ada out of exile and proclaimed her Queen of all Caria.

On returning to the car, it's worth taking time to explore the derelict houses on the outskirts of the town, some whitewashed with blue shutters, others with wooden overhanging balconies. Many have courtyards

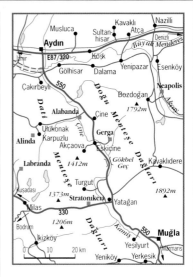

littered with carved blocks from the ancient ruins.

The atmospheric ruins of Alinda

THE AEGEAN

Cultural capital

Izmir has built quite a reputation for itself as Turkey's second cultural capital after Istanbul. The Cultural Centre hosts opera, theatre, ballet and concert performances, with the additional high points of the International Arts Festival in June and July and the International Fair in August and September. Many of these events are staged in the huge and beautiful Kültür Park in the city centre.

Its strategic position at the end of the peninsula leading to Izmir means that the attractive town of Çeşme has always been an important naval base; now, thanks to its spa and beaches, it is a busy resort as well

▶▶ Izmir (Smyrna)   100B3

Izmir is the modern successor to Miletos and Ephesus as the major port of the Aegean; it is also Turkey's third city, after Istanbul and Ankara. Attractively set on the hillsides that line the sweep of its bay, Izmir is a typically Levantine city, overpopulated, lively, dusty and colourful; this is especially true of its old quarters, where little houses painted in shades of green, yellow, blue and ochre crowd together beneath red-tiled roofs. If you want to get away from the bustle of the city, stay in Foça to the north or Siğacık to the south.

Earthquakes and the disastrous fire which took place in 1922, during the War of Independence, have destroyed most of Izmir's buildings of historic interest, leaving only the Roman market place (open 8:30–5:30 daily), the **bazaars** inland from the elaborate **Ottoman clock tower** on the seafront, and the flat-topped **Kadifekale**, the ancient acropolis. From here there is a superb view over the town and harbour, especially at sunset. If you are just passing through, try to stop for lunch at one of the excellent seafront **fish restaurants**, which serve specialities such as lobster and sea bass.

Environs of Izmir Çeşme▶ The biggest and most famous of the beach resorts around Izmir, Çeşme is an essentially Turkish resort and thermal spa (Çeşme means 'spring'), dominated by its 14th-century Genoese fortress with a labyrinth of twisting back streets behind. The attractive promenade is lined with restaurants. The long sandy beaches where most of the hotels are concentrated lie a little outside the town.

Foça▶ Very well placed for Izmir airport, this pretty fishing village has a lively harbour front with excellent seafood restaurants. Club Med has a village nearby, but otherwise there are just a few hotels. With its whitewashed houses and cobbled streets, it retains a very Turkish feel.

119

Yali Mosque, Izmir

Rich as Croesus
Croesus, last and greatest of the Lydian kings, became phenomenally wealthy as a result of the gold deposits discovered in the River Paktolos. The Lydians are believed to have been the earliest people to mint coins, using gold taken from the small stream which flowed through Sardis. The gold was collected by laying sheepskins in the water to catch the particles: the origin of the Golden Fleece.

Revolting ancient wine
The famous Pramnian wine, described by Homer as the drink of heroes, is said to have come from Smyrna. Mixed with sea water or honey, chalk and powdered marble (thought to make it sweet), it must have been truly revolting in its original, undiluted state in order to have warranted such adulteration.

Sart (Sardis)►► Rarely visited (because its location 90km east of Izmir makes it difficult to incorporate into an itinerary), **Sardis**, wealthy capital of the ancient Lydian Empire, is one of the most impressive sites in Turkey. The unusual rock formations in the nearby hills lend it a uniquely strange atmosphere, and this curious pointed landscape shelters hundreds of Lydian tombs, some dating back to the 7th century BC. It is the **Roman ruins** of Sardis, excavated by American teams since 1958, which are particularly impressive now, consisting of a road lined with shops, a gymnasium and a synagogue (originally a basilica). Throughout there is lovely marble and mosaic flooring.

The other part of the site lies a kilometre or so away, around the most striking monument in Sardis, the **Temple of Artemis**. Of the original 82 columns only two remain intact, with parts of 13 others still standing. The Ionic capitals on these columns are among the most beautiful known. Sacrifices to the goddess were made on the altar at the top of the flight of steps.

Sığacık► This little resort, 75 minutes' drive south of Izmir, has a headland on either side of which lie two small sheltered bays with camping and hotels. Nearby is the ancient site of **Teos**, picturesquely lost among the olive groves, and the village of Sığacık has a fine Genoese fortress rising above its little fishing harbour and yachting marina.

Carnival time in Izmir

■ In cinemas throughout Turkey, mass audiences enjoy films featuring goodies versus baddies with lots of fights, or cloyingly romantic tales of rural teenagers whose love is thwarted by their families and the world in general, but who triumph in the end and live happily ever after. Since the 1960s, however, there has appeared a group of bolder directors, prepared to explore more realistic subjects, such as the consequences of the drift of the rural population to the cities and the breakdown of traditional lifestyles......■

Heart of Turkish cinema
Beyoğlu is where cinema began in Istanbul. The first showings were in 1897, and the Luxembourg Cinema, the first in Turkey, opened a few years later. A series of extravagantly decorated cinemas then followed: Pathé (1908), Cine Palace (1914), Electra (1920) and Elhamra (1922). Turkish cinemas are now concentrated on Istiklal Caddesi and Yeşilçam Sokağı.

Istanbul's annual film festival is a showcase for new work

Yılmaz Güney Of these by far the best known – and possibly the only one to have established an international reputation – is Yılmaz Güney. He produced his first major film in 1970; called *Umut* (*Hope*), it is the tale of a desperate and gullible taxi driver who loses his house, his horse, and finally his mind. The final scene, in which the blindfolded hero circles a hole in the ground to the accompaniment of haunting music played on the reed flute, makes an unforgettable impression.

In 1971 Güney made two more films, *Ağıt* (*The Elegy*), about a man driven to smuggling by abject poverty, and *Acık* (*Sorrow*) on the subject of lost love and revenge. After the 1971 coup Güney was put in prison and not released till 1974, only to be imprisoned again on the charge of murdering a judge.

It was during this spell in prison that Güney managed to produce his best work, writing the scripts in his cell and passing them out secretly to friends, along with exact instructions on how to film each scene. These scripts tended to revolve around Güney's abiding interest, the problems of the rural poor, a theme which he developed further in each film.

1979 saw the release of *Sürü* (*The Herd*), written from prison and directed in Güney's absence by Zeki Ükten, which follows a Kurdish family taking their sheep to market in Ankara, and shows their total bewilderment at the world in which they find themselves. Güney's most famous film, *Yol* (*The Road*), also written from prison and directed this time by Şerif Gören, was finally released in 1982. It follows the fortunes of five prisoners allowed out on parole for one week, each of whom encounters a changed and alien world and finally meets with tragedy. Having escaped from jail, Güney was able to edit the film himself while in exile in France. He died of cancer aged 46.

New developments Political turbulence and censorship imposed severe restrictions on Turkish cinema in the late 1970s and 1980s, but a few notable films did nevertheless emerge. One of these was *A Season in Hakkari* by Erdan Kırel, a West German co-

Much allegory
Fairly strict censorship is applied to films in Turkey, and many western films are banned for being too sexually or politically explicit. Turkish film-makers face the same con-straints, with the result that they are often obliged to deal with their subjects obliquely, using allegorical characters and plots.

121

Released in 1979, Sürü (The Herd), which follows the fortunes of a Kurdish family taking their sheep to market in Ankara, was written by Yilmaz Güney from his prison cell

production, which follows the experiences of a young schoolteacher sent to work in a remote Kurdish village.

Other subjects treated for the first time during this period include the position of women in Turkish society, social hypocrisy, and the problems faced by migrant workers in Germany. Of these the best is *Forty Square Metres of Germany,* directed by Tevfik Başer and released in 1987.

There are indications in the 1990s that government censorship may be easing off. A recent film, *Blackout Nights* by Yusuf Kürçenli, even has as its subject the shortsightedness of censorship and political oppression: a hopeful sign for the future of Turkish cinema.

Güney himself (on the left) starred in his first major film, Umut *(Hope), as well as writing and directing it*

The island which gave Kuşadası its name, now linked to the mainland by a concrete causeway

MILET, AYDIN-TÜRKIYE

The great Medusa's head is an indication of the grand scale of Didyma's ruins

► **Kuşadası (Bird Island)**   100B2

This is the most overdeveloped resort in the Aegean, for one simple reason – its proximity to **Ephesus**. Coaches flood in from Izmir airport, 90 minutes away, and cruise ships disgorge their passengers at the harbour. The result, predictably enough, is a resort which has lost most of its original charm, and in which the local people have lost their souls to tourism and touting. Even other Turks express their dislike of it. That said, its location still makes it a good base for excursions inland, and there is a wide selection of nightlife, entertainment, restaurants and shops. There is also a new and well-equipped yachting marina.

In summer boats run daily across to the Greek island of **Samos.** The public beach on the main Kuşadası bay is rather overcrowded and most prefer the sandy **Kadınlar Plajı** (Ladies' Beach) 3km away, where hotels such as the Imbat are to be found. Kuşadası gets its name from the former island now linked to the mainland by a concrete causeway. The Genoese castle on the island has been converted into discos and cafés.

Environs of Kuşadası

Priene►► This modest Greek city dating from the 4th century BC, in its setting which is unquestionably the most spectacular of all the ancient Ionian cities, forms a telling contrast with the grandiose Roman monuments of nearby Ephesus. Once a flourishing port, it now languishes a full 15km away from the Aegean, owing to the silting up of the Maeander river. A steepish 10-minute climb leads from the ticket kiosk (open 8:30 to sunset daily) to the ancient city centre, where the Temple of Athena once stood. A thorough exploration takes two hours or more and involves quite a lot of climbing.

Milet (Miletos)►► Like Ephesus and Priene, the ancient port of Miletos was marooned by the retreating sea and ruined by the consequent loss of its trading role.

The ticket kiosk (open 8:30 to sunset daily) stands in front of the magnificent **theatre**. Note the remarkably well-preserved vaulted passages leading to the seats at either side. From the crumbling **Byzantine fortress** on the acropolis above the theatre, you can make out the contours of the **old harbour** to the east. Much of this area is marshy or even under water today and a raised dirt track has been constructed to give easier access to the ruins in the former city centre. The major monuments here are an *agora* (market place) with **baths** and **gymnasium** alongside, a *buleterion* (council chamber) and a *nymphaeum* (monumental fountain). Also impressive are the **Roman Baths of Faustina**, a complex of rooms with walls still standing 15m high.

A powerful sculpture of a lion from Didyma

Didyma▶▶ Site of the great **oracle temple of Apollo**, Didyma is at its most impressive at sunset, striking in its sheer scale. Seven high steps lead up to the main platform; this originally had 120 colossal columns, 103 of which still stand today. Many have decorated bases and capitals, though the most memorable carving by far is the huge cracked head of Medusa (1st century BC) lying on the ground, having fallen long ago from the frieze.

Before issuing a prophecy, the oracle priestesses were said to fast for three days, then inhale the sulphur fumes from the spring until they swooned in a state of divine inspiration. Their utterances were then translated into hexameter verse by the oracle priests.

123

Ancient theatres
Turkey has more than 200 ancient Greek and Roman theatres: the finest Greek example is at Priene; the best Roman one is at Aspendos (see page 146). The most outstanding Graeco-Roman example, holding no fewer than 15,000 spectators, is at Miletos.

Sage of Miletos
The most famous citizen of Miletos was Thales, one of the Seven Sages of Antiquity, who was born in the 6th century BC. He thanked the gods for three things: that he was human and not an animal; a man and not a woman; and a Greek and not a barbarian. His most famous dictum 'Know thyself', is inscribed on the temple at Delphi.

The ruins of the oracle temple of Apollo at Didyma still inspire awe through their sheer size and grace

Drive Kuşadası to Lake Bafa and Heracleia

This drive makes an exhilarating day trip from either Kuşadası or Bodrum, offering the chance to enjoy the lakeside setting of Bafa, sample its fish, swim in its waters, and explore the romantic ruined city of Heracleia ad Latmos on its shores.

The distance from Bodrum is 107km, a 90-minute drive, and from Kuşadası 83km, taking just an hour. The main road from Ephesus and Kuşadası to Bodrum and Marmaris passes along the southern lake shore, where you come to a clutch of simple restaurants and a campsite/motel. Lunch can be had either here or at a restaurant on the opposite shore, below Heracleia ad Latmos itself. Choose the excellent Bafa fish.

Continuing towards Bodrum and Marmaris you will reach the village of Çamiçi, from where a yellow sign points left to Heracleia (9km). The narrow track winds back to the eastern lake shore, where the ancient ruins lie in their dramatic setting beneath **Mount Latmos** (1500m). The mystery and charm of the lake's atmosphere are enhanced by the remains of a **Byzantine church** and **convent** on its little islands. Over the centuries a number of religious communities sought refuge from persecution here, but all their buildings fell into ruin after the Turkish conquest. By the restaurant at the foot of the site it is just possible to swim through the reeds to the islet.

In antiquity Heracleia stood on the coast, and what is now a freshwater lake was then an inlet of the Aegean,

Looking over Lake Bafa from Heracleia

A rural scene on one of the quiet roads near Heracleia

afterwards cut off by the silting up of the Maeander river. The ancient city's fortifications are its most remarkable feature, for from 300BC it was enclosed by extensive **defence walls**, which still climb to a ridge some 500m up the slopes of Mount Latmos and cover a total distance of 6.5km. Many of the towers, windows, gates and stairways up to the parapets are still in excellent condition.

According to legend, this is the spot where the handsome demi-god Endymion was sleeping when the moon goddess Selene saw him and fell in love with him. Zeus, jealous of a rumoured amour between Endymion and Hera, had decreed that Endymion should sleep forever on Mount Latmos, and in his dreams Selene slept with him and bore him 50 daughters. In Christian times Endymion was adopted as a local mystic saint, and Christian anchorites pronounced an ancient tomb discovered here to be Endymion's and made it a sanctuary.

This **sanctuary** can still be seen to the right of the road as you approach. Walk on beyond it to the headland where the ruins of a fortified **Byzantine monastery** stand.

Continuing towards the mountain, you will come to the most prominent building of ancient Heracleia: the **Temple of Athena**, a simple edifice with beautifully crafted masonry walls

perched on a promontory. Inland from this lies the *agora* (market place), where the school of the adjacent village of Kapıkırı now stands. On the south side of the agora is a well-preserved **market building** divided into shops. A little further inland is the charming *buleterion* or council chamber, poorly preserved but in a fine setting among the trees on the edge of the village. There is also a **theatre** about 300m away to the right up the mountain, again poorly preserved, as are the unidentified **temples** above it.

The afterglow of sunset adds to Lake Bafa's atmospheric charm

Fish in earrings

A mysterious marble building at Labranda is thought to have housed a sacred pool in which there once swam fish adorned with necklaces and gold earrings. These were used as a primitive oracle, capable of giving only yes or no answers; morsels of food were thrown into the pool and if the fish ate them the answer was yes.

Among the many attractions of the Marmaris area is its delicious honey

►► Marmaris   100B1

The resort of Marmaris boasts Turkey's largest yachting centre and is the embarkation point for many *gulet* cruises. Despite the damage caused by the 1958 earthquake it remains a pleasant town, with more of a Turkish feel than Bodrum.

The attractive harbour is lined with palm trees and crammed with cruise boats, and a walk along the length of the promenade makes an enjoyable hour's stroll. The older part of town is now pedestrianised, and parking along the main promenade has been prohibited in order to reduce noise and congestion (this sometimes means the nearest parking for seafront hotels is 15 minutes' walk away). Colourful restaurants and cafés line the front, and the market and shops sell an excellent selection of Turkish crafts, including jewellery, leather and carpets. Look out, too, for the delicious local honey. The town's only relic of any great antiquity is its crumbling **Ottoman castle**, built in 1522 by Süleyman the Magnificent, which appears to squat on a hillock jutting out into the bay in the old quarter.

The town beaches are not to be recommended: your best bet is to take a day trip by boat to sandy beaches nearby, such as **Sedir Adası** (Cedar Island) and **Ingilizlimanı**.

Boats run daily to Rhodes, which lies directly opposite, a journey of 2–3 hours. The transfer time from Dalaman airport is 1½ hours.

► Milas (Mylasa)   100B2

A busy market town set at a natural crossroads, Milas offers a few unusual and surprising monuments that are worth seeking out. The first, which stands on the western outskirts of the town, is a relic of ancient Mylasa: a large Roman mausoleum known in Turkish as **Gümüşkesen**. It is all the more interesting for being a replica in miniature of the Mausoleum in Halicarnassus, a famous Wonder of the Ancient World of which nothing now remains. The second is the **Firuz Bey mosque**, built in 1394 from pinkish marble blocks borrowed from ancient Greek temples. Most impressive of all, however, is the splendid castle, **Peçin Kale**, originally Byzantine but adapted by the 14th-century Menteşe emirs, and set 5km south of Milas on an unmistakable flat-topped rock. Within this small walled citadel are houses, a little *medrasa* (theological school) and a mosque. The castle itself is open from 8 to sunset daily and can be reached by a dirt track.

Environs of Milas Euromos►► The elegant columns of this temple to Zeus stand by the road some 15km north of Milas. This is one of the best-preserved temples in Asia Minor today, still with many of its original architraves, possibly as a result of its sheltered position in the lee of three

Men playing dominoes at a bar in Muğla

127

wooded slopes. The temple was originally part of an ancient city, the ruins of which lie over the hill, still unexcavated and lost among the trees and scrub.

Labranda►► The atmospheric ruins of Labranda make an unusual excursion from Milas, 17km away to the north. Site of a hilltop sanctuary of Zeus, Labranda belonged to Mylasa, and used to be linked to it by a paved sacred way, used for religious processions. Festivals including athletics contests used to be held here, and the ruins of a stadium have recently been located by the site's Swedish excavators. The ruins of the sanctuary area are impressive, with gateways, monumental tombs and baths as well as the temple itself.

► ■ **Muğla**   *100B2*

This large town, capital of Muğla province, merits a brief stop to visit the picturesque winding streets and bazaar area of its old Ottoman quarter.

The picturesque old town of Muğla

THE AEGEAN

Walk Gerga

See map on page 117.

A rarely visited hilltop settlement set in a rugged landscape that is in sharp contrast to the coast, Gerga makes an unusual excursion from Kuşadası or Bodrum. The ruins here are the only known surviving example of an early indigenous town, untouched by Greek or Roman influences, and quite different from the sophisticated cities of the Aegean coast. The modern Turkish name for Gerga, Gavurdamları, means 'infidel-roofed sheds', a reference to the strange rural architecture here. The drive from Kuşadası or Bodrum takes about 90 minutes, and the walk about 3 hours. Take your own picnic, as local facilities are scant.

After passing the **Seljuk mosque** in Eski Çine, look out for a driveable track to the right leading to the village of Ovacık (4km), then on a further 7km to reach the village of

Kırksakallar (Forty Beards). Park beside the school here and follow the walled path out into the fields. When the path stops, keep going in the same direction, watching out after about half an hour for a large toadstool-like rock bearing the inscription GERGA in huge Greek letters. Over the next 20 minutes you will stumble upon a number of such ancient signposts.

A descent down a ridge brings you in sight of the first of Gerga's remains, a stone-roofed hut with two lion's heads projecting beneath the roof. Further along the shady man-made terrace, shored up by impressive buttresses, stands Gerga's most famous building, an extraordinary little **temple**, with a gabled roof of stone slabs, and the name 'Gerga' carved on its pediment. Scattered about near by are various fallen statues, olive presses and some weird obelisks.

The monolithic temple at Gerga

128

Drive **Marmaris to Knidos (Cnidos)**

The beautiful theatre at Knidos

This pretty and scenic drive leads from Marmaris to the tip of the peninsula, where you can walk round the extensive and atmospheric ruins of Knidos, lunch at one of the simple fish restaurants, and swim in the still waters of the sheltered headland bay.

The total drive of 86km takes about 2 hours, climbing up through wooded hills, with some spectacular hairpin bends and perpendicular precipices, before descending to lush fertile meadows. At the fork to Datça, follow the yellow sign to Knidos; after Reşadiye the tarmac road gives way to a dirt track which continues to the tip of the peninsula. This track is by no means always straightforward, and driving here needs care. At two intersections on the track there is no yellow sign: take the left fork in both cases.

About 2km from the tip of the peninsula the drive takes you past an extensive **necropolis** scattered on the hillside. Round a bend after this you catch your first sight of the twin harbours and lighthouse of Knidos, with restaurants set down on the bay. The road now leads through the middle of the ruins of this important city founded in 400BC, and you can clamber up the original steps to reach the **Sanctuary of Demeter**. Lower down is a relatively well preserved **theatre**, from the 3rd century BC.

The most interesting remains now lie to the right, up on the hillside above where the road ends. Here are the foundations of temples, including the circular marble base stones of the **Temple of Aphrodite**, discovered in 1969 by the aptly named American archaeologist Dr Iris Love. Fragments believed to be of the famous statue of Aphrodite by Praxiteles, declared by Pliny to be the finest statue in the world, were found near by.

A walk out over the lighthouse headland will be rewarded with the discovery of the **Lion Tomb**, whose lion now resides in the British Museum in London.

THE AEGEAN

Pamukkale's peculiar calcified waterfalls

130

Festive mood
The very strangeness of the landscape and thermal spa at Pamukkale, so unlike any other place, seems to put most visitors in festive mood. Turks and foreigner visitors alike are generally overcome by the urge to wallow like hippos in the overflowing rock basins, splashing and paddling in as many streams as they can find.

The detailed theatre of Hierapolis

▶▶▶ **Pamukkale (Cotton Castle)**   *100C2*

One of the natural wonders of Turkey, the thermal spa of Pamukkale has abundant supplies of remarkable hot spring waters laden with calcareous salts; as the waters have spilled over the plateau edge down the centuries, they have deposited their salts to created a bizarre network of fantastical rock formations, gleaming white stalactites, cataracts and basins.

The spot is now highly commercialised, with rubbishy souvenir stalls and touts abounding even in the area below the plateau. If you are fortunate enough to spend the night here, do try to stay up on the plateau, preferably in either the **Tusan Motel** or the **Turizm Motel**, which have the best pools. The Tusan's pool is right on the edge, so that you can gaze down the extraordinary hillside as you wallow, while the Turizm has a shallower pool made memorable by the Roman columns and drums which litter the bottom.

Historically the waters' chief virtue seems to have lain in their ability to make fast the colours of dyed sheep's wool. Nowadays they are also claimed to benefit heart and circulation complaints, as well as digestive disorders and rheumatic and kidney diseases. Certainly nobody can dispute their excellent stress-relieving properties: a half hour wallow cannot fail to leave you feeling relaxed and benign.

Ancient Hierapolis▶▶ Many visitors, carried away with the search for more pools and basins, barely notice that the high plateau is also the site of the ancient spa of Hierapolis, built here by the Romans to dominate the spring waters and harness their reputed religious and mystical qualities. Most of the ancient ruins are set quite a way back from the plateau edge; the first group you come to as you walk 'inland' are the original **Roman baths**

consisting of two tall vaulted rooms now housing a small museum. Beside this is a *palaestra* or open courtyard for exercise, and behind that lie the remains of a vast **basilica** with three naves, thought from its size to have been the cathedral erected in the 6th century, when Hierapolis became a bishopric.

Beyond the Turizm Motel stands a recently restored *nymphaeum* (monumental fountain), and close by is the **Temple of Apollo**, recognisable by its wide flight of steps. The modern road follows the course of the original main street for 2km until it reaches the **monumental gate** to the north, passing on the right the colossal **theatre**, still well preserved, with some magnificent carvings and reliefs. Outside the city, the road leads up to a vast building on the hillside; Italian excavators have discovered that this housed the tomb of the Apostle Philip, who was martyred here in AD80. Do not miss the tombs which line the old road out to Ephesus from this northern gateway. Over 1,200 have been counted, making this one of the most extensive ancient cemeteries in Asia Minor.

Environs of Pamukkale Ak Han▶ Standing by the main road to Dinar is this impressive 13th-century Seljuk caravanserai faced in pinkish marble. The door is elaborately carved, as always, and you can still walk up on to the roof.

Laodiceia▶ This ancient city some 14km from Pamukkale is the site of one of the seven churches mentioned in the Revelations of Saint John. Known in ancient times as the 'City of Compromise' because of its indecisiveness, it was rebuked by the saint for its lukewarmness: 'I know your works; you are neither hot nor cold... So because you are lukewarm. and neither hot nor cold, I will spew you out of my mouth.' The main surviving monuments are the stadium, a large gymnasium, an *odeon* (originally a roofed theatre used more for music than drama), a *nymphaeum* and two theatres, both poorly preserved.

Noxious grotto
In a chamber below the Temple of Apollo lies the infamous Plutonium Grotto, the noxious fumes of which were described as deadly by ancient historians such as Strabo. The exhalations were said to kill anyone who breathed them; eunuchs, however, were able to enter the grotto unscathed, according to the Greek historian Dio Cassius, as they were particularly good at holding their breath. When the grotto was discovered by Italian archaeologists in 1957 the foul fumes seriously impeded their excavations, though no deaths were reported.

131

Some of the hotels at Pamukkale have their own private pools, complete with Roman remains

Fury of the dead
Many of the tombs in the necropolis at Hierapolis bear inscriptions in the form of curses of various kinds, including this particularly all-embracing example: 'May he who commits transgression, and he who incites thereto, have no joy of life or children; may he find no land to tread nor sea to sail, but childless and destitute, crippled by every form of affliction, let him perish, and after death may he meet the wrath and vengeance of the gods below. And the same curses on those who fail to prosecute him.'

THE AEGEAN

Origin of books

Jealous of Pergamum's challenge to his cultural supremacy, Ptolemy, creator of the mighty Library at Alexandria, banned the export of papyrus from Egypt. In response, the king of Pergamum ordered that animal skins should be used instead. The results came to be known as 'Pergamum books', from which the English word 'parchment' is derived. As the skins were too thick and heavy to be scrolled like papyrus, they were cut into pages which were laid on top of each other.

The vast ruins of the city of Pergamum

▶▶▶ Pergamum   100B3

So extensive are the remains of this spectacularly sited ancient Greek city that just to walk between the three main areas would take all day, and even with transport a visit takes a good 3 hours. One of the most pleasurable ways to see Pergamum is to arrive in time to see the sunset from the acropolis, then to stay the night and explore the rest of the site in the morning.

After Athens lost its political importance in the 2nd century BC, Pergamum and Alexandria became the two main – and competing – centres of ancient civilisation. Pergamum's famous **library** and the **Temple of Zeus** were constructed at this time, along with the vast **artificial terraces** on the hillside which allowed the city to spread downwards. All its rulers were devoted patrons of the arts and sciences, with the exception of the last, Attalus III, who in an act of extraordinary eccentricity bequeathed his entire kingdom to Rome. Pergamum thenceforth became the capital of the Roman province of Asia, which stretched as far south as Caunus.

German excavators have reconstructed enough of the acropolis area today to give an impression of how the upper city would then have looked. The most spectacular and impressive structure remains the **theatre**, a remarkable piece of engineering built into an exceptionally steep hillside.

The lower terraces are best explored from the car park at the foot of the acropolis. Here are to be found a vast **gymnasium**, the **Temple of Demeter** and Hellenistic houses and shops on streets rutted by chariot wheels. The lowest part of the city is now largely covered by the town of **Bergama**, with an attractive old quarter. Above rises the colossal Roman **Red Basilica**, originally a temple to Serapis and later converted to a church by the Byzantines. Finally comes the **Asklepieion**, the foremost medical

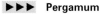

Excavating a dream
The discovery of the site of ancient Troy became a romantic obsession for a 19th-century German businessman named Heinrich Schliemann. In 1870 he obtained permission to excavate here, using money he had amassed in the Californian goldrush. Schliemann devoted the next 20 years of his life to the excavations, and was rewarded with the discovery of no fewer than four Troys, one on top of the other. He also found the fabulous 'jewels of Helen', which he kept for his wife's use for 20 years before bequeathing them to the Berlin Museum (they disappeared after the Russians entered the city in 1945). Despite his success, Schliemann never gained the acceptance he craved from the academic world, who scorned him as an amateur who had destroyed much valuable evidence.

centre of the ancient world, founded primarily on the fame and reputation of Galen, the greatest physician and medical writer of late antiquity who was born here in Pergamum in AD129.

▶ **Truva (Troy)**   100A4

Those who come to Troy cherishing visions of Homer's great fortified city are bound to be disappointed by the series of mounds and ditches that are Troy today. For others it is enough that a city so powerfully linked with legend should exist at all. But there can be few for whom the name of Troy does not conjure up images of ancient romance and heroism, and a visit here takes on the quality of a pilgrimage to the place where western literature had its beginnings, with Homer's *Iliad* and *Odyssey*.

The excavations that followed Schliemann's work have now uncovered nine major layers of habitation, the favoured contenders for Homer's Troy being Troy VI (1800–1275BC) and Troy VIIa (1275–40BC). The layers are clearly labelled and the recommended circuit is signed, but by its nature the site remains confusing.

At the site entrance is a gigantic wooden horse, a slightly absurd gesture towards the legendary climax of the siege of Troy, when the Greeks tricked their way inside the walls concealed within a wooden horse.

Troy is open daily (fee) from 8:30 to sunset.

The wooden horse guards the entry to Troy

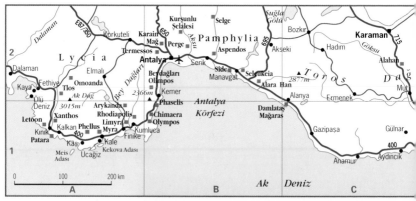

Right: popular with Turkish familes and foreign visitors alike, Alanya is one of the liveliest resorts on the beautiful coastline of the Turkish Riviera

Far right: the spectacular scenery of Selge Canyon, in the Köprülü Kanyon National Park inland from Antalya and Side, makes one of the most exciting excursions in the Mediterranean area

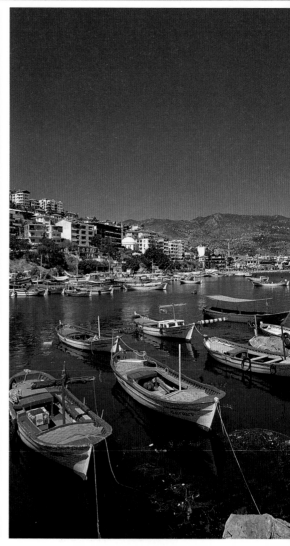

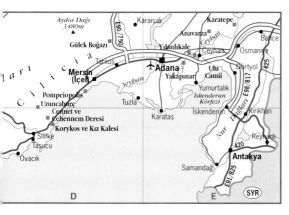

The Mediterranean Served by the airports of Dalaman, Antalya and Adana, Turkey's southern coastline, known as the Turquoise Coast or the Turkish Riviera, stretches for some 600km from Fethiye in the west right through to Antakya and Iskenderun, near the Syrian border, in the east. This is without doubt one of the most beautiful stretches of coastline anywhere in the Mediterranean, with many fascinating excursions to be made inland as well.

Landscape The coastline falls into several quite distinct regions. The first of these, known as **Lycia**, stretches from Fethiye to Kemer and is Turkey's wildest and most beautiful stretch of coastline, with dramatic mountains tumbling right down into the sea. The beaches, including

THE MEDITERRANEAN

135

THE MEDITERRANEAN

the famous **Ölü Deniz** (Dead Lagoon), are the most glorious in Turkey, and inland there are spectacular ancient Lycian ruins to visit.

From Antalya eastwards lies the region known as **Pamphylia**, a flat and fertile coastal plain that runs as far as Manavgat, with mountains rising further inland. In antiquity this plain supported the five great cities of **Attaleia** (Antalya), **Perge**, **Aspendos**, **Sillyon** and **Side**.

Further to the east, from Alanya to the Syrian border, is **Cilicia**. The first section, round the headland to Silifke, is rugged and sparsely populated; the second part is the Cilician Plain, a monotonous but fertile flatland devoted to rice and cotton crops. The scenery along the coast between Alanya and Silifke is magnificent, with cliffs dropping away into the sea, but the coastal road – winding endlessly over wooded headlands and round deep bays – makes for tiring driving. The vegetation is subtropical, and lush orange groves and banana plantations line the road.

Resorts Within Lycia the main resorts are **Fethiye**, **Kalkan**, **Kaş** and **Kemer**, though mercifully tourist development is still relatively small in scale here in comparison with the giant resorts of Kuşadası, Bodrum and Marmaris.

Ölü Deniz is one of the most popular destinations on the Mediterranean coast of Turkey

Solitude on one of the long sandy beaches at Side

Perfect for pirates
The rugged coastline of Cilicia was notorious for the piracy and brigandage that plagued it in ancient times; its numerous tiny inlets and coves made perfect hiding places from which to launch attacks, and the heavily wooded terrain inland protected the robbers from pursuit. Assaults on ships plying the important trade route from Syria to the Aegean were so relentless that they seriously weakened the economy of Syria's mighty Seleucid Empire.

137

The tarmac road linking the towns and villages of Lycia's coastline was not completed until 1981, so the charms of the region have been generally accessible only for the last 10 years. Kemer is the only resort with hotels of 200 rooms and over; in the other resorts the emphasis is more on smaller family-run *pansiyons*. All the resorts now have yachting marinas.

Antalya has put a lot of money into its development as the premier resort of the south coast, completely reno-vating its old harbour to turn it into a chic new yachting marina with classy hotels. The main beaches are 5km out of town at **Lara**, where large hotels stand on the water's edge. In **Cilicia**, both **Side** and **Alanya** are lively tradition-al resorts, very popular with Turkish families. Both have long sandy beaches lined with hotels, large and small, though Side retains more of a village feel with its narrow winding streets in the old centre. East of Alanya the only place that could qualify as a resort is **Silifke**, with a few beach hotels. From Mersin eastwards the coastline is largely agricultural or industrial.

A 20-minute drive inland from Side are the waterfalls at Manavgat, with an unusual restaurant near by, making a refreshing change from the tourist beaches

No escape from fate
According to the local legend, Kız Kalesi (Maiden's Castle) was built out to sea by a king who wished to protect his only daughter, after it was predicted that she would die of a snakebite. One of her admirers unwittingly sent her a basket of fruit in which a snake was lurking, however, and so she was bitten and died.

The imposing black and white marble minaret of the 16th-century Ulu Cami, or Great Mosque, in Adana

Adana
135E2

Turkey's fourth largest city, with a population that is growing fast, is the centre of the prosperous cotton industry, set in the heart of a rich agricultural plain. The River Seyhan runs through the middle of the city, whose sole ancient monument of note is the **Taş Köprü** (Stone Bridge) built by Hadrian. Near by is the only notable Turkish monument, the **Ulu Cami** (Great Mosque), built in 1507 of black and white marble, with surprisingly fine tiles inside. Adana offers many good hotels, and the city would make a comfortable base from which to visit the places described below.

Environs of Adana Anavarza (Dilekkaya)▶ This pleasant detour, 72km northeast of Adana, takes you to a **Roman-Byzantine** city in a lovely setting at the foot of a mountain. The remains consist of a Roman triumphal arch and theatre, from which a stairway cut out of the rock leads to the upper town. The well-preserved fortress at the summit encloses a funerary church of the Cilician Armenian kings, still with traces of frescoes inside.

Discovered in 1945, the remote and unusually beautiful neo-Hittite site of **Karatepe**▶▶ involves a well-signposted detour of a good 3 hours from the main Adana–Maraş road. It is well worth it, however, for in a lovely wooded setting overlooking the Ceyhan lake you will find neo-Hittite stone reliefs *in situ*, in a quantity and state of preservation unique in Turkey – or, for that matter, in the world (see also pages 28-9). On the way you will pass to the left the site of **Hieropolis Castabala** (1st century BC) with its fine castle on the hilltop and rows of columns marching across the fields.

Kız Kalesi (Maiden's Castle)▶ This much-photographed castle consists in fact of two buildings: the first, built in the 12th century by Armenian kings, stands on the sandy beach, while the other rises from its own island in the sea (see panel) and was originally reached by a causeway. The beaches here are popular for camping.

The largest town as you drive east along the coast from Anamur, **Silifke**▶ has a pleasant open feel, set as it is on the banks of the wide Göksu river. A Roman bridge crosses the river, but apart from this the only monument is the large Crusader castle on the hill. Built originally by the Byzantines in the 7th century as a defence against Arab raiders, it was rebuilt by the Crusader knights of Rhodes, complete with 23 towers and bastions. Now it is wild and overgrown: take care if you decide to walk the crumbling battlements. On the hill to the west of Silifke stands the Byzantine church of **Haghia Thekla**, dedicated to Saint Paul's first convert, who was also the first female Christian martyr.

One of the two castles at Kız Kalesi, isolated on its island

Uzuncaburç (Diocaesarea)►► This is a very worthwhile detour, for the drive itself – 30km north of Silifke along a winding road – is attractive and the ancient site is one of the most impressive along this coast. After parking in the centre of the small village that lies among the ruins, you walk through a monumental Roman arch to reach the Temple of Zeus Olbius, built by Seleucus I in the 3rd century BC and the oldest-known temple of the Corinthian order. Most of its columns still stand, and it was converted to a church in the Byzantine era. Other monuments are a theatre, the Temple of Tyche, and a powerful Hellenistic tower nearly 25m high.

Yakapınar (Misis)► A sign 25km east of Adana points to these early mosaics, housed in a makeshift 'museum'. The main mosaic is said to represent Noah's Ark and the animals, though sadly its poor condition makes this hard to discern.

Yılanlıkale (Castle of the Snakes)►► Some 39km east of Adana, look out for this magnificent 12th-century Armenian castle set up on a hill to the right of the road. Inside, the dungeons and living rooms are well preserved.

Cennet and Cehennem (Heaven and Hell)
The names of these two caves give a clue to the contrasting nature of their character. Fortunately only Heaven can be visited, a huge natural chasm on the edge of a field of Roman and Byzantine ruins. Descent is via an easy path to the chasm bottom; from here a trickier, slippery path continues to a cave where a pretty church dedicated to the Virgin has stood since the 5th century. Inside, you will hear the roar of an underground river, said to be the Stream of Paradise. Hell, by contrast, is a frightening narrow pit accessible only to potholers. Superstitious locals tie rags to nearby trees and bushes in order to ward off any evil spirits who might escape from below.

139

Street vendors in front of the great stone bridge built by Hadrian across the River Seyhan in Adana

■ **From their origins on the steppes of Asia, the Turks arrived in Asia Minor in the 10th century, having adopted the religion of the Arabs *en route*. Fierce fighters and horsemen, these nomadic tribesmen were descended from the Tu-Kin tribes of Mongolia: hence the modern name 'Turk'......**■

Different values
'The life of insecurity is the nomad's achievement. He does not try, like our building world, to believe in a stability which is non-existent; and in his constant movement with the seasons, in the lightness of his hold, he puts something right, about which we are constantly wrong...'
Freya Stark, 1956

140

Nomad women and children near Antalya

The Seljuks The first nomads settled with apparent ease, founding what became known as the Seljuk Empire of Rum with its capital at Konya. Their stable and enlightened rule over the following two centuries led to the first flowering of a Turkish civilisation.

The Seljuks encouraged large numbers of nomads to settle in areas as far west as **Lycia**, where they remained in effect semi-nomadic, migrating with their flocks and herds from their summer pastures (**yaylas**) in the mountains down to the coastal towns in the winter. Travellers who visited these parts in the 19th century have given us colourful descriptions of the caravans setting off for the mountains in about May, the men riding horses or camels in front, the women generally on foot and herding the flocks of sheep and goats, the donkeys laden with pots and pans, and the children playing about behind with the dogs and chickens.

To this day there are still a surprising number of villages up in the Lycian mountains which are empty in winter, the houses left just as they are, with no thought of theft. But now, increasingly, the villages remain empty in summer too: as the advent of tourism in towns like Kaş and Kalkan brings in a more lucrative income in the summer months, the semi-nomadic tradition of centuries is breaking down.

Eastern nomads Most nomads remaining in Turkey today live much further to the east; many are Kurds

(known officially as 'mountain Turks'), especially in the regions south and southeast of **Diyarbakır**. The authorities persist with resettlement programmes, trying to persuade nomadic Kurds to give up their age-old practice of growing only what they need to survive, and gaining a small income by selling their livestock from time to time in order to purchase the other essentials of life. Instead they are being encouraged to do some farming, and so to help supply food for the big cities.

The distinctive black goat-hair tents of the *yürük* ('walkers'), as they are known, are today to be seen most frequently in the foothills of **Ararat** and the valleys of the Zap river in **Hakkari**. The women remain unveiled, and they and the children still dress in colourful clothes, often with a lot of gold jewellery. The sheepdogs, wearing spiked collars, are savage in the extreme and should be avoided at all costs.

Nomadic traits of the modern Turk Turks remain extremely proud of their nomadic heritage, and their attachment to the tenets of this way of life shows itself in many ways, including their special love of woven carpets, once the most important piece of tent furniture and now given pride of place in many Turkish houses. Those houses themselves also often appear flimsy, less solid and less lavishly furnished than those of purely sedentary peoples. All over Turkey you will be struck, too, by the number of museums with ethnographic displays, showing the costumes worn by the nomads, the layout of their tents and their chattels. Far from being for the benefit of tourists, these exhibitions are intended for the Turks themselves, anxious not to forget their nomadic origins.

A Kurdish nomad woman in front of a traditional goat-hair tent, or yürük

Tax evasion
The Turkish authorities used to experience great difficulty in collecting taxes from the nomadic Kurds. Whenever a visit from the tax-collector was in the offing, they would simply pack up their chattels and migrate to the mountains, returning to the plains only when their spies told them the coast was clear.

Problems of settling down
The nomadic life can be viewed as a relatively easy one, free of responsibilities and involving little hard physical toil. The prospect of settling down to an agricultural life can therefore seem like a prison sentence, an endless drudge of exhausting manual labour, with no escape through movement and change.

Licentious Antioch
In Roman times the city of Antioch was a great cultural, artistic and commercial centre which became notorious for its depravity and its indulgence in life's pleasures. For this reason it was chosen by St Peter for his first mission to the Gentiles, and his converts here were the first to be called Christians. Out of town on the Aleppo road is a grotto with a secret escape tunnel where St Peter is said to have founded the first Christian community. The church here was built by Crusaders in the 13th century.

▶▶ **Alanya** *134C2*

The approach to the town of Alanya is unmistakable, its great rock crowned by the crenellated red fortress that dominates the coast from afar. By virtue of its impressive site and good beaches Alanya has in recent years become the most developed resort along this southern coast after Antalya. Hotels have mushroomed, and there is a clear divide between the old town, perched in the fortress up on the rock, and the modern sprawl of development on the two beaches beneath it. In the 13th century, under the Seljuks, the fortress was used by the Sultan as his winter quarters, and the town was a naval base protected by the prominent **Red Tower** (Kızıl Kule). A remarkable and unique structure, octagonal in shape and with five internal storeys, this is the major monument of the lower town, along with the old **Seljuk dockyard** beside it, still in use today. You can drive all the way up to the old fortified town, quietly dilapidated but still partially inhabited, to reach the citadel at the top and the remains of the sultan's palace. A platform at the very edge of the cliff gives a magnificent view. This was the spot from which condemned prisoners or women convicted of adultery used to be hurled on to the rocks below.

At the foot of the rock promontory, approached from the beach to the west, is the stalactite grotto of **Damlataş**, whose very high levels of humidity are thought to be beneficial to asthma and bronchial sufferers. From here boats can be hired to explore the many caves which honeycomb the foot of the rock.

▶▶ **Anamur** *134C1*

This medieval castle is the largest and best preserved on the southern coast of Turkey, with all its walls and 36 towers still intact. Known locally as Mamure Kalesi (Marble Castle) it stands right on the water's edge, with the waves lapping at its outer walls.

The castle was the last foothold of the Cypriot Lusignan kings, this being the southernmost point of the coast,

The mighty Seljuk fortifications and harbour at Alanya, dominated by the great octagonal Red Tower

directly opposite Cyprus which is only 65km away. The Ottomans expanded the castle and continued to use it until the last days of the empire in 1921. The guardian sells tickets (open daily except Mondays 8:30–12:30 and 1:30–5:30), and there is a handful of simple restaurants and motels near by; the unexceptional modern town of Anamur is a few kilometres away inland.

On a hillside 2km to the west of the castle are the interesting ruins of ancient **Anamurium**, a Byzantine city deserted in the 7th century when the wave of Arab incursions began from Damascus. So complete are the remains, including many private houses, with traces of mosaic and painting, that it gives the impression of being a ghost town deserted just a few years ago.

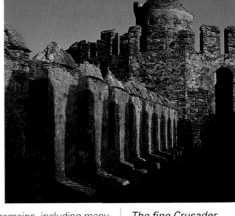

The fine Crusader castle at Anamur

Hand-painted dolls from Alanya

143

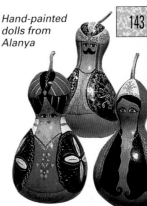

►   **Antakya (Antioch)**   *135E1*

This city close to the Syrian border is the site of ancient Antioch; though only a shadow of its former self it is still picturesque enough, with its narrow lanes leading down to the Orontes river, and its segregated districts inhabited by different religious communities in Ottoman times. The outline of the ancient city walls, 30km long in total, give an indication of the extent of the city in its heyday.

In Antakya today the only ancient monuments are the **Roman bridge** and the **Mosque of Habib Haccar,** originally a church. The **Hatay Museum,** however, should not be missed for its collection of Roman floor mosaics, the finest in the world, from the villas of ancient Antioch and nearby **Daphne**, home to many wealthy Romans.

The Friday market at Alanya: a fascinating opportunity to observe local life and sample the produce of the region

A red Gibraltar
The mighty red fortified town of Alanya, a splendid example of Seljuk military architecture with its 146 towers, is unlike anything else to be seen along this coast. In its general appearance the rock on which it sits, jutting out to sea, has been compared with Gibraltar.

■ **Alexander the Great's extraordinarily swift conquest of Asia Minor and the whole of the Persian Empire brought an enormous region under Greek control, creating conditions in which ideas and cultures could cross-fertilise, resulting in a tremendous flowering of thought and art that was to transform the civilised world......■**

144

Marching on its stomach
Just 22 years old when he entered Asia Minor, Alexander possessed political vision and military genius combined with a youthful energy and enthusiasm for adventure. A master tactician with a superb grasp of logistics, he always made sure his army was well provided with food and drink. Later, when he had amassed the wealth to pay for them, he made considerable use of mercenaries.

Above right: a tetra-drachm (a coin worth four drachmas) showing the head of Alexander the Great

Below: a mosaic from Pompeii depicts Alexander (left) defeating Darius at Issus in 333BC

The man Born in 356BC, Alexander was the eldest son of Philip II, King of Macedon (359–336BC); the philosopher Aristotle was one of the young Alexander's tutors. When Philip was assassinated, Alexander first consolidated his position in Europe, then set out with the express purpose of liberating the Greek cities to the east and overthrowing the Persian Empire of Darius the Great. It was in 334BC that he crossed the Hellespont into Asia Minor, together with an army of 32,000 infantry and 5,000 cavalry.

In some cities, such as Ephesus and Phaselis, Alexander was greeted as a liberator; in others, notably Halicarnassus (modern Bodrum), Miletos and Aspendos, he was resisted as a conqueror. After campaigning in Asia Minor for just one year, Alexander won his first major battle, defeating Darius at Issus in 333BC; he then pressed on into Egypt, where he was accepted by the priests as the land's new ruler. Next he swept on eastwards, across the Persian Empire to the edge of the Himalayas, beginning – as he moved ever further from Greece – to enlist Persian soldiers and to appoint Persian nobles to posi-

tions of authority. After a mutiny by his exhausted Macedonian soldiers in 324BC he turned back, only to die of a sudden fever in Babylon the following year, at the age of just 32. In 10 years he had built up the largest empire the world had ever known (see also pages 116–17).

The problem of succession On his sudden death Alexander left no clear successor. His wife Roxana was pregnant when he died, and a regent was therefore appointed, but both mother and child were murdered in the disputes among Alexander's generals that ensued after his death. After 20 years of squabbling, three main kingdoms emerged under three generals: Ptolemy in Egypt; Seleucus in Syria; and Antigonus in Greece. The Seleucids and the Ptolemies, supposedly descended from Apollo and Dionysus, were worshipped as gods, and throughout all three kingdoms Alexander himself was honoured as a god, from whom all the kings claimed descent. In spreading Greek culture and ideas throughout his empire. Alexander founded many cities, endowing a number of them with his name. Some, such as Alexandria in Egypt, survive to this day. Throughout all three kingdoms it was these cities which became the centres of wealth and power, often free to administer their own affairs with an unusual degree of independence.

The Hellenistic legacy The period from Alexander's death until the gradual extinction of his successor kingdoms – largely absorbed by the Roman Empire in the 2nd and 1st centuries BC – is known as the Hellenistic Age (from the Greek *hellenistes*, meaning 'imitator of the Greeks'). It was an era marked by an extreme competitiveness of spirit on all levels. Cities rivalled each other for power and trade, while their citizens competed to amass great fortunes, flaunting their wealth by financing the construction of splendid monuments for their cities. It was also a period of great cultural activity, stimulated by the cross-fertilisation of oriental and western cultures and marked by great scholastic innovation. The two outstanding centres of learning were Alexandria in Egypt and Pergamum (see page 132); both left an immense legacy of learning, the influence of which cannot be overstated.

The spectacular theatre at Pergamum, one of the many remarkable surviving buildings of this ancient centre of learning

The Gordian knot
According to a prophecy in the Central Anatolian town of Gordion, whoever could untie the Gordian knot would be master of Asia. The knot had been tied by the Phrygian king (who was of peasant stock) to fix the yoke of his ox-cart to the pole. Alexander, hearing of the prophecy, could not resist the challenge. Stopping off at Gordion, he simply sliced through the knot with his sword. The significance of the knot remains in dispute: some say it represented the importance of the peasantry to the kingdom; others that it symbolised Gordion's strategic value as the key to the ancient road network.

146

*The new marina at
Antalya, converted
from the old harbour*

T.C. KÜLTÜR BAKANLIĞI

ANTALYA MÜZESİ GİRİŞ BİLETİ   № 195649

Waterfalls and caves
Near Antalya are two sets
of waterfalls, the Düden
Şelalesi on the road to
Lara, where the river hur-
tles over the cliff edge into
the sea, and the Kurşunlu
Şelalesi, inland on the
Isparta road, a spectacular
sight set in mountainous
scenery.
  There are also two sets
of caves: the Karain cave,
inhabited in neolithic
times, on the Burdur road;
and, on the same road
further north, the Insuyu
caves, a series of
interlinked chambers with
underwater lakes, stalac-
tites and stalagmites.

▶   **Antalya**   *134B2*

Antalya is the main port on the southern coast of Turkey,
as it has been for the last 2,000 years. The town is set on
a natural harbour with its industrial port area lying to the
west, while large US Navy ships are often to be seen in
the bay. The tourist hotels are concentrated round
the pretty, newly restored yachting marina in the
town centre, and out on the beaches of **Lara** to the
east. Half a day is enough to see Antalya's sights;
these consist of the 13th-century **Yivli Minare**
(Fluted Minaret), in typical Seljuk red brick, the
Karaalı Park up on the clifftop, with some remains
of fortifications, and the modern **museum** (open
daily except Mondays, 8:30–12:30 and 1:30–5:30 in
winter; 9–6 in summer) on the western outskirts,
noteworthy for its impressive sarcophagi from Perge.
  The sites around Antalya merit far more time: a
stay of three nights would be needed to visit the places
described below.

Environs of Antalya Aspendos▶▶ boasts the finest
example of a Roman theatre – indeed of any ancient
theatre – in the world. Under the Roman Empire
Aspendos prospered, producing salt from the nearby lake
which dries up in summer, cultivating vines and corn, and
producing coarse Pamphylian wool from the local sheep.
The site of the ancient city lies 30 minutes' drive east of
Antalya on the banks of the Eurymedon river, which is
crossed on the approach to the site by a lovely 13th-cen-
tury Seljuk bridge, still in use and perfectly sound. Before
arriving at Aspendos proper, fork left to reach an extraordinary aqueduct behind the acropolis, with a tall water
tower which provided enough pressure to force water to
flow up to the main city on the acropolis.
  The main track leads to the parking area directly in front of
the stupendous theatre, built in the 2nd century AD and still
nearly intact. A scramble up the hillside above the theatre
will reveal the ruins of a market hall, a *nymphaeum* (monumental fountain) an *agora* (market place) and a council

chamber, all of them invisible from the theatre below.

Perge► Set uninspiringly on the flat plain 5km west of Antalya, the ruined city of ancient Perge nevertheless has some striking features, notably its tall round Hellenistic gates, and its evocative main street complete with chariot ruts. It also has a fine stadium, the best-preserved in Asia Minor after that of Aphrodisias (see pages 104–5).

Sillyon► Lying between Perge and Aspendos, the acropolis of Sillyon, jutting up from the coastal plain, is visible from a long way off. Following a severe landslip in 1969, half its monuments toppled over the cliff, leaving the other half on the edge; these are still extensive, however, and about 3 hours should be allowed for a visit. Notice in particular the impressive southern and northern ramps leading up into the city, remarkably well preserved and with handsome paving.

Termessos►►► A visit to the ancient ruin of Termessos is one of the most exciting excursions in all Turkey. Known as the eagle's nest, it is set high in the mountains behind Antalya. The journey takes a full day, so take a picnic. Exploring the site involves some steep climbing, and sturdy, comfortable footwear is important. Despite being overgrown and never properly excavated, the ruins of the city have a grandeur rarely equalled anywhere.

A well-signed path leads up through the defences of the lower and upper city walls to reach the first main monument, the gymnasium, built in the impressive dark grey stone that is characteristic of Termessos. Higher up, the theatre has the most impressive setting of any in Turkey, with splendid views across the mountains. A complex of temples lies a little higher up by the market place, and beyond this on the hillside lies the extraordinary necropolis, littered with hundreds of sarcophagi from the first three centuries AD, presenting an apocalyptic vision.

Missing goddess
Despite extensive excavations, the whereabouts of the cult temple of Artemis Pergeia, the dominant goddess here, remain a mystery. Although it was known to be rich with the offerings of her worshippers, thorough searches of the hilltops and hillsides of the area have revealed no trace as yet of the famous temple.

The ancient theatre at Aspendos: the finest example in the world

Formidable ferocity
Inhabited in ancient times by people of legendary ferocity – known as Solymians after Mount Solymus, under which the city lies – Termessos also has some of the most formidable natural defences of any ancient city in Turkey. Alexander the Great took one look and decided to waste no more time, moving on to easier prey. Homer tells us that one of the trio of seemingly impossible tasks allotted to the young Bellerophon was the slaying of the Solymi.

The ruined city of Perge

■ In high season and on public holidays, when the beach resorts of the Aegean and Mediterranean are crowded, it is worth remembering the freshwater lakes of Beyşehir, Eğridir and Burdur, which lie just two hours' drive inland from Antalya. Set in magnificent scenery, surrounded by greenery and mountains, they offer excellent swimming in a peaceful environment, along with a few simple but surprisingly pleasant hotels and restaurants. The lakes may be approached on a circuit from Konya as well as from Antalya, and they make a delightful change in atmosphere from the tourist resorts of the coast......■

Kovada National Park
This wild forest centred on Kovada Lake is rarely visited but beautifully tended. The lake is rich in carp and bass, and the forests are said to shelter bears, wolves and wild boar. The roads are almost empty, and the only signs of habitation are the black goat-hair tents of the nomads who bring their flocks to pasture here in summer. Camping is permitted at the lakeside and the area is excellent for hiking.

Eğridir's unrivalled lakeshore setting

Beyşehir The easternmost of the three, just 90km from Konya, this is a shallow freshwater lake rich in carp. The main town of the lakeshore, also called Beyşehir, is at first sight a rather scruffy, sprawling place, but it repays a closer look. The overnight accommodation here is not good, but aim to have lunch either by the lake or at the pretty Beyaz Park in town, and then visit the 13th-century **Eşrefoğlu mosque** and *türbe* (tomb), an unusual pair, the mosque with a forest of columns and some lovely carpets. You can hire a boat to explore the 20 or so islands in the lake and, if you have the time, the unique 13th-century Seljuk **Kubadabad Palace**, on the western shore and accessible only by boat. On the beautiful **Kızkalesi Island** opposite is another Seljuk palace.

Another nearby excursion, this time by car, takes you to the enigmatic Hittite sanctuary of **Elfatun Pınarı**, 21km from Beyşehir on the Isparta road. The approach road to the site is bad but drivable with care; you are rewarded by the sight of these deserted and atmospheric ruins, with

Inland lakes

huge carved blocks covered in Hittite reliefs showing monsters and sun discs, symbols of the divine force.

Eğridir The most beautiful of the lakes and the best for swimming, Eğridir should be first choice for a base from which to explore the other inland lakes, as it offers the best hotels in the area. Cars can also be hired via the Tourist Information Office. The water of the lake is cold except in the height of summer (the altitude is 1,000m), but its clarity and blueness are delightfully inviting. The mountain setting is exceptionally lovely, the trees and vegetation making a welcome contrast to the bleak Anatolian plateau if you have arrived from Konya.

The town itself is set on a little promontory forming a peninsula on the lake. Here the remains of a Seljuk castle with a minaret enclose an amazing series of old Turkish houses, perched in precarious positions on the edge. A pebble-built causeway now links the promontory with two little islands, also covered with houses. A Greek basilica stands on the far island, its roof still intact. To find deserted beaches from which to swim, drive north along the lakeshore towards Barla.

Burdur and Salda On Lake Burdur is Cendik Beach, 2km from Burdur town, 5km long and good for swimming, though the water here is very saline. Salda, the westernmost of the lakes, is better for swimming: the water is a lovely crystal green, and the shore is lined with campsites, picnic areas and restaurants.

The most interesting excursion in the area is to the ancient ruins of **Sagalassos**, near Ağlasun, south of Isparta. The remains are impressive for their remarkable setting high on a plateau, and their good state of preservation, especially the theatre. Virtually a whole day is needed for a visit as the city can only be reached on foot, a 1½-hour walk, signposted from Ağlasun.

Lake Eğridir

Local delicacies
As might be expected, the local fish, on offer in all the restaurants, is a culinary highlight. Carp (*sazan*) and bass (*levrek*) are abundant, and Eğridir also specialises in baby crayfish. The food in the lakes area is generally of a very high standard, and is also much cheaper than in the coastal resorts.

The timeworn entrance to the old bazaar in Eğridir

Who were the Lycians?
The origins of the Lycians remain mysterious. Most scholars are now agreed that they were not an indigenous people, but that they came from Crete in about 1400BC under the leadership of Sarpedon, brother of King Minos. They always remained distinct from their neighbours, and Lycia was the last region in Asia Minor to be incorporated into the Roman Empire. They had their own language, even now not fully understood, which bears some resemblance to Hittite – according to one theory they are the Lukka referred to in Hittite records.

The bustling town of Fethiye, set on a large sheltered bay backed by mountains, was always the principal port of Lycia. In the last 10 years it has developed considerably as a resort, with a new yacht marina, and hotels lining the bay known as Çalış Beach, on the western approach to the town. The town seafront is crowded with caiques offering day trips to other nearby beaches, and the wide promenade has a string of cafés. The cobbled streets inland are full of colourful shops and restaurants, and the daily open-air food market is always humming with life.

There are three main sights: the rock tombs cut in the cliffs above the town, involving a steep climb, but worthwhile, especially at sunset; the medieval castle attributed to the Knights of Saint John, now crumbling, set on the old acropolis; and the superb sarcophagus set in the middle of the road in front of the town hall, left there by the earthquakes of 1856 and 1957. One of the finest in Lycia, it represents a two-storey Lycian house, and has a curved arch-shaped lid decorated inside and out with splendid reliefs of warriors.

Environs of Fethiye Kaya▶ Until the exchange of populations in 1923 (see pages 16–17), Fethiye had a large Greek

The lagoon at Ölü Deniz: Turkey's most beautiful beach and now a conservation area

population; extraordinary evidence of this can be seen in Kaya, the largest Greek ghost town in Turkey, once home to 3,500 Greeks and a few kilometres inland, about 20 minutes' drive *en route* to Ölü Deniz. A walk among the deserted houses and churches is an eerie experience.

Ölü Deniz▶▶ This is Turkey's most beautiful beach, to be seen decorating the front of numerous brochures, and the serene splendour of the lagoon (the Turkish name means 'Dead Sea') lives up to all expectations. Mercifully, the lagoon has now been designated a conservation area and development in the beach area is very strictly controlled: the bulk of development is now at **Ölü Ata** at the top of the valley, about 4km inland from the beach. Cheap *dolmuş* taxis run constantly between Ölü Ata and Ölü Deniz, and Ölü Ata has the advantage in high summer of

Lycian magic
Fethiye is the western gateway to the region known as Lycia, the bulge in Turkey's southern coastline between Fethiye and Antalya. An isolated and mountainous region, Lycia has always held itself aloof from its neighbours. Until 1981 the tarmac road stopped at Fethiye, leaving the region beyond inaccessible except to four-wheel-drive vehicles and horses. Freya Stark explored the coastline by boat (*The Lycian Shore*, 1956), and George Bean, the redoubtable explorer, classicist and academic, visited most of the area on foot. Despite the development now affecting some parts, the landscapes of Lycia have retained their savage beauty; the mountains, the remote and ancient hilltop ruins and the lovely Xanthos valley all exert a magic unequalled elsewhere in Turkey, and are possessed of a bewitching quality that will draw many under its spell.

151

being cooler than the beach. An entry fee is charged to the lagoon beach itself, but there is another long pebbly stretch to which access is unrestricted. The resort appeals to a young crowd, and nightlife is quite a feature. A 20-minute walk along the coast road brings you to **Kudrak**, Paradise Beach, still relatively unpopulated, even in high season.

Tlos▶ The 5-hour round trip from Fethiye to Tlos makes an exciting day's outing, preferably with a picnic. Set on a rocky outcrop dominating the valley of the Xanthos river, this ancient Lycian fortress on its summit is visible from afar, with characteristic tombs cut into the rock face below. The castle was used as a winter palace by the local feudal ruler in the 19th century, and Tlos was one of the very few Lycian cities to remain inhabited right through to the 19th century.

Of the various rock tombs, make sure that you do not miss the tomb of Bellerophon, with carvings of the mythological hero mounted on the winged horse Pegasus, his right arm raised to slay the Chimaera (see pages 164–5).

Lying in the flat lee of the acropolis is the charmingly overgrown theatre, with many carved blocks depicting actors' masks still to be found lying amongst the ruins; beyond stands the memorable baths building, with its wonderful seven-arched windows overlooking the Xanthos valley.

Lycian rock tombs at Tlos

Lycian ruins
The ruins of some 40 ancient Lycian cities have now been identified. Many are extremely remote, perched up on rocky outcrops and accessible only by arduous walks from the nearest road or village. The sites mentioned here (pages 150–65) repay the effort and are also accessible by car; sometimes reaching the site involves a short walk, but never more than half an hour.

Finike   134A1

Now a thriving agricultural town with an active harbour, Finike is set at the western edge of a fertile plain. A handful of small hotels and *pansiyons* make it a good base for exploring the Lycian sites of the area.

Environs of Finike Half an hour's drive inland from Finike on the Elmalı road is the splendid hillside site of **Arif (Arycanda)►►**. A 15-minute walk leads to the lowest building, thought to be the ancient citadel. Further on are scattered Roman temple tombs, some with carvings. Above them tower the colossal baths, and beside these stands the gymnasium, with an open-air exercise courtyard in front. The path now crosses the stream bed, dry in summer, to reach a large sunken oblong *agora* (market place), connected by archways to a small *odeon* (theatre). The magnificent theatre looks out over the valley, with the cliff as its natural backdrop, and above it a crumbling stairway leads to the stadium, the highest building in Arycanda.

Just a few kilometres inland from Finike, **Limyra►** has a remarkable necropolis, the most extensive in Lycia, rising up the mountains behind. On the plain below, a road leads to the small theatre, opposite which is a pleasant stream with the picturesque ruins of a Byzantine nunnery on its banks. On the hillside behind the theatre stands the famous 4th-century BC tomb of Catabura, an elaborate sarcophagus and plinth covered in reliefs of the judgement of the dead and a funeral banquet. Further up and the most dramatic of all is the tomb of Pericles, also 4th-century BC, set on a natural rock platform with fabulous views some 250m above the plain. Its unique reliefs and caryatids display both Greek and Persian influences. The 20-minute approach is from a small village to the west: the local children will undoubtedly show you the way.

Part of the ruins of Arycanda in their impressive hillside setting

Legacy of tombs
The most striking legacy of ancient Lycia is its tombs; tombs are everywhere, scattered over hillsides, cut into cliff faces and even submerged in the sea. Veneration of the dead and the associated custom of building important funerary monuments were universal throughout the ancient world, from the pyramids onwards. Much care was taken to protect these monuments and the bodies they contained, and Lycian tombs frequently carried inscriptions threatening to bring down fines and curses upon anyone violating them. The oldest and rarest of Lycian tombs, and also the most characteristic, are the pillar tombs, as at Xanthos. Uniquely Lycian are the numerous house tombs, at Myra, imitating the houses of the ancient Lycians.

The spectacular Lycian rock tombs – many of them house tombs – at Myra

Delicate carvings on one of the rock tombs at Myra

► **Kale**   *134A1*

A dusty, sprawling town, Kale (formerly known as Demre), is not somewhere you would choose to linger, were it not for the surprisingly beautiful and unusual sights that are to be found near by.

Environs of Kale The little harbour of Kale lies some 3km from the town centre; in ancient times, when it was known as **Andriake** (now **Cayağzı**)►, this was the port to the Lycian city of Myra (see below). The ruins now stand in the swampy estuary. Do not miss the vast grey stone building known as **Hadrian's Granary**, a 10-minute walk from where the drivable track ends. Over the central doorway are busts of Hadrian and his empress Faustina. The road ends by a pretty beach with good bathing in the icy estuary waters, and a footbridge over the river leads to some fish restaurants.

The necropolis and Roman theatre of the ancient Lycian city of **Myra**►► are truly spectacular and not to be missed. The ruins nestle at the foot of the cliff behind Kale (open 8:30 to sunset daily).

The theatre still has its vaulted entrance passages below the seats, trodden by audiences so many centuries ago. A path leads up to the cluster of tombs cut in the cliff face, most of which are of the house type. The main tomb has beautiful reliefs showing a funeral banquet.

FOCUS ON *Wildlife*

■ Turkey is blessed with huge tracts of virgin landscape, which in recent years have been preserved by the creation of numerous national parks throughout the country. Most of these are in heavily forested areas, often with lakes and rivers, and all are rich in flora and fauna......■

Hunting

Hunting has long been a popular pastime in Turkey, as in most Mediterranean countries, with the result that many species – such as the brown bear – have been hunted virtually to extinction. Popular game birds include wild duck, wild goose, quail, partridge and pheasant. Foreigners may hunt only in parties organised by Turkish travel agencies; these agencies will provide all relevant information on seasons, authorised zones, permits and weapons. In non-prohibited regions, tourists can fish for sport without obtaining permits.

Cistus albidus, a native Turkish rock rose

National parks In the Aegean region the **Dilek Milliparkı**, on Dilek Burnu south of Ephesus and close to Priene (see pages 122-3), combines a spectacular area of 1,200m-high jagged mountains with flat marshland rich in birdlife. The mountains are home to many birds of prey, as well as to jackals, striped hyenas, wild boar and even the very occasional leopard.

Abundant wildlife is also to be found in the **Olympos Milliparkı** on the Lycian coast near Antalya (see pages 162-3), with its 2,000-m high mountains covered in Calabrian pines. On the coast here you may see shearwaters flying in long formations, and Cory's shearwaters are also common. April and May are the loveliest months, with flowering shrubs such as lavender and rock roses attracting hosts of butterflies.

In inland parks, such as the **Kovada Milliparkı** between Lake Eğridir and Antalya, the forests provide shelter for red and roe deer, wild boar, wolves and even a small number of brown bears. In the **Yedigöller Milliparkı** (the name means 'Seven Lakes'), 50km inland from Zonguldak on the Black Sea (see pages 246-7), the deciduous and coniferous woodland of the national park is home to a similar range of wildlife.

Turtles The beach at **Dalyan**, near Dalaman airport on the Aegean coast (see page 112), is the biggest nesting beach for loggerhead turtles (*Caretta caretta*) in Turkey, and the second most important, after the Greek island of Zakynthos, in the whole Mediterranean. The turtles are threatened because the sandy beaches where they come to lay their eggs are increasingly being developed for tourism. During their two-month incubation period, the eggs are vulnerable to disturbance from digging and trampling. When they hatch, at night-time, the baby turtles scurry down to the sea, attracted by the natural luminescence of the surface and the reflected light of the moon; bright lights from hotels confuse them, and as they hesitate they are easily picked off by scavengers, while many others simply die of exhaustion before ever reaching the sea.

Birdwatching Birdwatching in Turkey can usually be combined with sightseeing or even lazing on the beach: armed with a pair of binoculars and a field guide, you can add a whole new dimension

Wildlife

to your holiday. Because of its geographical position on the edge of Europe, Asia and Africa, Turkey has a tremendously wide range of birdlife. Spring and autumn are the most exciting times because of the great north-south migrations of colossal numbers of birds – from sparrowhawks and eagles to black and white storks – visible even from Istanbul itself, especially from the Çamlıca hills on the Asiatic side.

May is probably the best month of all for birdwatching, when even the inexperienced may spot well over 100 species on a typical touring holiday. No one can fail to notice the tall storks which build enormous nests on minarets, rooftops and telegraph poles, or the vultures and birds of prey which hover overhead. On the road, the bird which is always running up under the wheels of the car is the crested lark, while on the telegraph wires you can usually spot yellow black-headed buntings, colourful bee-eaters and bright blue rollers.

Turkey also boasts several bird sanctuaries, notably **Kuş Cenneti** (Bird Paradise) by the Sea of Marmara, and **Birecik** near the Syrian border. Here you can see among other species the monstrously ugly and near-extinct bald ibis, the subject of a Worldwide Fund for Nature rescue operation.

Loggerhead turtles are threatened by tourist developments which disrupt their nesting beaches

155

Dangers to the explorer
In summer, the most aggravating form of wildlife you will encounter in the Aegean and Mediterranean regions is the mosquito, so go equipped with repellent, especially if you intend to eat outdoors. Scorpions and snakes are not abundant, but it is worth being careful when walking off the beaten track in sandals or with bare legs.

The short-toed eagle (Circaetus gallicus) is one of the many species that can be spotted in Turkey's bird sanctuaries

One of Kalkan's picturesque narrow streets

A Lycian house tomb at Xanthos

▶▶ **Kalkan** 134A1

A good base for exploring Lycian sites inland, Kalkan is an attractive town climbing up the hillsides that encircle its fishing harbour. There is a growing number of small family-run hotels in renovated village houses, many of which have characteristic roof terraces, and the narrow cobbled streets have relatively sophisticated souvenir shops and restaurants.

Environs of Kalkan Xanthos▶▶ Reached from unsavoury Kınık, 18km inland from Kalkan, Xanthos is a magnificent site, as befits the remains of Lycia's greatest city. It is also very extensive: a thorough visit takes a good 3 hours, with a fair bit of walking and scrambling. In the 19th century the British plundered 70 huge crates of sculptures, most of which are now in the British Museum in London. No serious excavations were carried out until a French team arrived in 1950. Any tour should begin with the theatre and its extraordinary pair of pillar tombs, 8m high. The reliefs (plaster casts, as the originals are now in London) depict amazing creatures, half-bird, half-woman, carrying children in their arms, thought to represent either the Harpies or Spirits carrying off the souls of the dead. On the acropolis stand the remains of a Lycian **royal palace**, overlooking the river valley. On the other side of the car park is an extensive Byzantine basilica with mosaic flooring, and further uphill is the necropolis, with a cluster of house tombs dominated by another pillar tomb. At the top of the hill are the remains of a Byzantine monastery and large Roman temple.

Boat trip Kekova

An enjoyable day trip combining a swim with a simple lunch at a village restaurant, and calling off at several partly submerged ancient Lycian settlements around the island of Kekova.

Tickets can be bought at Kaş harbourfront, and the boat generally leaves at 9am and returns by 6pm. Boats also run from the little harbour of Demre, called Çayağzı. Private boats are more flexible but more expensive. Bring a mask and flippers, so you can snorkel round the underwater ruins. Skindiving is forbidden.

After setting off from Kaş and passing the Greek island of Castellorizo, 90 minutes' cruising brings you to the ruins of **Aperlae**, a Lycian town of the 4th century BC. In the shallow waters of the bay you can discern the outlines of streets and buildings submerged as a result of earthquakes over the centuries.

After another 45 minutes you reach a pretty cove on Kekova island, where the ruined apse of a Byzantine church stands on the beach. This is a good swimming spot; look out for the foundations of houses at the far end of the bay. Watch out too for occasional sea urchins.

The boat now hugs the shoreline of Kekova island, where you will see

Kekova's ruins: Byzantine above and Lycian beneath the waters

more ruins beneath the turquoise water. The final port of call is the village of **Kale** (Turkish for castle), named after the Byzantine fort whose crenellated walls crown the hilltop, enclosing a tiny, charming ancient theatre with seats cut into the rock. A few simple fish restaurants have grown up on the waterfront, overlooking more submerged ruins.

The return journey to Kaş takes about 2½ hours.

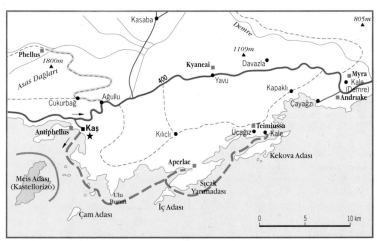

*Local leather goods
on sale at Kaş*

*A near-deserted
beach at Karayellari,
near Kaş*

▶ **Kaş** *134A1*

Like Kalkan (see page 156), Kaş is an excellent base for exploring the Lycian sites, but whereas Kalkan still feels like a village, Kaş is definitely a town, offering a good choice of shops and restaurants and a range of hotels and small family *pansiyons*. Set in a lovely bay encircled by high mountains all around, it retains quite a traditional feel, with an attractive harbour frequented by fishermen and yachting enthusiasts alike. Much development has taken place on the snake-like headland to the west; the rocky beaches are not so good for children, however.

A few fragments of the ancient site of **Antiphellus** remain, including the small theatre above the town and a number of huge sarcophagi strewn about the streets and harbourfront. The whitewashed mosque is recognisable as a former Greek church, a relic of the days before 1923, when Kaş had a thriving Greek community.

Environs of Kaş Kekova Adası (Kekova Island)▶▶ See page 157.

Letoon▶▶ Try to visit this site at sunset, when it is at its loveliest. The principal remains of this ancient Lycian sanctuary to Leto and her two children Artemis and Apollo (see panel) consist of three temples and a *nymphaeum* (monumental fountain). The only other major building is a theatre, reflecting the Letoon's other role as a central meeting place for the Lycian League (see page 162). Leto, Artemis and Apollo were the national deities of Lycia, and national festivals were held here, the ceremonies conducted by the chief priests of the League.

The greater part of the site is underwater, which lends a particular charm – especially at sunset, when the frogs in the sacred pools croak for all they are worth.

▶▶ Patara   134A1

This ancient site, with its natural harbour, once served as the port for Xanthos. Now the river disappears into marshland, and an immense sandbank has accumulated over the centuries to silt up the harbour, but also to give Patara its superb 22km-long sandy beach. No development is allowed on the beach because of the proximity of the historical site, but a small cluster of hotels has grown up a kilometre inland. The ancient city itself has never been excavated and the theatre, buried in sand to the waist, makes a strangely attractive sight. The distances involved in exploring the ruins are considerable and the terrain is tricky, with sand and occasional marshy areas. From the top of the theatre you can assess the effort required to reach each part. A small temple buried in sand and undergrowth is probably the closest monument, remarkably well preserved and with a beautifully decorated lintel. The indefatigable may not be able to resist a trek right across the silted-up harbour to **Hadrian's Granary**, a colossal building which serves as an evocative reminder of how these outlying parts of the empire served as bread baskets to feed the citizens of Rome.

▶ Phellus   134A1
See pages 160–1.

▶ Üçağız (Teimiussa)   134A1

The drive to this village at the end of the Kekova peninsula is an interesting one, through rural, sparsely populated countryside. The remains of a number of ancient cities lie on these wild, remote hillsides, but it would take many days and a great deal of stamina to explore them all.

The road ends at Üçağız, a surprisingly sophisticated little place, more visited from the sea than from the land. Right on the water's edge, by the football pitch, lie the remains of ancient Teimiussa, with a little fortress on a low summit and many sarcophagi scattered about, some of them with fine carvings.

The harbour at Kaş attracts fishing boats and yachts alike

The legend of Leto
In ancient times the cult of Leto was widespread in this part of Turkey. According to legend she was loved by Zeus, who was father to her twins, Artemis and Apollo. Persecuted by Hera, the jealous wife of Zeus, she was forced to flee while still pregnant. Many cities refused her entry, fearing the gods' wrath, and she finally arrived in a land known as Termilis, where she gave birth to her twins. As she was bathing them in a spring near where the Letoon now stands she was driven away by local shepherds; she turned them into frogs in punishment, and it is their descendants that we hear today (see page 159). Wolves then guided her to the River Xanthos, where she bathed her children and drank. In gratitude, she dedicated the river to Apollo and renamed the land Lycia (from *lykos*, the Greek word for wolf).

Walk Mountain ridge from Kaş

See map on page 157.

The starting point for this walk is reached by a short drive inland to the village of Çukurbağ. From here there is a wonderful ridgetop walk with superb sea views, ending in the rarely visited Lycian ruined town of **Phellus**. Allow 3 hours altogether.

Head out of Kaş inland on the Finike road for 10km until you reach the village of Ağullu, then take the easy dirt road that forks back to the west (refer to the map on page 157). On reaching the village of Çukurbağ, pass the village spring to the left and continue on a broad track that sweeps up the hillside in a loop. It then winds in and out of thick forested patches, affording superb views down over Kaş, Castellorizo and the coast. After about 5km the road ends at a forest look-out post at the crest of the ridge. The total distance from Kaş is no

more than 20km, and the drive takes about half an hour.

The Turkish name for Phellus is Felandağ (the name of the mountain); if anyone is at home in the forest station you can ask for directions. In fact you need only head along the ridge-top in a westerly direction before coming almost immediately upon a little path, usually clearly visible, sometimes a bit prickly and boulder-strewn.

A delightful walk of no more than half an hour brings you to the first signs of the ruined town, in the shape of some fine sarcophagi bearing reliefs and carvings. The finest of all lies down the hillside to the south, raised up on a solid base and with reliefs on three sides. The long south-facing side shows the deceased reclining on a couch drinking from a cup, waited upon by servants.

Most exciting of all is the area at the far end of the ridge, set down in a hollow which is surrounded by what were clearly the fortified city walls.

A typically fine Lycian landscape

Here, heavily overgrown with scrub, are two enormous house tombs, carved from colossal free-standing boulders at least 3½ metres high.

In a corner near by, there seems to have been a small sanctuary, with a low semi-circular wall recalling the apse of a church. On a large flat rock-face beside it is a carved bull, twice life-size: this is one of the few pieces of evidence to support the existence of a bull cult in ancient Lycia.

The position of Phellus, commanding a view in all directions, conveys the feeling of a fortification rather than a settlement. Extensive sections of the beautifully crafted wall remain. There are also two wells, still in use, with cool, clear drinking water: this is the only ancient hilltop town in Lycia still with an abundant water supply. In the far southeastern corner is a small watch-tower, and more sarcophagi can be found scattered down the north-facing side of the valley.

An ancient rock tomb on the route of the walk

A crescent-shaped bay on the coast south of Kemer

The Lycian League
The Lycians always had an instinct for unity, an unusual phenomenon in an age of constant warfare between city-states. To defend their region, the Lycians formed themselves into a league of 23 cities in the 2nd century BC. They even introduced a system of proportional representation: at their meetings, which rotated from city to city, the chief cities had three votes, the middling ones two votes and minor ones a single vote. Taxes were levied in the same proportions. Peace meant that the country prospered and huge fortunes were amassed by private citizens, many of whom lavished money on public building works.

Kemer   134B2

This holiday resort for Antalya (see page 146) is the most easterly town in Lycia and also probably the most developed, with a wide range of hotels, holiday villages, restaurants and shops. Its setting is very attractive, backed by wooded mountains tumbling right down into the sea, and its sand and shingle beaches are immaculately maintained. There is a busy yachting marina and the atmosphere is of a popular yet sophisticated family resort. The **Moonlight Beach** complex offers excellent sporting facilities and watersports for a small fee. In the **Yürük (Nomad) Theme Park** you can watch traditional crafts being practised. Kemer is also well placed for excursions to nearby Lycian sites and to places near Antalya, such as **Termessos** and **Aspendos** (see pages 146-7).

▶▶   **Olympos**   134B1

Set in its own National Park, Olympos probably enjoys the loveliest site in all Lycia. Allow at least 3 hours for a visit to this remote spot, or – better still – make it a day's outing with a picnic so as to allow plenty of time to enjoy the ancient ruins, the beach and the wonderful scenery.

The approach to the site is along a dirt track which follows the river valley lined with pink-flowering oleander bushes. The ruins – many of them covered in dense undergrowth, or partly submerged – are quite difficult to explore, but the persistent will be rewarded by the discovery of the collapsed ruins of a theatre, baths, a basilica and a fine temple doorway dating to the 2nd century AD.

A short drive or long walk from the Olympos beach brings you to the **Chimaera** (see pages 164–5).

► **Phaselis** *134B1*

Just 30km from Antalya (see page 146), Phaselis is a popular destination for school outings and picnics. It has been extensively excavated, and a new complex of buildings by the entrance includes a souvenir shop and tea house. This is one of the very few Lycian sites to have a formal ticket office and an entry fee, but, like all the others, it is effectively open throughout daylight hours. The site has three natural harbours, all of which can be used for swimming – a memorable experience while looking back at the pine-clad mountains tumbling down to the sea.

The track leads to a Roman aqueduct among the trees. Foundations of shops line the paved main street, and there are extensive baths, complete with underground central-heating systems. A stairway leads off the main street to the pleasantly overgrown and shady theatre. The street then continues across the headland to the far harbour and a large gateway erected in honour of a visit by the Emperor Hadrian in about AD130.

► **Rhodiapolis** *134A1*

A full day with picnic should be allowed for a trip to the ruins of this ancient city, high in the hills above Kumluca. It is difficult to reach without a guide, and involves about an hour's walk up through the forest from the nearest drivable track, yet the walk itself is so enjoyable and the ruins themselves so charmingly buried in the forest, that the exertion is well worth it. The city's claim to fame is its funeral monument to Opromoas. A citizen of Rhodiapolis, Opromoas amassed a great fortune, and on his death bequeathed large sums of money for the construction of public monuments here and elsewhere in Lycia. The walls of his funeral monument are covered in inscriptions narrating the honours poured upon him, amounting to the longest single inscription in Lycia, and perhaps even in Asia Minor. The tomb is now in ruins, its carved blocks scattered about the forest floor by treasure-seekers convinced that a mighty hoard must lie within.

Phaselian tricks
Demosthenes described the Phaselians thus: 'They are clever at borrowing money in the market, then as soon as they have it they forget it was a loan, and when called on for repayment think up all sorts of excuses and pretexts, and if they do repay it they feel that they have been done out of their own property; and in general they are the most scoundrelly and unscrupulous of men'.

163

One of the three harbours at the Lycian site of Phaselis at sunset: a wonderfully romantic setting for swimming

Walk The Chimaera

This short but dramatic walk leads up through forest, inland from Olympos, to reach the extraordinary flames that burn eternally on the hillside above Olympos, the home of the legendary fire-breathing Chimaera.

The starting point for the walk, which takes about an hour each way, is the site of Olympos, on the eastern Lycian coast between Kemer and Finike (see pages 162–3). Boat trips run daily from Kemer in season. Bring a picnic if you intend to be here over lunchtime. The pebbly beach offers excellent swimming, against the lovely backdrop of the mountains and constantly flowering oleander bushes; and there is good paddling for chil-

dren in a river estuary. If you swim round the bay you can examine the full extent of the castle crenellations up on the cliffs, part of the defences erected by the den of pirates who made this their base in ancient times. As early as the 5th century BC pirates plagued the whole southern Turkish coast, preying on trading ships from Syria and the Aegean, and selling their captives into slavery in wealthy Roman households. In the 1st century BC Olympos became the head-quarters of the pirate chief Zeniketes.
Begin the walk by heading northwards along the beach towards

A curl of flame licks up as it has done for centuries on this site

some huts, then follow a dirt road through a small village. Continue north through the village, asking for *ateş* (literally 'fire') if in doubt.

Beyond the village the track comes to a dead end in a cleft between two hillsides. Red paint on rocks and tree trunks now mark the path, which climbs gently from this point to reach the Chimaera in less than 30 minutes.

Suddenly the character of the hillside undergoes a curious change, becoming strangely bare. Issuing from it in at least a dozen places are flames the size of camp fires. These were the eternal flames which inspired the ancient pirates of Olympos to hold secret rites to Mithras, the Zoroastrian god of light whose cult they must have encountered in their eastern exploits. Visible far out to sea, the flames also served to guide sailors round the cape, which was notorious for its violent storms and shipwrecks.

In antiquity this was believed to be the home of the Chimaera, a mythical beast described in the *Iliad*: 'in front a lion, and behind a serpent, and in the midst a goat, and she breathed dread fierceness of blazing fire'. Homer describes how the King of Lycia set Bellerophon, the youthful suitor for his daughter's hand, the task of slaying the Chimaera.

Over the ages the flames have fluctuated greatly in their intensity, from a huge fire that the ancients claimed could not be extinguished, to a few feeble flames easily put out with handfuls of earth. In the 19th century travellers used to come here to wallow in the waters of a nearby sulphurous pit, supposedly good for skin diseases, while their servants boiled tea and cooked food on the flames of the Chimaera.

At the lowest part of the bare mountainside stand the remains of the pirates' temple, where the citizens of Olympos later came to worship Hephaistos, the Roman Vulcan, god of fire and forging.

165

The ruins of the shrine to Hephaistos

The vast 2nd-century theatre at Side affords magnificent views over the ancient site and to the sea beyond

The Manavgat falls, a cooling alternative to the seaside with a refreshing breeze

▶▶ **Side** 134B2

Side, where the ruins of the ancient city mingle with the new, is the most charming resort on Turkey's southern coast. It offers an ever-increasing number of hotels, motels, *pansiyons* and campsites, most of them lining the excellent long sandy beaches. Despite the development, Side nevertheless succeeds in retaining its special identity and atmosphere. It also serves as an excellent base for combining a beach holiday with excursions to inland sites – and it is less than an hour's drive from Antalya airport.

Side lies on a promontory 3km south of the main coastal road; a fine Roman aqueduct, which used to bring water a distance of over 32km from the mountains, heralds the outskirts of the town. All cars must be left in the parking area beside the site museum.

Of all the ancient cities on Turkey's southern shore, Side is the only one to have been excavated systematically. It flourished under the Roman Empire, and most of the extant monuments date from this period. In the 10th century it was abandoned after a fire, and the present town on the site dates only from the beginning of the 20th century, when it was founded by a group of Greek-speaking Muslim exiles from Crete. After the earlier abandonment of the town, sand drifted in to block the old harbour and cover many of the ruins. Somewhere under this sand there probably lies buried Side's stadium, of which no trace has yet been found.

A tour of the site can take anything

from 2 to 4 hours. The museum (open 9–12, 1:30–3 daily) is housed in the 5th-century Roman baths, still with their original room plan. It now makes an effective display area for all the significant sculpture found on site. Many of the statues are headless, having been decapitated by over-zealous Christians soon after their conversion by Saint Paul.

The restaurant at Manavgat makes an unusual lunch stop

Directly opposite the museum is the *agora* (market place), from which you can climb into the theatre, built in the 2nd century and one of the largest in Asia Minor, seating about 17,000. From here there are fine views over the rest of the site and its Hellenistic defence walls and on towards the sea.

Environs of Side Manavgat▶ Lunch at Manavgat makes a very pleasant change, only a 20-minute drive from Side. There is a nominal admission fee to the waterfall area, which is laid out with crass souvenir shops. Beyond this is the unusual restaurant, with tables scattered about beneath the trees, or perched on individual platforms built out on the edge of the rushing river. Even in the height of summer there is always a cooling breeze here, and the staple fare is the river trout, helped down by refreshing white Turkish wine.

Seleukeia (Seleuceia)▶ A half-day outing from Side to the ruined city of Seleukeia is a good opportunity to see the landscapes inland and do a little walking. The site is rarely visited – surprisingly, given its closeness to Side and its good state of preservation. It is reached from the village of Şıhlar, from which you can either drive carefully on the rough track or walk for about an hour to reach the hill on which the ruins stand. At the entrance is a narrow hollow with a cave on the left which shelters a fine and very welcome spring. Just above this are the baths, the city gate, flanked by rectangular towers, and the *agora* (market place) beyond. Beside the *agora* is the market hall, Seleukeia's most impressive monument.

Selge▶▶ See pages 168–9.

Communal latrines
In the western corner of the *agora* (market place) in Side, against the theatre, are the ancient public latrines, consisting of a semicircular arched passage, lined with marble and originally containing 24 seats above a water channel. In classical times one's daily achievements were not, as now, private affairs to be performed in solitary confinement, but rather an excuse for social gatherings and a chat.

Walk Selge Canyon

This trip inland into the magnificent scenery of the Köprülü Kanyon National Park, culminating in the ascent to the ancient town of Selge, is not to be missed by anyone using Side or Antalya as a base. Unquestionably one of the most exciting excursions on the Mediterranean coast, it merits a whole day. There is a simple restaurant at the bottom of the canyon, but if you plan to venture all the way to Selge take your own provisions.

Turn off the main Antalya to Side road and drive inland 37km to Beşkonak,

The magnificent mountain scenery of Selge Canyon makes an unforgettable day's excursion

also signposted Köprülü Kanyon Milliparkı. From Side the drive takes one and a quarter hours, winding through forest with glimpses down over the wide Eurymedon river. At Beşkonak the tarmac stops and an easy dirt track continues north for 6km to reach the stone Roman bridge that spans the canyon over the river. Just before this is the attractive **Kanyon Restaurant,** right on the river's edge.

Follow the signs to Altınkaya ('golden rock' in Turkish), the new name for the small settlements 14km away on the plateau, where ancient Selge and the modern village of Zerk lie.

Cross the Roman bridge. If you wish to limit your walk to the canyon and river area, take the left fork for a kilometre or so to reach a second Roman bridge beside a picnic area.

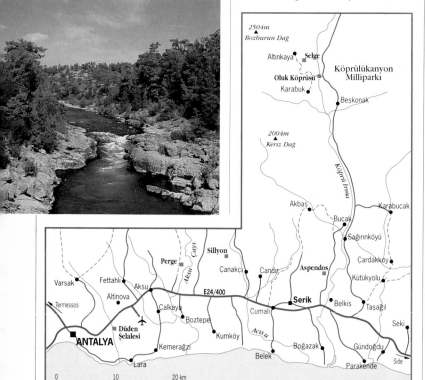

The fork right to Altınkaya is pretty rough in some places, but recent improvements mean most saloon cars can now make it. From the bridge to Selge is 13km, so you can stop the car at any point and walk if you prefer. The scenery along the way is very dramatic, with weird rock formations called 'fairy chimneys' in the higher parts, and in all directions the deep gullies and precipices which successfully defended ancient Selge against successive conquering armies.

The plateau at the end of the road is 900m high, and the temperature here is noticeably cooler than on the coast. The cultivated fields of Zerk are quickly followed by the first sight of Selge's ancient theatre, standing in the middle of the village, against the backdrop of the impressive snow-covered peaks of the **Kuyucuk** range (2500m).

Park in the designated area and children will doubtless appear and escort you round for a small tip. Walking up through the village, passing the remains of a *stoa* (colonnade of shops) on your right and a barely recognisable stadium (for horse races) on your left, you emerge at the back of the well-preserved theatre.

From the top of the theatre a small path leads off to the hill where the Temples of Artemis and Zeus, now just heaps of rubble, have been iden-

The wild terrain acted as an impregnable defence for the ancient town of Selge

tified. Following the course of the main street (with traces of the drainage system still visible), the path eventually reaches the fine paved courtyard of what was once the *agora* (market place), littered about with fragments of carved marble blocks. A short climb up the second hill brings you to the scant remains of a Christian church, and from here a scramble down the hillside affords good views of the extensive walls that encircled the city in its heyday, when 20,000 fiercely independent citizens lived here.

Traditional cooking in Selge Canyon

CAPPADOCIA

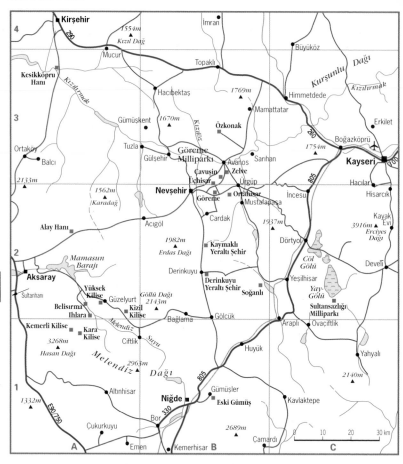

Above right and far right: troglodyte dwellings hollowed out of the soft tufa

Fairy chimneys
These extraordinary rock formations which have become the symbol of Cappadocia can be found in greatest numbers in two valleys close to Ürgüp. Four kilometres north of Ürgüp is the Devrent Valley, where you can park and walk down among the pink fairy chimneys, and 2km west of the town is the Çatalkaya Valley with its mushroom-shaped formations.

A scene typical of the Göreme Valley

Cappadocia This extraordinary region of Central Anatolia has now become justly famous for its weird volcanic landscapes and painted churches, unique in the world. It was largely unknown in the West until a French priest, Guillaume de Jerphanion, decided to devote his life to the study of its churches, publishing the results of his vast research in the 1930s and 1940s.

Landscape The natural agent responsible for the famous Cappadocian landscapes was the (now extinct) volcano **Mount Erciyes**, which rises behind the town of **Kayseri**. Thirty million years ago, the volcanic ash it spewed forth consolidated into a layer of the soft porous rock known as tufa, covering an area of about 4,000 square kilometres. Over the millennia, the soft tufa was eroded by wind, snow and rain, but where it was protected above by a deposit of harder stone, the result was the curiously shaped rock cones that we see today, often still capped by the protective block of hard stone, which gives them a toadstool shape. The fanciful epithet 'fairy chimneys' derives partly from local folk tales of men being carried off by *peris*, or fairies, after venturing into old churches in the rocks. Whereas the usual colours in volcanic landscapes are harsh greys and blacks, the rocks here are in soft

CAPPADOCIA

The 'fairy chimneys' of Cappadocia

Alternative transport
Cappadocia's landscape is well suited to horse riding and cycling, and local travel agencies can arrange sorties into the countryside, sometimes involving camping out. Hot-air ballooning has also become popular recently; the best time for this is in the early morning, when the air is still clear enough for superb aerial views.

shades of pale grey, yellow, mauve, pink and umber, the colour variation reflecting the variety of metal ores and minerals emitted over the millennia during countless different eruptions.

Changing seasons Cappadocia lies in the triangle formed by the three main towns of **Nevşehir**, **Kayseri** and **Niğde.** The best place to base yourself is probably the attractive rural town of **Ürgüp**, which has a good range of hotels. The tourist season begins in earnest in April and continues until the end of November; in high season, the area is subject to a major invasion of tourists from all parts of Europe, almost all of them in organised coach tours. The **Göreme heartlands** have been particularly hit by tourist development, with forests of signs and billboards advertising hotels and restaurants. As an independent traveller it is possible, however, to get off the coach tour routes and visit some of the less well-known valleys, such as **Soğanlı** and **Ihlara**, where you can still enjoy relatively untouched Cappadocian landscapes and churches.

A winter visit is in many ways the best, when the whole region is frequently lightly covered in snow, and when all the sites stay open but there are few or no coach tours. Even in spring the region remains remarkably cold, and snow is not unusual as late as early May. The swimming pools of most of the hotels do not function until June, when the really hot weather starts. Autumn is probably the most colourful season, when the leaves of the apricot and poplar trees turn to lovely yellows, reds and oranges under clear blue skies.

Cave paintings

The moving and beautiful wall paintings in the rock churches and monasteries of Cappadocia constitute an essentially provincial art form, described by the art historian Steven Runciman as 'expressions of an intense but unsophisticated piety'. Dating from the Iconoclastic period (8th and 9th centuries) to the 11th century, the paintings are characterised by crudely drawn figures, strongly outlined to produce an immediately powerful effect. Some of them reflect the artistic traditions of Egypt, Syria and Palestine, while others show the influence of the Byzantine capital, Constantinople. As so few works of art from this period survive outside Istanbul, these cave paintings are an exceptionally important record of Byzantine cultural history.

Itineraries Cappadocia covers a large area, and the sheer number and variety of places to visit can be bewildering on first arrival. To help plan your stay, here are some detailed excursions which can all be done from Ürgüp (or from **Nevşehir** or **Avanos**), each excursion taking a day.

1 Ortahisar, Üçhisar (lunch), Göreme Valley.
2 Çavuşin, Zelve (lunch), Avanos, Sarıhan, Özkonak, Peribacalar Valley.
3 Ürgüp, Mustafapaşa, Soğanlı (lunch), Derinkuyu, Kaymaklı, Nevşehir.
4 Ürgüp, Avanos (lunch), Hacıbektaş, Gülşehir, Nevşehir.
5 Nevşehir, Ihlara (lunch), Güzelyurt (Sultanhanı, if you are going on to Konya, see pages 204–5).
6 Ürgüp, Mustafapaşa, Soğanlı (lunch), Eski Gümüş, Niğde (from where you can go on to reach Adana the same day if you wish, see pages 136–7).

Typical Cappadocian villages combine cave dwellings with surface-built houses

CAPPADOCIA

► **Avanos** *170B3*

North of Göreme on the road to Özkonak, Avanos is a pretty little town on the banks of the **Kızılırmak**, the Red River, the longest river in Anatolia. The distinctive deep red soil which tinges the water also colours the clay used to make the famous local pottery, which was exported even in earliest times to Greece and Rome.

On the southern outskirts of the town, a yellow sign points to **Sarıhan**, the Yellow Caravanserai. The *han* itself is remarkable for the soft colour of the stone used to face its exterior and for its very small proportions. It is presently being restored.

► **Çavuşin** *170B3*

As the landscape flattens out between Avanos and Göreme, you reach Çavuşin Church, slightly set back to the right of the road (entrance fee). The front section of the church has been eroded away, exposing frescoes of the archangels Gabriel and Michael guarding the entrance. The frescoes inside, in clashing orange and yellow, are rather different from those at Göreme (see pages 176–7), and some experts believe they are the work of Armenians. Outside, steps lead up to the monastery next door, with four carved tombs inside. In the village of Çavuşin itself (some 400m before this church) is the **church of Saint John the Baptist**, dating back in part to the 8th century and generally regarded as the oldest in Cappadocia. Its façade has recently collapsed and the exterior is heavily damaged, but the interior still has fine paintings.

Avanos, famous for its pottery since Classical times

▶▶ Derinkuyu   170B2

A yellow sign in a muddy carpark in the dirty little village of Derinkuyu announces this underground city (open daily 8–6), offering no clue from the outside to its scale and extent. Discovered by accident in 1963, this is one of the most extensive of Cappadocia's 37 known underground cities, and was home to at least 20,000 people (see panel). The full number of storeys is still not known, but is thought to be as many as 18 or 20, of which only the top eight are open to the public.

No one is sure who the original builders were, but the current belief is that the first level was probably built by the Hittites in about 1400BC as a store area: Hittite seals have been found by locals digging foundations for their houses, and certainly the Hittites built a surface city 20km southwest of Derinkuyu at Göllü Dağı. It is thought that the air chimneys, 70 to 80m deep, were dug first until water was reached, and then horizontal passages were cut between them. The volcanic tufa was very soft to cut, as it hardens only on contact with air, and the tufa chambers make surprisingly pleasant living areas, with good air circulation, constant temperatures and humidity and, very importantly, no insects.

The first two storeys consist of communal kitchens, areas for eating, sleeping and storage, wine cellars, stables and toilets, while the lower levels contain hiding places with wells (Derinkuyu means 'Deep Well'), chapels, armouries, dungeons, burial places and a meeting hall. The villagers at Derinkuyu still depend on these wells for their water. Several of the tunnels have large cartwheel-shaped stones to seal them off, and some of them were intended to serve as escape routes – one tunnel, leading to the underground city of Kaymaklı, is astonishing 9km long.

Part of the network of subterranean corridors in the underground city of Derinkuyu

Underground congestion
Throughout history the people of Cappadocia have used their underground cities as refuges from the invading hordes which regularly poured across the Anatolian plain. As recently as 1839 the locals hid here from the invading Egyptian army, under Ibrahim Paşa. Today, they are invaded by the tourist hordes who pour underground by the busload. Derinkuyu has eight storeys open to the public, with only one single-file stairway to the bottom. If you encounter a tour group on the second storey, your chances of reaching the eighth storey within the hour are small, and if two tour groups going in opposite directions encounter each other on the stairs, complete paralysis of the system ensues.

CAPPADOCIA

Iconoclastic zeal
In the 8th and 9th centuries much religious art of the Byzantine world was destroyed by zealots known as Iconoclasts (from the Greek 'image-breakers'). Fearing that the veneration of images would lead to idolatry, some emperors not only prohibited the creation of religious art, but also authorised the wholesale destruction of church images already in existence. The paintings in Cappadocia were among the few to escape the Iconoclasts' fervour.

Frescoes inside the Çarıklı Kilise, or Shoe church

Some farmers use old rock dwellings as pigeon cotes

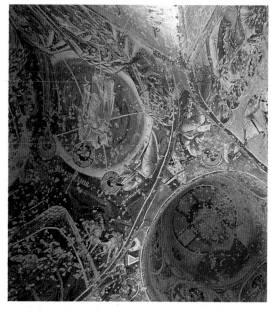

▶▶▶ Göreme 170B2

The churches of the Göreme Valley contain unquestionably the most spectacular paintings of the region; as a result, this area has been designated the Göreme National Park, a huge open-air museum. The inevitable corollary is heavy development of the site for tourists, with high entry and parking fees, a bank and shops at the entrance, and a definite sense of being 'processed' round, as you follow the arrows in a one-way system. Try to visit out of season or very early in the day in order to avoid the worst of the crowds. Alternatively, choose the relative freedom of less well known sites such as **Soğanlı** (see pages 186–7) and **Ihlara** (see pages 182–3).

The tour begins with the **Elmalı Kilise** (Apple Church), named after either the dwarf apple trees growing near the entrance, or a round object held by Jesus in one of the frescoes, thought to resemble an apple, though it is probably the Earth. After a narrow arcaded tunnel entrance, the church opens up into the usual dome over four pillars. The 11th-century frescoes depict the Baptism of Christ, his Entry into Jerusalem, the Last Supper, the Crucifixion and the Betrayal of Judas.

Next is the **Church of Saint Barbara**, cut into the back of the same rock as the Apple Church and decorated with the unexciting geometric red lines of the Iconoclastic period (726–842), when the use of images was forbidden. These churches are curiously small, in compliance with the views of Saint Basil, the founder of eastern monasticism, on the importance of keeping monastic communities small.

After this you reach the **Yılanlı Kilise** (Snake Church), one of the most interesting, with a vaulted ceiling with frescoes on its sides. The name derives from one of these, showing Saint George on horseback fighting the dragon, which is depicted as a serpent with the damned trapped in its coils.

Passing through a series of rooms and refectories, part of a monastic complex cut in the rock, you next reach the **Karanlık Kilise** (Dark Church). This originally had only one window, making it very gloomy inside, but the façade has now fallen away to expose the interior. The 11th-century frescoes here – depicting the Last Supper, the Adoration of the Magi and the Betrayal of Judas – have retained the freshness of their colours through having been protected from the light for so long.

Next is the **Çarıklı Kilise** (Shoe Church), reached by an iron staircase. *Çarık* means a kind of moccasin, referring to the shoe-prints at the bottom of one of the frescoes of Christ. Finally you reach the **Kızlar Kilise** or convent, thought to have housed some 300 nuns.

The loveliest church, the **Tokalı Kilise** (Buckle Church), lies on the other side of the road from the car park. The guardian comes with you to turn on the lights, revealing a magnificent interior, still in excellent condition. The frescoes depict the Miracles of Christ and other scenes, such as the Last Supper, the Flight into Egypt, the Nativity and the Entry into Jerusalem, all against a superb deep blue background. This is the largest of the Göreme churches, and its paintings are the most sophisticated. Near by is a scattering of other churches with frescoes, generally kept unlocked.

Miraculous brew
Much of the damage to the frescoes in the Göreme Valley is known to have been inflicted by the Greek Christians themselves, who apparently believed in the medicinal powers of a brew made by adding fragments of broken frescoes to water. The perpetrator would then carve his name and the date beside the chunk he had chiselled out, just to make sure that God had registered who he was.

Dating problems
The precise dating of the churches and monasteries in Cappadocia is frequently very difficult. Most were built before the 11th century, and only a few after the 13th. The architecture tends to conform to standard Byzantine arrangements of dome, arches and pillars, the latter being purely decorative in function. As a general rule the paintings within the churches are considered to be of greater significance than their architecture.

Its beautiful frescoes make the Tokalı Kilise, or Buckle Church, the loveliest of all the churches in the Göreme Valley

Christian Turkey

■ **Turkey was one of the first countries to which Christianity spread from the Holy Land, with Saint Peter the Apostle founding the first Christian community in Antioch between AD47 and 54. It was here that the followers of Jesus first became known as Christians......■**

Conflicting doctrines

Early Christianity was dominated by numerous battles against heresy. Three Church Councils were held in Asia Minor to resolve critical issues. In 381 the Council of Constantinople confirmed the Nicene Creed of 325, which had rejected the Arian heresy concerning the precise nature of Christ's relationship to God the Father. The Nestorian heresy, which stressed Christ's human nature, and so questioned his divinity, was denounced at Ephesus in 431. Lastly, the Monophysite doctrine, in which God the Father and God the Son share a single nature, was rejected in 451 at the Council of Chalcedon.

The Jewish influence

An important feature of the area in which Christianity emerged in Asia Minor was its Jewish communities, founded in past centuries by the Seleucids. When Saint Paul arrived in the cities of Asia Minor, he began his preaching among these Jewish communities. They enjoyed many privileges and their religion was tolerated on the whole, despite the Roman requirement of universal allegiance to the imperial cult. Sardis had a large Jewish community, hence the synagogue which is now a major monument.

The grotto of Saint Peter at Antakya (Antioch), perhaps the first Christian church in the world

Ephesus became the chief centre of Christianity in Asia Minor, principally because Saint John is said to have lived there from AD37 to 48, accompanied by the Virgin Mary, who had been entrusted to his care by Christ when on the cross. When Saint Paul of Tarsus arrived there in 53, he thus found a small group of converts already in existence. The success of his preaching gave rise to a riot against the Christians by local people who claimed that the new teachings were challenging the greatness of Artemis. After this Paul left Ephesus, later writing his celebrated letters to the Ephesians.

The Seven Churches of Asia As Christianity gradually became established, the 'Seven Churches of Asia Minor' referred to in the Revelation of Saint John, were founded at Smyrna, Ephesus, Pergamum, Thyatira, Sardis, Philadelphia and Laodicea. Over the next two centuries the Christians were routinely persecuted by the Roman authorities for their staunch refusal to comply with the imperial cult.

Then in the 4th century the Roman Emperor Constantine the Great converted to Christianity, and at the Council of Nicaea (Iznik), Christianity was proclaimed the official religion. When Constantine founded his new Eastern Empire in Constantinople, five years later, he set out to make it a Christian city, the first time Christianity had ever been actively embraced, rather than merely tolerated, by a Roman emperor.

Christianity in Cappadocia Monasticism began to develop in Cappadocia in the 4th century, when followers of the order of Saint Basil (329–79) built hermitages in the rocks. In the 7th century, when the area became an important frontier province with the onset of Arab raids on the Byzantine Empire, Christians may well have resorted to these caves in order to avoid persecution. The soft tufa had by then been tunnelled into the chambers and passages of underground cities, in which life could continue during difficult times. When the Byzantines re-established secure control, between the 7th and 11th centuries, this troglydyte population resurfaced to carve their churches into the rock faces and cliffs of the **Göreme** and **Soğanlı** areas, now so celebrated. Their churches and monasteries were many and small: the landscape was well suited to recluses in quest of spirituality, and the region was far distant from the contending doctrines of orthodox Constantinople and monophysite Syria. Saint Basil, a 4th-century monk from **Kayseri** (see pages 180–1) held that small, intimate and disciplined communities were the most conducive to religious feeling, and such communities flourished here. Icons continued to be painted after the Seljuk conquest of the province in the 11th century, and even under the Ottomans, Christian practices were tolerated in Cappadocia, where the population was largely Greek, with some Armenians. Decline eventually set in, however, and Göreme, Ihlara and Soğanlı lost their early influence. The Greeks finally ended their long history here with the mass exchange of populations between Greece and Turkey in 1923 (see pages 16–17).

The church of Saint Saviour in Chora (Kariye Camii), which originally stood outside the walls of Constantinople, contains 14th-century Byzantine mosaics of exceptional beauty and spirituality

Christian symbolism
When images based on the human form were forbidden during the Iconoclastic period, they were replaced by other images with secret symbolic meanings, including the following:
fish: pious followers
vine: Jesus
palm: heaven and eternal life
deer: eternal being and healing
rabbit: sexuality, the devil and magic
lion: victory and salvation
peacock: the resurrection and transfiguration of the body after death
pigeon or dove: love, peace and innocence

CAPPADOCIA

Caveat emptor
The traders of Kayseri are notoriously shrewd: one story tells of a merchant who sold a neighbour a white donkey, then stole it from him in the night and painted it black. The next morning the neighbour told his tale to the merchant, who sympathised with him and promptly sold the donkey to him once more. Tourists should be wary of Kayseri silk, which is known as rayon in most people's vocabulary.

180

► **Hacıbektaş** *170B3*

If you want a change from the Cappadocian landscapes and churches, make a half-day excursion to the north, to the Hacı Bektaş Monastery. Prettily set among gardens, the monastery was opened as a museum in 1964. Beyond the main courtyard, with its soothing running water, lie a mosque and two *türbe* (tomb) shrines: one to Hacı Bektaş himself, and the other to Balim Sultan, the secondary founder. Shoes must be removed inside all the buildings of the Bektashi Dervish order (see panel), and visiting Turks speak in awed whispers and kiss every tomb in sight. The abundant local onyx, used by the disciples to make everyday implements, is now used to make the many onyx souvenirs in the area.

►► **Ihlara** *170A2*

See pages 182–3.

►► **Kaymaklı** *170B2*

The region's major underground city after Derinkuyu (see page 175), Kaymaklı is open from 8–12 and 1–6 daily, and has a pretty entrance with steps leading up to a honeycombed mound. Discovered in 1964, it has only four underground storeys open to the public, compared with Derinkuyu's eight, but they are arranged in a more interesting fashion, with bedrooms, food warehouses, wine cellars, ventilation chimneys, water depots, and a church with a double apse and stone doors that could be rolled shut from the inside.

► **Kayseri** *170C3*

The approach to Kayseri is somewhat insalubrious, though things improve a little as you reach the main square, with its inevitable equestrian statue of Atatürk and the black walls of the citadel looming to the left. The monuments that have managed to survive the town's changing fortunes are the 13th- and 14th-century Islamic buildings of the Seljuks and the Turcoman emirs, now in uninspiring settings surrounded by ugly modern buildings. The **Sahibiye Madrasa**, off the main square, was built by the famous Seljuk architect Sahip Ata in 1267; the citadel, with its 19 black basalt towers, has been renovated and turned into a shopping precinct. Opposite the citadel and near the tourist office stands the **Huant Foundation**, the first mosque complex to be built by the Seljuks in Anatolia. Consisting of a mosque, a *türbe* (tomb), a bath and a *çeşme* (fountain), it is now a museum of local ethnography and crafts. See also the drive on page 184.

 Nevşehir *170B2*

The main town of Cappadocia, Nevşehir is an unexciting place with little to detain you. Its name, meaning 'New Town', was given to it in Ottoman times, when the now largely ruinous crenellated citadel in the centre was built.

► **Ortahisar** *170B2*

The main attraction here is the huge honeycombed cone fortress. In the village are the Harın Church, with its huge columns, and the Sarıca Church, with a good fresco of the Annunciation.

► **Özkonak**   *170B3*

To the north of Avanos (page 174) a small road forks west to Özkonak, the largest of Cappadocia's underground cities, once housing 60,000. Recently opened, and lying slightly off the beaten track, it receives fewer visitors.

T.C. NEVŞEHİR VALİLİĞİ

308450

Bird-rich marshes
To the south of Kayseri lie the Sultan Marshes (Turkish Sultan Sazlığı Milliparkı), much frequented by bird-watchers, especially in April and May. If you arrive early in the day at the village of Ovaçiftlik, the villagers will take you through the marshes by boat to watch the birdlife.

Ortahisar is remarkable for its colossal tufa cone which has been honeycombed into a maze of tunnels, stairways and refuges

The Bektashi Dervishes
The Bektashi Dervish order, founded by Hacı Bektaş in the 13th century and closely connected to the Janissaries, was extremely popular because of its sceptical and irreverent attitude to religion. With a reputation for free-thinking and loose ways, including permitting women to participate unveiled in their ceremonies, it enjoyed its major following among the rural poor of the villages. Centuries ahead of his time, Hacı Bektaş declared that a nation which did not educate its women could not progress. The order survived the abolition of the Janissaries in 1825 and was dissolved only in 1926, along with the Mevlevis and other Dervish orders.

CAPPADOCIA

Walk The Ihlara Gorge

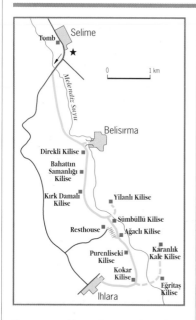

Far removed from the crowds at the main sites in Cappadocia, this walk combines magnificent scenery with a chance to explore some early rock-cut churches in the gorge. The whole valley is estimated to have 4,500 manmade caves and 105 churches or

A Cappadocian shepherd silhouetted against the setting sun

shrines. Most of the painted churches are thought to date to the 8th and 9th centuries, therefore constituting a rare example of this period that escaped the wrath of the Iconoclasts.

If you have the whole day free, begin your walk at Selime, the village at the head of the gorge; from here you can walk all the way along the river, through the exceptionally pretty village of **Belisırma**, to reach Ihlara village, a total distance of some 10km, taking 3–4 hours. At Ihlara you can easily get a taxi to take you back to Selime. If you have less time, drive to the clifftop resthouse just before Ihlara village and descend the steep concrete steps 150m into the gorge to explore the main churches in around 2 hours. Though shorter, this is the more energetic option, which also takes you to the busier part of the gorge.

If you are using **Nevşehir** as your base, set off on the Aksaray road, then fork off for 30km along a narrow tarmac road dominated by the **Hasan Dağ** volcano (3,268m). Melted snow from the volcano formed the Melendiz river which in turn eroded a passage through the soft volcanic tufa to create the deep Ihlara Gorge.

Setting off from Selime along the southwest river bank you immediately enter a different world, a hidden valley with no sound except the wind in the poplar and willow trees and the rushing shallow water. Wildlife is abundant, with birds, frogs and lizards at every turn, and more butterflies than anywhere east of Ankara. The contrast with the bleak and featureless Anatolian plateau is complete.

The first church of note, just beyond Belisırma, is the 11th-century **Direkli Kilise** (Church with the Columns), with fine frescoes. Next come the small **Bahattin Samanlığı Kilise** (Church with a Granary) and the **Kırk Damalı Kilise** (Church with Forty Roofs), the latter set 50m up the hillside. Inside, a fresco shows Saint George with the 13th-century benefactor and his wife.

One of the frescoes in the Yilanlı Kilise, or Church of the Snake

The next landmark is a pretty wooden bridge; cross this and follow the path up to the **Yilanlı Kilise** (Church of the Snake), perhaps the most interesting of the churches, shaped like a long cross. One of its frescoes depicts the Archangel Michael consigning sinners to a grizzly end in the coils of the snake.

Now cross back over the bridge to visit the **Sümbüllü Kilise** (Church of the Hyacinth), with blind arches and an elaborate rock-cut façade that give it one of the most attractive exteriors of any of the churches. A little further on, concrete steps descend from the clifftop restaurant. Up a few steps is the curious **Ağaçlı Kilise** (Church under a Tree), cross-shaped with a central dome, and with frescoes depicting biblical scenes.

Next along the path towards Ihlara is the **Purenliseki Kilise** (Church with a Terrace) with fragmentary frescoes, followed by the **Kokar Kilise** (Fragrant Church), which contains scenes of the Annunciation, the Nativity, the Flight into Egypt and the Last Supper. If you have the courage to ford the river at this point, you can seek out the **Karanlık Kale Kilise** (Dark Castle Church), with fragmentary paintings, and **Eğritas Kilise** (Church with a Crooked Stone), a set of large interlinked chambers with extensive but eroded frescoes; both are set high above the river.

183

The contrast with the emptiness of the Anatolian plateau is clear

Drive Kayseri to Mount Erciyes

A short drive (26km) from Kayseri brings you part of the way up Mount Erciyes and from the point where the road ends you can take a picnic for a magnificent walk up the mountainside. Allow half a day.

Kayseri itself lies on the eastern fringes of Cappadocia, dominated in fine weather by Mount Erciyes (3,916m), snow-capped for most of the year. It was this now extinct volcano, known in antiquity as Mount Argaeus, which in an eruption aeons ago spewed out the volcanic tufa that was to be moulded over the centuries, by wind, rain and man, into the fantastical shapes for which Cappadocia is now famous.

Armed with supplies of the local speciality, *pastırma* (thinly-sliced beef dried in the sun and rolled in garlic and herbs, with a slight flavour of aniseed), head out of town on the road due south from the black basalt citadel, passing Kayseri's most famous tomb, the *Döner Kumbet* ('Revolving Kumbet'), on the right

about a kilometre from the centre. This tomb of a Seljuk princess dates from 1276; its external walls are decorated with tree of life symbols, a pair of winged leopards, a griffin and a two-headed eagle, the Seljuk sign of royalty, and it now looks rather lost in its suburban setting.

After 14km you reach the village of Hisarcık, from where a track continues to **Kayak Evi,** where there is a council-run mountain hut with 100 beds. Climbers come here in summer to enjoy the fabulous volcanic scenery, with numerous small cinder cones scattered about. The altitude at Kayak Evi is 2,150m, and the temperature is noticeably cooler than in the town. There is skiing here from December to May, with a chair-lift operating from Kayak Evi up to the slopes. In summer bring plenty of liquid; if you feel inspired to climb to the top, you will also need a guide, ice-axe and crampons, all of which can be hired from Kayak Evi.

Kayseri's Döner Kumbet

Turkish puddings and pastries

■ Names such as 'nightingale's nest', 'lady's navel' and 'lips of the beautiful beloved' sum up the Turkish attitude to desserts. The abundance of *pastahanes* (pastry shops) positively bursting with every conceivable gooey concoction betrays the Turkish sweet tooth. Milk, nuts, honey, eggs and pastry are the basic ingredients of Turkish puddings, of which the best-known are sticky pastries such as *baklava* and *kadayıf*......■

Pastries *Kadayıf* uses long, finely shredded strands of dough to enclose a mixture of ground hazelnuts and honey. *Baklava* is generally bought from the *pastahane*, as it takes an expert pastry chef to prepare these sticky, syrup-sodden triangles of flaky pastry filled with ground walnuts. *Dilber dudağı* ('a beautiful woman's lips') are little oval-shaped pastries soaked in oil, with fresh cream and crushed pistachio nuts tumbling from a small slit down the middle.

185

Noah's Pudding

Aşure is the food which the Bektashi Dervishes use to break their 10-day fast, on the 10th day of the Islamic month of Muharram. It is said to contain 40 ingredients, in honour of the traditional belief that after the Ark had sailed its 40 days and 40 nights, Noah ordered a stew to be made of the remaining supplies in celebration of the end of the Flood. These days you can buy ready-made *aşure* mix in Turkish supermarkets, but this tends to have a mere 20 ingredients.

Milk puddings and jellies The classic Turkish milk puddings are *muhallabi*, a type of rice pudding with cinnamon, sometimes flavoured with rose-water, and *keşkül*, a smooth mixture of milk and ground almonds and pistachios, garnished with dried coconut and pistachio. *Aşure* (see side panel) is the classic jelly dessert, a rose-water jelly full of chickpeas and dry beans and decorated with dried figs and apricots, raisins, walnuts, pine nuts and pistachios. When using fresh fruit in their puddings, the Turks favour delights such as black cherry bread and peach bread, pumpkin with nuts and banana rice pudding.

Of all Turkish sweets the best known is undoubtedly Turkish delight (*lokum*), made from solidified sugar and pectin flavoured with rose-water, lemon or pistachio and dusted with icing sugar.

Baklava, halva and Turkish delight are just a few of the temptations awaiting visitors with a sweet tooth

CAPPADOCIA

*A precarious rock
dwelling in the
Soğanli Valley*

*A single cone might
once have sheltered
an entire community
in a picturesque
hotchpotch of super-
imposed chambers
and tunnels*

▶▶   **Niğde**   *170B1*

Do not miss the unique 10th-century rock-cut monastery
of Eski Gümüş, discovered by an English professor only in
1963, right on the southern edge of Cappadocia, 2km
north of Niğde. Before that it had been used as stables by
the villagers; as a result the condition of the frescoes here
is almost perfect, far better than those at Göreme (see
pages 176–7). The monastery church is especially lovely,
with fine tall pillars and a vaulted roof. Look out, too, for
the extraordinary wall paintings of deer, ostriches and
men hunting with bows and arrows in the monks' bedrooms, reached now by a metal staircase.

In Niğde itself, with its 11th-century citadel rising up in
the centre, are a handful of interesting Seljuk and
Mongolian monuments, notably the superb 16-sided
Mongolian conical *türbe* (tomb) of Hudabend Hatun
(1312).

▶▶   **Soğanlı**   *170B2*

Soğanlı Valley, 33km away to the south, makes a pleasant, quiet excursion from Ürgüp. The drive is a delightful
one, through wooded valleys and colourful villages. The
pretty troglydyte village of Soğanlı is set in a huge table-
topped mountain; either side of this lie the valley's
churches, some 60 of them in all, though many have been
filled up with earth or turned into pigeon-cotes by the villagers. The most interesting ones are along the right-hand
side of the valley, especially **Yılanlı Kilise** (Snake Church),
Saklı Kilise (Hidden Church) and the amazing three-
storey **Kubbeli Kilise** (Domed Church) in its own curious
domed rock formation.

▶   **Üçhisar**   *170B3*

This scruffy village is dominated by a tall cone fortress
similar to the one at Ortahisar (see pages 180–1). From

the top there is an impressive view over the whole Göreme Valley, and at night the cone is illuminated, looking like a colossal hollowed-out Halloween gourd.

▶ Ürgüp 170B3

The best base for a few days in Cappadocia, Ürgüp is an attractive rural town set at the heart of the main valleys. The cobbled streets that wind up and down its hills are lined by many grand old Greek houses, with fine loggias and carved decoration round the doors and windows. Many of the houses are set partly into the cave-riddled cliff-faces, and the locals use the caves as garages, storerooms and stables. A curiosity particular to the Ürgüp region is the travelling library, carried on the back of a donkey, which tours the far-flung areas of the town.

▶▶ Zelve 170B3

Just north of Çavuşin (see pages 174–5) a fork in the road leads to Zelve, a pretty series of three valleys peppered with troglydyte dwellings. There is no village here any more: the Greeks left in 1923, and the Turks who moved in after them also had to leave in the 1950s because of landslips and erosion. A walk round the Zelve valleys, involving about an hour of strolling and clambering, is one of the most enjoyable in Cappadocia.

Head first into the main right-hand valley, going past a little mosque to reach the monastery complex, a huge bowl cut out of the rock. A gallery runs round it halfway up, from which a tunnel leads up steep steps to the very ceiling of the dome. You need a torch to explore the deeper recesses of the monastery rooms. Scattered about in the second and third valleys are more churches and even a rock-cut mill with grinding stone. A host of little footpaths run up and down the hillsides to aid your explorations.

Good souvenirs
Ürgüp's cobbled main street, by the museum, has a number of very good souvenir shops, offering silver jewellery set with semi-precious stones such as amethyst, lapis lazuli, jade and garnet, along with good carpets, elaborate woodwork and metalwork boxes. Colourful knitted woollen socks and gloves are also on sale at government-regulated prices.

187

Evening light at Üçhisar

CENTRAL ANATOLIA

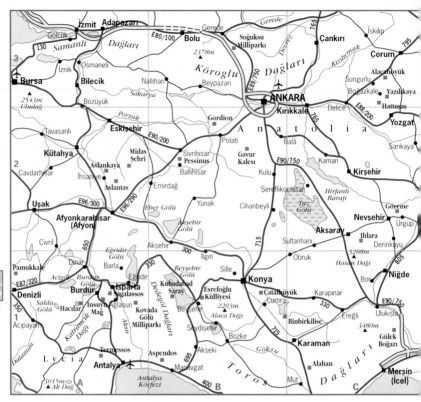

Itineraries
One week:
Ankara
Afyon (two nights)
Konya (two nights)
Ürgüp (two nights)
Ankara

Two weeks:
Ankara (two nights)
Boğazkale
Amasya
Sivas, Divriği
Elazığ
Diyarbakır
Şanlıurfa
Nemrut Dağı
Antakya
Adana
Göreme
Ürgüp
Ankara

*A detail of the
intricately carved
portal of the mosque
at Divriği*

Map labels:
Merzifon, Amasya, 180, E80/100, Kuzey, Niksar, Anadolu, Dağları, Gümüşhane, 885, Comana Pontica, Kelkit, Turhal, Tokat, Yeşilırmak, Suşehri, Sebinkarahisar, Yıldızeli, Zara, E88/200, Refahiye, E80/100, Erzincan, 850, Sivas, Fırat, Akdağmadeni, Divriği, Mercan Dağları, 3368m, Kızılırmak, 260, Kangal, Keban Barajı, Gemerek, 890, Kanesh, Hekimhan, Keban, Elazig, Kayseri, Pinarbaşı, Gürün, Darende, 300, 3916m, Erciyes Dağı, 815, Fırat, Malatya, Cappadocia, 825, Elbistan, 850, 2583m, Nemrut Dağı, Göksun, Arsameia, Kâhta, 3756m, Feke, Gölbaşı, Adıyaman, Tahtalı Dağları, Kozan, Ceyhan, Kahramanmaraş, Atatürk Barajı, 885, Karatepe, Narlı, 825, Şanlıurfa, Yılanlıkale, Sehan, E90/400, Gaziantep, Osmaniye, Birecik, 850, Adana, 850, Harran (Altınbaşak), İskenderun Körfezi, İskenderun, Kilis, SYR, E, 0 50 100 km, E98/827

Central Anatolia This heartland of Turkey, dismissed by foreign visitors until recently as a bleak featureless plateau, is now beginning to be appreciated as the cradle of the extraordinary Hittite civilisation (1500–1200BC), contemporary with the river cultures of Egypt and Mesopotamia. Turkish civilisation can be said to have originated in these central steppelands, where the Seljuks also chose to base themselves, in their capital Konya.

Landscape The prospect of inhospitable steppeland stretching to the horizon is a forbidding one, and many balk at this entry to a different Turkey, far removed from the familiar, semi-European resorts of the Mediterranean. Once you have overcome the initial shock, however, this 1,000m-high plateau holds some curious surprises, some man-made, others natural. After adjusting your eye to the barrenness of the landscapes, you come to notice detail of a different sort: the fascinatingly sparse villages clinging to the edges of the hills; soil changes and weird rock colourings, reflecting the mineral deposits in which Turkey is so rich; and above all the abundant birdlife. The plateau is crossed by a number of large rivers, such as the Kızılırmak and the Yeşilırmak. The mountains encircling it isolate the plateau geographically and climatically from all maritime influence, and the small amount of rainfall is concentrated in a very short period in the spring. The central depression around Tuz Gölü (the Great Salt Lake) – 'shining waters of saline deposit', as the Victorian

189

CENTRAL ANATOLIA

How to travel
Car and bus are the best
ways to travel: the bus network runs as efficiently
between main towns here
as it does elsewhere in
Turkey. A railway runs from
Eskişehir to Ankara, then
continues southeastwards
to Kayseri on the edge of
Cappadocia; if you are not
fortunate enough to have a
car, this train route makes
an exciting journey, following as it does the many
dramatic river gorges of
the plateau, notably that
between Divriği and
Erzincan.

*Characteristic river-
side houses at
Amasya*

explorer Gertrude Bell described it – is virtually uninhabited, and the most barren place in Turkey.

Towns Ankara will be the most likely base for any stay in
Central Anatolia, not least because of its airport, the only
international one in the region. For a capital city Ankara
has a remarkable lack of signposts, but it is nevertheless
a relatively straightforward place to find your way round. It
has little charm, and most people stay only long enough
to visit the museum before setting off into Central
Anatolia proper.

*Typical backstreets in
Afyon*

The two most attractive cities of the region are **Amasya**
and **Afyon**, by virtue of their settings: Amasya lies on a

One of the mosaics in the Kariye Camii (St Saviour in Chora)

river bank with a cliff-face behind, and Afyon lies below a rocky citadel. They both make good bases for an exploration of the surrounding area, and Afyon in particular is a far better choice than the rather dull and faceless Eskişehir or Kütahya. There is no obvious base for a visit to the Hittite heartlands round **Boğazkale**, so the best bet is perhaps to stay in the simple accommodation that is provided at Sungurlu.

Distances between major towns can be great, and as petrol stations are scarce it is very important to fill up before your tank drops below the quarter-full mark. The dearth of good accommodation also makes it imperative to plan an itinerary.

Itineraries Two weeks is the maximum most people would allow to visit all sites of interest in Central Anatolia; usually a fortnight would also cover Cappadocia, or perhaps the Black Sea coast or the inland lakes of Eğridir and Beyşehir. To reach parts of eastern Turkey from Ankara, you would need three weeks. See panel on page 188.

Hittite relief from Yazılıkaya, near Boğazkale

CENTRAL ANATOLIA

Origins and angora
Although we tend to think of Ankara as a new city, its origins go back to the 2nd millennium BC, when it was a Hittite settlement called Ankuwash on the royal road from Hattuşaş to Sardis. The prefix *ank* is known to mean gorge or ravine in early Indo-European languages, an obvious reference to the town's setting. In the 11th century Ankara was in the hands of the Seljuks, who brought with them the long-haired angora goats which gave the city its modern name.

One of the traditional buildings of old Ankara

T.C. KÜLTÜR BAKANLIĞI

FIYATI : 12.500 TL.

ANADOLU MEDENIYETLERI MÜZESI GIRIŞ BILETI № 09036

Parts of Ankara remain deceptively like simple rural communities

► **Ankara**   *188B3*

The capital of modern Turkey has many new roles to play, and it is the conflicts between these roles that make the city so intriguing today. When Atatürk declared it the capital of the new republic in 1923, he was making a calculated move away from the Byzantine and Ottoman associations of Istanbul and its past, and back to the original Anatolian heartlands.

Role dilemma When Atatürk first moved his headquarters to Ankara in 1919, at the beginning of the War of Independence, the town had a mere 30,000 inhabitants. Ankara's present population is close to four million. The contrast between the old town and the new city centre contributes to Ankara's strange character and points to its split identity, which is more marked than that in any other city in Turkey. The main boulevard is lined with luxury high-rise hotels and impressive new embassies and government buildings, while in the old streets around the citadel and the Ulus Meydanı (the People's Square) you could be forgiven for thinking you were back in a simple and traditional Anatolian town. It is a split which symbolises the curious dilemma of Turkey as a whole, as it tries on the one hand to project itself as a semi-European state with a face acceptable to doubting western observers, and on the other hand to cling to customs and values unchanged for centuries.

Sights It is fitting that Ankara's two major sights should reflect its ancient and modern ties: the **Museum of Anatolian Civilisations**, and Atatürk's mausoleum, known as **Anıtkabir**. One day should be sufficient to visit Ankara's attractions; even an energetic half-day is enough for you to spend two hours in the museum, take a brief stroll round the citadel and visit Anıtkabir, then leave for the Hittite heartlands after lunch.

Arkeoloji Müzesi (Museum of Anatolian Civilisations)►►► For most people this museum, with the most spectacular and comprehensive display of Hittite and Urartian finds in the world, is the main reason for visiting Ankara. Set in a renovated 15th-century Ottoman *bedesten* (covered market hall with courtyard), the museum is small but beautifully laid out. It is open 8:30–12 and 1:30–5:30 daily except Mondays. The most notable exhibits to look out for are the 8,000-year-old murals of the Çatalhüyük cave sanctuary; the Alacahüyük royal tomb jewellery and bronze sun discs; the huge Hittite sculptures; the Urartian gold and silver work; and the world's first coin, from Sardis, dating from 615BC.

Medieval and Roman Ankara► See pages 194–5.

Anıtkabir (Atatürk's Mausoleum)►► The precincts of this extraordinary monument occupy an entire hill over a kilometre square in the centre of Ankara. It is open daily except Mondays 9–5 in summer and 9–4 in winter. Four evenings a week in summer there are also 'sound and light' dramas enacting Turkey's transformation into a modern state. A visit to the mausoleum cannot fail to impress on you the extent of the personality cult built around the memory of Atatürk, who died over half a century ago. Parking is at the summit of the hill, from where a colossal avenue, 300m long and flanked by mock Hittite lions, leads to a vast open courtyard, at the highest point of which stands the monumental limestone mausoleum itself, completed in 1960. The marble interior is stark and empty; the colossal stone of the sarcophagus weighs 40,000 kilograms. Armed guards stand everywhere, and an atmosphere of reverence pervades the place.

A fine display in Ankara's spice market

Fat is beautiful
The Museum of Anatolian Civilisations in Ankara houses one of the earliest known examples of the Anatolian earth mother figure, grotesquely fat by modern standards, with colossal arms, legs, breasts and belly. Female corpulence was much admired in Turkey until relatively recently. An Ottoman saying observes: 'She is so beautiful she has to go through the door sideways.'

Hittite sculptures in the Museum of Anatolian Civilisations

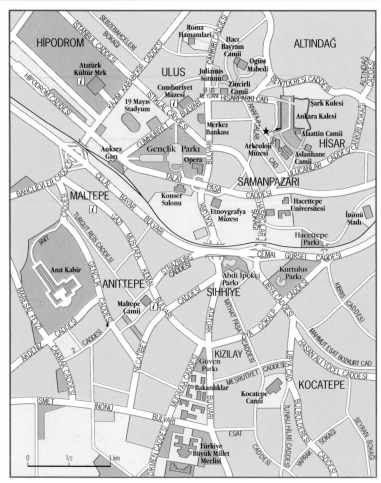

Walk Ankara

Starting from the Arkeoloji Müzesi (Museum of Anatolian Civilisations), this 4km walk of about 2½ hours takes you through the poor quarters of the medieval citadel, then down to explore the remnants of Roman Ankara. Refer to the Ankara city map for directions.

From the museum, walk up the hill to the right to find the **Aslanhane Camii**, the only mosque worth visiting in Ankara. Tucked up a little side street in the old bazaar quarter, this 13th-century Seljuk mosque is memo-

rable for its 24 wooden columns supporting a beautifully carved wooden ceiling.

Doubling back to the museum road, continue uphill to reach the **citadel** (see Hisar on the city map) to catch a glimpse of the contrast between Turkey old and new. As you climb through the powerful gateway you step back into medieval times. Cars can barely penetrate here, and children play barefoot in the dusty narrow streets between the decaying houses.

The citadel walls as they stand

today are of mainly Byzantine construction, with much subsequent Turkish addition. Ankara's long, eventful history is reflected in the fabric of the citadel walls and the houses within it, a hotchpotch of re-used stones and fragments from different eras.

Head over to the eastern walls and to the ruined tower of Şark Kulesi, from which there is an extraordinary view over the city, especially the *gecekondu* (literally 'night lodgings'), squatter settlements of rural migrants seeking a better life in the city. These have been responsible for an astonishing surge in population in the last 25 years. A legacy of the Ottoman law decreeing that anyone who could build a house on unused land in a single night had legal ownership, today they are colourful, established neighbourhoods with their own schools and utilities.

Leave the citadel by the western side and descend the steps through the terraced gardens below, to enter **Hisarparkı Caddesi**, a lively cobbled street that brings you down into the city again. Turn up a side street to the right, just before the Zincirli Camii; take the right-hand fork to reach the unmistakable **Temple of Augustus** (Ogüst Mabedi), the most prominent of Ankara's Roman monuments. The mosque beside it is dedicated to Ankara's favourite saint, Hacı Bayram, whose adjacent *türbe* (tomb) is still a

The remarkable Museum of Anatolian Civilisations, set in a 15th-century bedesten

popular place of pilgrimage.

Return now to the fork and take the left-hand one to reach the **Column of Julian** (Julianus Sütunu), erected in AD362 in honour of the Emperor Julian's visit to Ankara. Head along the side street behind the column to reach the main Atatürk Bulvarı, then follow this to the north a short way to reach the **Roman Baths** (Roma Hamamları) to the left of the road. Discovered by chance in 1926, they contain central heating pipes, marble paving and fragmentary statues.

Ankara's extensive Roman remains reflect a significant period in the city's long history

Atatürk

■ **While all nations have their great men, the cult of Atatürk in modern Turkey is unique. His monolithic tomb in Ankara (see pages 192–3) is a kind of secular Mecca, signifying the virtually divine status he has achieved – for many, indeed, a substitute for religion......**■

Undying respect
Each year on the anniversary of Atatürk's death, at 9:05am on 10 November 1938, a minute's silence is observed and all traffic comes to a standstill.

Childhood and background Atatürk's background was humble. Born in Salonica in 1881, the young Mustafa Kemal inherited his determined and domineering nature from his mother Zubeida, a profoundly religious woman. His father, Ali Reza, a former customs official who had a small business dealing in wood, inclined towards liberal ideas, and in his autobiography their only son recalled the battle that took place between his parents over whether to send him at the age of seven to a religious school or a new science establishment. Eventually a compromise was reached: Mustafa spent six months at Islamic school, before going on to the more liberal alternative. When Mustafa was just nine Ali Reza died, and the boy had to leave school and go with his mother to live on her brother's farm near Salonica. Here he adapted quickly to his new country life, cleaning out stables and looking after the animals. He also gained two qualities that were to prove essential to his later development: robust health and an abiding love of the peasantry, among whom he would afterwards find his most ardent supporters in the fight for independence.

Military matters At the age of 12, Mustafa was allowed by Zubeida to continue his studies, and, at his own insistence, to prepare for a career in the army. Having passed his exams at cadet school with distinction, he went on to progress quickly through the ranks. At the same time he developed a strong and active interest in the opposite sex which, as is so often the case with men hungry for power, continued throughout his life. In 1911, at the age of 30, he accompanied an army general to Paris, where he followed the diplomatic manoeuvrings of the French with fascination. After the outbreak of war he acquired some practical experience of battle in Tripoli, against the Italians, and in 1915 came his great opportunity. As Lieutenant Colonel controlling the zones where the Allies landed *en masse* to take the Dardanelles in April of that year, he took the initiative, surprising the Allies with

Atatürk depicted as military hero

the strength of his tactics and going on to paralyse their offensive. His role in the Dardanelles campaign earned him the admiration even of his enemies.

Political involvement At Staff College Atatürk had met many like-minded young men who regarded with fierce impatience the clumsy machinery of the decaying Ottoman Empire which they were being trained to serve. It was at this time that he was introduced to the writings of Voltaire, who denounced the mingling of the secular with the religious – the very factor which Atatürk viewed as being responsible for drawing the allegiance of the ignorant masses to the sultan. Throughout his military training he had been politically active, even setting up a secret society and being arrested by police spies. His frequent quarrels with Enver Paşa, Commander-in-Chief of the Turkish forces, and his vociferous criticism of his masters in general saw him consigned to several peripheral commands in Libya and Syria. Thus by the age of 37, Kemal had shown himself an efficient and energetic military commander but no more, and he had seen his Staff College contemporaries such as Enver Paşa rise to much higher positions than himself. It was not until May 1919, when the Greeks were landing in Smyrna and he was appointed as Inspector-General in the interior, that his position changed. The date of his landing at Samsun to take up this appointment, on 19 May 1919, is generally considered as the start of the four-year-long War of Independence. This was the moment when Atatürk turned his back on Istanbul and the decadent Ottoman authorities, and instead sought the foundations of the new Turkey in the interior, making direct appeals to the Anatolian soldiers and peasantry to rise up and defend their nation (see pages 42–3 for what happened next).

An equestrian statue in Ankara: every town has its effigy

Atatürk's words
'There are two Mustafa Kemals. One is that sitting before you, the Mustafa Kemal of flesh and blood, who will pass away. There is another whom I cannot call "Me". It is not I whom this Mustafa Kemal personifies, it is you – all you present here, who go into the furthermost parts of the country to inculcate and defend a new ideal, a new mode of thought. I stand for these dreams of yours. My life's work is to make them come true.'

The face of modern Turkey
The face that hangs in every office and house in Turkey tells of the character of the man: determined, capable and without illusions; energetic, burning all his candles at both ends; an originator and a force for change, not an administrator; a man who inspires devotion and whose leadership created modern Turkey.

CENTRAL ANATOLIA

189D3

The Pontic kingdom
Amasya was the capital of the Pontic kingdom, founded in the 3rd century BC by the adventurer Mithridates. The kingdom survived more than two centuries of turbulence before being crushed by the Romans, under Julius Caesar, in 47BC. The tombs of the Pontic kings, cut into the rock above the town, are Amasya's most memorable relic today.

Amasya's setting under a rocky outcrop on the banks of the Yeşilırmak river is exceptionally picturesque

►► **Amasya**

Set under a dramatic rock outcrop on the banks of the Yeşilırmak river, Amasya is a pretty town which makes an excellent stopover between the Hittite heartlands of Boğazkale and the Black Sea. To explore the town, walk from the main square to the bridge across the river, admiring the picturesque timbered Ottoman houses overhanging the water: one of them, the **Hazaranlar Konağı** (Museum House), has been converted into an ethnographic museum (closed Mondays). Yellow signs point the way to **Kralkaya** (King's Rock), a steep 10-minute climb up steps between houses, passing on the way the **Kızlar Sarayı** (Maidens' Palace or Harem), all that remains of the Pontic kings' palace. A remarkable tunnel with steps cut into the bare rock leads round to the two largest royal tombs.

In the town the Islamic buildings worth looking at are the **Seljuk Gök Madrasa** on the main street; the **Fethiye Camii**, originally a 7th-century Byzantine church; and the remarkable lunatic asylum built on the river bank by the Mongols in 1308, only the elaborate façade of which remains today.

A short way outside the town on the Samsun road, a roughish track leads up 2km to the **citadel**; the surprisingly large and dramatic ruined castle makes a lovely picnic spot. Some of the towers date back to Pontic times, but the walls are thought to be of Byzantine or Turkish construction. During Ramadan an old Russian cannon is fired here at sunset.

▶▶ **Boğazkale (Hattuşaş)** *188C3*

If you have come from Ankara to visit these ancient Hittite heartlands, the contrast between city and village lifestyles will strike you forcibly. Here geese meander across the dirt street, and heaps of circular dung cakes lie drying in the sun to be used as fuel.

The huge fenced-in site of the Hittite capital is open daily except Mondays until dusk, sometimes as late as 7:30 or 8:00pm. A car tour of the site takes about 1½ hours; on foot it would take more like 3–4 hours, as distances are considerable, and they involve steep climbs. The remains consist largely of foundations and low walls, but the scale of the site's conception cannot fail to impress. The earliest surviving example of a walled city, Hattuşaş covered an enormous area: the defence walls were 6.5km long, with nearly 200 towers. At the highest point you will find the three city gates – the **Lion Gate**, the **Sphinx Gate** and the **King's Gate** – all set about 500m from each other. At the Sphinx Gate you can still walk through the extraordinary 70m-long postern tunnel that runs through the hillside, then climb the monumental stairways which were used in peacetime for access to the city, and in wartime for attacking the enemy.

Continuing downhill, you reach the signposted **Büyükkale** (Great Fortress), the palace of the Hittite kings. At the bottom is the **Great Temple of the Weather God**, the largest and best-preserved of the Hittite temples on the site.

Environs of Boğazkale **Alacahöyük▶** This small fortified Hittite city about 30km northeast of Boğazkale is the source of many of the stupendous finds displayed in the Museum of Anatolian Civilisations in Ankara. As you enter through the monumental Sphinx Gate and walk along the main street, you have the real feeling of being in a town. Do not miss the wonderful postern tunnel.

Yazılıkaya▶▶ Just 3km beyond Boğazkale lies this 13th-century BC rock-cut sanctuary formed from two natural rock galleries, the only open-air Hittite temple to have survived. The inner walls are carved with reliefs of the gods and goddesses of the Hittite pantheon.

The two stone lions of the Lion Gate have been guarding the Hittite fortress at Hattuşaş for over 3,000 years

Defensive mentality
The most remarkable feature of Boğazkale is the clever manner in which the natural contours of the land have been incorporated into the city's fortifications. The modern name Boğazkale, meaning 'fortress of the narrow mountain pass', reflects this unusual topography.

Comic art
The figures on the rock-cut façade at Alacahöyük could have been taken straight from a circus: while one entertainer is doing a sword-swallowing act, an acrobat climbs a free-standing ladder and another stands ready to catch him. The stumpy little figures are endearingly like comic-strip characters.

FOCUS ON *The Turkish language*

■ **A fiendishly difficult language in which the average westerner will recognise nothing familiar, Turkish does not have regional dialects. Instead you will notice a difference in pronunciation between the soft, cultured tones of Istanbul and the harsher Anatolian diction, which becomes more guttural as you move further east. ....■**

Ottoman to modern
Where the modern Turkish civil servant might write: 'I have been thinking about your suggestion', his Ottoman predecessor would have been more likely to declare: 'Your slave has been engaged in the exercise of cogitation in respect of the proposals vouchsafed by your exalted person.'

Posterior domes
The architectural term *kümbet*, applied to the distinctive conical mausoleums found throughout eastern Turkey, literally means 'dome'. Not inappropriately, it is also slang for the human posterior.

A calligrapher at work: calligraphy is a highly valued skill

Nomadic origins Turkish derives from a Turco-Tartar language group called Altaic, a distinction it shares with Mongol, Tunguz and possibly Korean. The migrations of the Turkish peoples from the central steppelands, and their consequent intermingling with other peoples of different languages over the course of history, has created a linguistic structure of great complexity which is still the subject of academic research. The original language of the nomadic tribesmen had a wealth of vocabulary for describing livestock and weather conditions, but was obviously inadequate to cope with the complexities of the civilised urban life that the Turks discovered in the countries they conquered. They therefore borrowed the majority of their words for abstract and intellectual concepts from Arabic (amounting to some 40 per cent of the language, similar to the proportion of French words in medieval English), and they borrowed from Persian most of their words to do with crafts, trades and associated matters. With the conversion of the Turks to Islam and their adoption of the Arabic script, their language became increasingly artificial and removed from its linguistic roots. The Arabic alphabet, in which vowels are not written and all words are based on three root consonants, was never suited to the Turkish language, in which vowels and vowel harmony are of critical importance.

200

Atatürk's reforms When Atatürk came to power in the early 1920s he set about removing foreign influences from the Turkish language, trying instead to find Turkish substitutes for Arabic and Persian words. The academic body he set up to oversee this process informed him that it would take at least six years to reform the language and adopt the Latin alphabet – he gave them six months. Not surprisingly, this led to many problems of adjustment, not least between the generations, as grandparents who had grown up with Arabic and Persian words struggled to communicate with their grand-children, who were taught a whole new vocabulary at school.

A mosque bookstall selling books in both Roman and Arabic scripts

The Turkish press in all its variety

The ultimate negative One of the most infuriating characteristics of Turks, as any traveller to Turkey soon discovers, is their way of saying 'no'. The famous Turkish negative, *yok*, accompanied by an upward movement of the head with eyes half closed, is the negative to end all negatives, as it also manages to convey an attitude of complete indifference. When the hotel is full, or there is no orange juice, no fish, no fruit, no whatever, this upward nod of the head and weary closing of the eyes conveys: 'No, there isn't any (and who cares anyway)'. Freya Stark described it as 'that eloquent gesture which is the Turkish equivalent of a blank wall'.

CENTRAL ANATOLIA

Goats in bras
The Anatolian plateau was not always as barren as it is now; centuries of deforestation by goats and man have transformed the landscape. The government tries to encourage people to breed cattle instead of the destructive goat, but old habits die hard. In some rural areas you can even still see goats wearing bras – not an expression of modesty or Islamic fundamentalism, but a practical way of stopping kids from suckling too long.

The wild mountain landscape that surrounds the remote Divriği mosque means that few visitors manage to reach this remarkable site

▶▶ **Çavdarhisar (Aizanoi)**   *188A2*

Near the village of Çavdarhisar is one of the largest and best-preserved temples in Turkey. Though accessible from Afyon or Kütahya, it is rarely visited because of its remote and difficult position. Built in the Ionian style in the 2nd century AD, the magnificent Temple of Zeus stands virtually intact on this barren plateau. Inside, you are surprised to discover a subterranean sanctuary dedicated to the worship of the Phrygian goddess Cybele, predecessor to Artemis. Notice the animal figures and hunting scenes on the stone blocks of the walls, which are thought to have been drawn by Turkish nomadic clans many centuries ago.

▶▶ **Divriği**   *189E2*

The famous Divriği mosque and *madrasa* (theological college) complex has been declared by UNESCO to be one of the most important centres of cultural heritage in the world. Its exceptional remoteness – two hours' drive from Sivas, with no tourist-standard accommodation in the town – means that any visit involves such a detour that it takes on the nature of a pilgrimage. Originally a Byzantine stronghold, Divriği was taken by the Seljuks and beautified with this lovely and unusual building. Commissioned in 1228 by the local emir, it has portals lavishly carved with floral and geometric motifs, with the occasional bird and animal concealed among the garlands and fronds of its decoration.

The beautifully carved 13th-century portal of the mosque at Divriği

Near Çavdarhisar is the magnificent Temple of Zeus

Eskişehir
188A2

A largely modern town in spite of its name ('Old Town'), Eskişehir has become prosperous through its position at the fork of the railway which arrives here from Haydarpaşa, Istanbul's Asian Station; here the line divides to head east towards Ankara, and south towards Kütahya and Konya. The town is famed today for its meerschaum, which comes from quarries 25km away on the Ankara road. The meerschaum keeps a large part of the population in work, and the famous pipes, walking sticks and other objects can be obtained more cheaply here than elsewhere in Turkey. In the old quarter of town, to the northwest, stands a Seljuk castle. The 16th-century **Kurşunlu Mosque** is attributed to the architect Sinan (see pages 64–5).

Kırşehir
188C2

One of Turkey's holy cities, Kırşehir became the centre of the influential Ahi Muslim brotherhood in the 14th century. In the town are several Seljuk buildings of interest, notably the **Cacabey Mosque** (1272), a former astronomical observatory, and the **Ahi Evran Mosque**, beside which stands the *türbe* (tomb) of the founder of the Ahi sect. On the road towards Kayseri, notice the attractive Mongol *türbe* of Aşık Paşa, dated 1333.

'Turkish pizzas' are a local speciality

Ramadan
Konya is Turkey's most religious city, and during Ramadan, the Muslim month of fasting, it is one of the few places in Turkey where you will experience problems in finding restaurants and cafés open during the day. The restaurants of the top hotels are about the only places where food and drink are available before nightfall.

Mevlana the mystic
Mevlana, the founder of the Whirling Dervishes, was a 13th-century poet and philosopher who believed that an ecstatic state of universal love could be induced by the practice of whirling round and round. This religious rite can be seen in Konya each December, the dervishes dressed in their white robes and tall conical hats, and dancing to the accompaniment of haunting music played on the *ney*, a reed flute.

▶▶▶ Konya 188B1

The very name of Konya – home to Sufism, a mystical sect of Islam, and to the famous Whirling Dervishes – conjures up for many visitors a certain magic and mystery. The city has a number of exceptionally beautiful Seljuk buildings in varying states of preservation, all dating from the 12th and 13th centuries, the period when Konya was the Seljuks' capital and a haven for Muslim art and culture, attracting many great men of learning.

Apart from these buildings, Konya is not very prepossessing; in fact many visitors are disappointed. Essentially a city of the steppe, it is a small oasis of relative greenery surrounded on all sides by vast bleak horizons. In the summer it is hot and dusty, like all cities of the plateau, and in winter it is perishingly cold. The major sights are concentrated within a square kilometre of the city centre; as it takes the best part of a day to see them, two nights is generally the minimum time to spend here.

Mevlana Tekke (Mevlana Monastery)▶▶▶ The highlight of any visit to Konya, this *tekke* (dervish monastery), with its unforgettable blue-green dome, lies in the heart of the city. It is this building which endows Konya with its special status as a religious city, for Mevlana himself is buried here, and it was here that the dervishes were based for more than six centuries until the Mevlevi Order was dissolved by Atatürk in 1925. In 1927 the *tekke* was opened as a museum, for it is crammed with precious works of art and opulent furnishings, even housing what purports to be a remnant of the Prophet Muhammad's beard. It is open to the public daily except Mondays 2–6.

The entrance leads to a courtyard containing the ablution fountain around which the dervishes used to perform their whirling dance. The heavily decorated tombs of Mevlana (died 1273), his father, his son and other distinguished dervishes lie in the main building, draped in richly embroidered cloth with the distinctive turban on top. Mevlana's tomb is an exquisitely carved sarcophagus inscribed with verses from his poetry, placed centrally beneath the blue-green dome covered on the inside with stars. The treasures on display were all gifts to the

Souvenirs on sale in Konya

The blue-green dome of the Mevlana dervish monastery

Mevlevi Order from wealthy patrons and converts. Next door to the tombs is the **Semahane**, the vaulted hall with fine carpets and chandeliers where the *sema* dance is still performed every December (see pages 24–5).

Alaeddin Camii (Alaeddin Mosque)► This 13th-century Seljuk mosque, the largest in Konya, took 70 years to build. It has an irregular groundplan and the sequence of construction is uncertain. Eight sultans are buried here.

Karatay Madrasa►► This theological college, built in 1251, is now a museum of Turkish tiles from the Seljuk and Ottoman periods. The most beautiful of the tiles, from the Seljuk palace on Lake Beyşehir (see pages 148–9), include representations of people, animals and birds, including the Seljuk symbol, the two-headed eagle.

Alaeddin Park► Laid out on the former acropolis in the heart of the ancient city, this park has a network of pathways and cafés, making it a pleasant place to stroll and linger. On the far side of the park from the Karatay Madrasa you can also visit the **Ince Minare** (Slender Minaret) and **Madrasa**, the **Sırçalı (Glazed) Madrasa** and the **Sahip Ata** complex of Seljuk mosque, *türbe* (tomb or shrine) and oratory.

Drive Konya to Çatalhüyük, Karaman and Alahan

This fascinating day's drive from Konya gives you a glimpse of Turkey's extraordinary variety, incorporating visits to the oldest known city in the world, a Seljuk oasis and a unique Byzantine monastery. The round trip is 335km long and takes a whole day, so bring a picnic.

Leave Konya on the Silifke road to the south to reach the first stop at **Çatalhüyük**, 60km away across the bleak Anatolian plateau. After Konya fork left to Çumra, a small town 12km off the main road; turn left in the centre of town in front of a modern mosque, then right 500m later, then immediately left again to cross a railway track. From here the road is sign-

The remote and beautiful Byzantine monastery at Alahan

The landscapes of this region combine a savage grandeur with colours of luminous clarity

posted. Discovered in 1961 by James Mellaart, Çatalhüyük is Turkey's most important neolithic and Bronze Age site, and the earliest known city in the world. The sophisticated tools, jewellery and sculpture found here, and above all the wall paintings decorating the shrines, all dating from 6800BC, indicate a remarkably advanced civilisation in Anatolia. These objects have been removed to the Ankara Museum of Anatolian Civilisations, but the site is nevertheless impressive for its sheer size. The complex houses, all crammed together without streets to separate them, were entered through holes in the roof via ladders.

The next port of call, again across the Anatolian bleakness, is **Karaman**, a surprisingly green oasis which was the capital of a powerful emirate from 1277 until 1467, when it was incorporated into the Ottoman Empire. There are two monuments in the town centre that merit a brief look: the Ak Tekke (1371), formerly a monastery of Mevlevi mystic dervishes, and the Yunus Emre Mosque (1349).

The Karaman region was inhabited for a long time by Turkish-speaking Orthodox Greeks who even wrote Turkish in Greek script. As a result there are many monasteries here. The most important monastic complex is **Binbir Kilise** ('A Thousand and One Churches') dating from the 9th to the 11th centuries, and the subject of a study by Sir William Ramsay (a Scottish archeologist) and Gertrude Bell (a

The wild scenery in and around the Göksu Gorge is typical of the arid mountains of Central Anatolia

Victorian traveller) in 1905. The churches are not easy to visit: 8km of rough dirt track leads to an impressive cluster of churches and monasteries, near the hamlet of **Değler**. The nearest town is **Maden Şehir**.

South of Karaman, the Silifke road leaves the plain and crosses a pass; beyond, a fork leads to **Alahan**, the site of a remote Byzantine monastery complex of great beauty. The scenery here is stunning, and the monastery itself stands on a terrace overlooking the lovely **Göksu Gorge** with wild mountains all around. It had two churches, and you arrive at the great western one, built at the end of the 5th century. Elaborate reliefs on its doorway depict the four Evangelists and the Archangels Gabriel and Michael trampling a bull and a priest of Isis underfoot, representing the triumph of Christianity over paganism. The eastern church, with its well-preserved and elegant façade and its graceful slender columns, was built some 50 years later. Hollowed out of the cliff behind are the refectory, kitchen, bakery and guest rooms, as well as an intriguing series of caves which served as the monks' cells.

On the return journey to Konya, you can vary the route by taking a left fork (close to the Çumra/Çatalhüyük fork) towards **Alaca Dağı** (2,203m). Here there is wonderful mountain scenery, as well as the pretty **May Baraji dam** and its lake.

CENTRAL ANATOLIA

Kütahya is famous for its ceramic ware

Kütahya
188A2

Kütahya is dominated by its Ottoman citadel and its ceramics factory. The city is now Turkey's leading tile producing centre, having taken over from Iznik (see page 61), its rival since the 16th century. Almost every street has shops selling tiles, china and porcelain, and even the *otogar* (bus station) is covered in tiles, while the main square has a huge ceramic vase as its centrepiece. You can drive to the citadel for fine views over the town.

Environs of Kütahya Afyon▶ Afyonkarahisar (the name means 'Black Castle of Opium') makes the best stopover place in the Kütahya area, being quite interesting in itself and also having reasonable accommodation. The town's skyline is dominated by a 225m-tall black rock with a ruined citadel on its summit, fortified by the Hittites, Phrygians, Romans and Byzantines in turn. A flight of 700 steps on the southern rock face leads up to the crenellated remains on top of the rock, at the foot of which sits the old town, a maze of narrow streets with many old Ottoman houses. Some of these still have the traditional wooden latticework on the overhanging upper storeys, designed to enable the women to look out while remaining unseen themselves.

The **Ulu Cami**, Afyon's oldest mosque (1272), stands directly opposite the steps up the rock and still retains its original wooden capitals with stalactite carving. Afyon was the second most important Mevlevi centre after Konya, and the Mevlevi Camii and adjoining hall near by have been turned into a **Mevlevi Museum** with displays

208

Opium in abundance
Afyon is Turkish for 'opium,' and this region does indeed produce 35 per cent of the world's legal opiates. In the 1960s there was a fair amount of illegal drug trafficking, with very lax controls on the harvest and who picked it. Now the poppy fields are patrolled, and while locals continue to sprinkle seeds liberally on bread and the leaves are used in salads, most of the harvest ends up in processed capsules destined for pharmaceutical factories. The other local speciality is *kaymak*, a thick clotted cream made from buffalo milk.

The golden touch
Legends of King Midas and the phenomenal wealth of his kingdom of Phrygia abounded in ancient times. The king's legendary gift by which everything he touched turned to gold was in fact inspired by a river rich in gold particles that ran through the kingdom.

Afyon boasts some unusually fine Ottoman houses

of ceremonial costumes and musical instruments.

Aslankaya and Aslantaş► These two Phrygian monuments (both names mean 'Lion Rock') are similar to Midas Şehri (below) and easily reached from Afyon. Both consist of two lions cut from a rock face and guarding the entrance to a niche containing a statue of Cybele. Aslankaya is the more impressive because of its enormous lions; it is to be found near Lake Emre in the small town of Döğer.

Midas Şehri (City of Midas)► The most impressive site west of Ankara, this monument is rarely visited because of its remoteness. Although the name implies the remains of a whole town, there is in fact just one monument here, a colossal gabled rock-cut building with an ornamented façade. The first western travellers to see it thought it was the tomb of King Midas, who was king of Phrygia during the prosperous 8th century; the mistake is understandable since the façade was inscribed with the word 'Midai'. It is now known that the monument is a temple to Cybele, the early Anatolian fertility goddess. Her statue once stood in the niche, flanked by attendant lions. Near by in the hills are further rock tombs and a monumental rock stairway leading up on to the acropolis.

The old town of Afyon is a picturesque maze of narrow streets lined with old houses

Local traditions and crafts survive in these remote provinces

Central Anatolia is an important carpet-making region, as can be seen from the goods on sale in the bazaar at Sivas

▶▶ Sivas *189D2*

As one of the principal cities of the Seljuk sultanate, Sivas was adorned with an abundance of beautiful Seljuk buildings. The jewel of the city is the **Çifte Minare (Twin Minaret) Madrasa**, built in 1271 and now set among the pretty gardens of the small municipal park. All that remains is the spectacular façade, giving a hint of what it would once have looked like. Close by is the restored **Şifaiye Madrasa**, a combined hospital and medical school and the largest and most elaborate medical institution ever built by the Seljuks. Inside, note the beautiful

The Gök Madrasa at Tokat, now an ethnographical museum

Ma's orgies
Ten kilometres north of Tokat is the great sanctuary of Comana Pontica, where the Anatolian earth mother goddess was worshipped under the apt name of Ma. Every two years her worshippers held a festival, a very popular kind of market fair-cum-orgiastic feast in which a statue of the goddess was paraded about, accompanied by frenzied worshippers.

tiles on the *türbe* (tomb or shrine) of Keykavuş, some with lions marching in relief, showing Hittite influence.

Another Seljuk masterpiece in the town is the **Gök Madrasa**, also of 1271, built by Sahip Ata, whose work is also prominent in Konya (see pages 104–5) and Kayseri (see pages 180–1). It is reckoned to be the most beautiful *madrasa* (theological college) ever built by the Seljuks. Near by stands the **Ulu Cami** (Great Mosque), the oldest Turkish monument in Sivas, with its leaning minaret and forest of pillars inside.

► **Tokat** *189D3*

In Tokat there is really only one major monument, the **Gök (Turquoise) Madrasa**, named after its blue tiles, most of them missing today. Blue is a holy colour in Turkey (the English word turquoise derives from 'Turkey'). The *madrasa* is now used as a museum to display a hotchpotch of Seljuk, Roman and ethnographic exhibits. A 19th-century house in the town, the **Latifoğlu Mansion**, has recently been restored and has opened its doors as a museum of Ottoman life.

► **Yassıhüyük (Gordion)** *188B2*

Lying some 100km west of Ankara, the site of the ancient capital of Phrygia is difficult to incorporate into an itinerary, and thus remains little visited, despite its importance. The site, which stands on a great mound nearly 500m long and 350m wide, includes foundations of the Phrygian royal palace, paved with pebble mosaics in geometric patterns of dark red, white and deep blue: the oldest mosaics ever discovered (8th century BC). Bordering the palace square are buildings called *megarons* (large vestibules opening on to an inner room with a round hearth near the centre). These *megarons* are known to have had gabled roofs, a feature first seen in Urartian buildings much further to the east, which spread from there via Gordion westwards to Greece and thence to the rest of Europe. Perhaps the most prominent structure on the site today is the great gateway, which was originally flanked by a pair of massive towers.

The Bee Goddess
Some 50km southwest of Gordion stand the remains of Pessinus, the religious centre of Phrygia, with its temple to Cybele, the Anatolian fertility goddess who was later adopted by the Greeks as Artemis. In Phrygia Cybele was worshipped as a bee, which explains the Turkish name for the site – Ballıhisar, meaning 'Honey Castle'.

The twin minarets of the Çifte Minare Madrasa, the jewel of the many Seljuk monuments in Sivas

211

EASTERN TURKEY

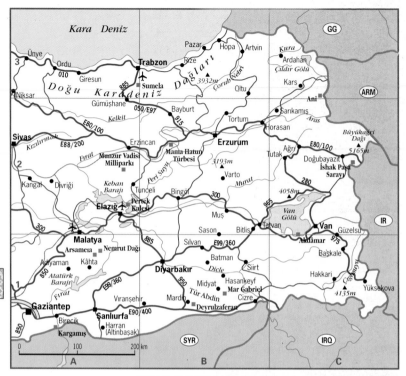

Kara Deniz

Ünye
Ordu
010
Giresun
Trabzon
Sumela
Gümüşhane
Doğu Karadeniz
Niksar
Kelkit
E80/100
Sivas
Kızılırmak
E88/200
Kangal
Divriği
Fırat
Erzincan
Munzur Vadisi
Milliparkı
Keban
Barajı
Tunceli
Bingöl
Elazığ
Pertek
Kalesi
Muş
Sason
Malatya
Arsameia
Nemrut Dağı
Adıyaman
Kâhta
Atatürk
Barajı
Fırat
Gaziantep
Birecik
Harran
(Altınbaşak)
Kargamış

Pazar
Hopa
Artvin
Rize
Dağları
3932m
Çoruh Nehri
Oltu
Bayburt
915
Tortum
Horasan
Erzurum
Mama Hatun
Türbesi
3193m
Varto
Murat
300
Diyarbakır
Dicle
Batman
Siirt
Silvan
E99/360
Midyat
Hasankeyf
Mardin
Tür Abdin
Mar Gabriel
Cizre
Deyrulzaferan
Viranşehir
E90/400
E99/360
885
050/E97

GG
Kura
Ardahan
Çıldır Gölü
Kars
Ani
Sarıkamış
Aras
Büyükağrı
Dağı
5165m
Ağrı
Tutak
E80/100
Doğubayazıt
İshak Paşa
Sarayı
280
4058m
965
Van
Gölü
Tatvan
Bitlis
Van
Güzelsu
Akdamar
975
Başkale
Hakkari
4135m
Yüksekova
ARM
IR
IRQ

Peri Suyu
300
850
SYR

0   100   200 km

A   B   C

212

Shepherdesses near Kars

Far right: The pleasure palace of Ishak Paşa Sarayı, set incongruously in the near wilderness at Doğubayazıt

Eastern Turkey This region remains for most people a complete unknown, and many are convinced that it is moreover effectively out of bounds. Until the Kurdish dissident problem is under full control again, after its escalation in 1993, you would be unwise to travel in the extreme southeast (that is, from Diyarbakır and Tunceli eastwards), but the Nemrut Dağı area remains safe, as do Malatya, Erzincan, Erzurum, Kars and all points northwards to the Black Sea coast.

EASTERN TURKEY

Earthquake zone
Earthquakes measuring
five points and over on the
Richter scale occur in this
part of the world every few
years. The main belt runs
northeast between Malatya
and Varto, but Erzincan and
Erzurum are also regular
targets.

*Traditional transport
near Nemrut Dağı*

Landscape The east of Turkey is very different geographically from the western and southern coastal regions. There are vast tracts of bleak wilderness, the climate is subject to harsh extremes of heat and cold, and facilities for eating and accommodation are generally meagre. Despite all this, the sheer scale and wildness of the country exert their own powerful fascination. Most surreal of all is the vast and eerie **Lake Van**, its thin piercing blueness ringed with snow-covered peaks.

The **Tigris** and **Euphrates** both have their sources here, and these majestic rivers rolling across the flat mudlands of Mesopotamia are indeed an awe-inspiring sight. South of the new Lake Atatürk, these mudplains are difficult to reconcile with the image of Mesopotamia as described by Robert Byron: '...once so rich, so fertile of art and invention, so hospitable to the Sumerians, the Seleucids and the Sassanids'. He goes on, 'The prime fact of Mesopotamian history is that in the 13th century Hulagu destroyed the irrigation system; and from that day to this, Mesopotamia has remained a land of mud deprived of mud's only possible advantage, vegetable fertility.' The great hope is that the irrigation schemes now possible as a result of the new Lake Atatürk will restore this area to its former fertility and prosperity.

Towns and Sites The high point of any visit to eastern Turkey is Van and its extraordinary lake. The towns of most beauty and note are **Diyarbakır** and **Mardin**. Otherwise, the major sites of eastern Turkey lie in remote spots such as the **Nemrut Dağ** mountaintop sanctuary near Adıyaman, and the **Ishak Paşa Palace** near Doğubeyazıt. Many of the other towns, such as **Kars** and **Erzurum**, give a poor first impression but improve after

you have had the chance to seek out their more interesting monuments. Because of the great distances involved, many Turks choose to travel by air, and all the main towns are connected by regular THY flights to Ankara and Istanbul. There are car-hire outlets at Adana, Erzurum, Diyarbakır, Malatya and Van, as well as at Samsun and Trabzon on the Black Sea.

A shoe shine at work in Erzurum

Potholes
Owing to the extremes of temperature, maintenance of tarmac roads is very difficult, and potholes are a near-permanent feature of the roads. It is therefore infinitely preferable to travel by bus or hired car than to take your own car.

Kurdish problems
Since early 1993 there has been an intensification of activity by the PKK Kurdish guerrillas, but this time hostile to tourists, part of a deliberate attempt to affect tourist revenues. In 1993 about 20 westerners were kidnapped. All were released in a few weeks, after an unpleasant experience in harsh conditions. The PKK have declared that anyone entering the area known as 'Kurdistan' without authorisation risks being kidnapped.

The Pool of Abraham at Şanlıurfa

EASTERN TURKEY

The valley of the Kinalicam river near Artvin

Georgian Mount Athos
The eastern valley opposite Artvin once contained such a wealth of monasteries that it became known as the Georgian Mount Athos. Some of these buildings are still relatively well preserved and can be visited on drivable tracks. The most commonly visited is the 10th-century church of Dolişhane, now in use as the village mosque of Hamamlıköy.

Free women for sale
In the 19th century a tribe was discovered in the remote village of Sason, to the east of Bitlis, whose members were neither Christians nor Muslims, and who spoke a mixture of Arabic, Kurdish and Armenian. They had no churches or mosques, and there was no institution of marriage. Women went free and unveiled, but could be bought and sold.

A farmer in the mountains of the Georgian heartlands around Artvin

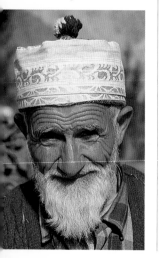

▶▶ **Artvin**   212B3

As you approach from a dramatic gorge in the Georgian valleys, the first glimpse of Artvin is unforgettable. As the gorge widens out you suddenly look up to see the houses of the town lying in a magnificent setting on the upper slopes of the valley. At its foot, on a jagged cliff with a sheer drop to the river below, there looms an impressive 15th-century castle. Described as the point where 'Turkey and the Caucasus meet', Artvin makes an excellent base for exploring these Georgian heartlands.

▶ **Bitlis**   212B2

Set on the outer fringes of the former Byzantine Empire, Bitlis is the gateway to another world. As you enter the steep black gorge with its curious houses set up on the cliffsides, you feel you are on the brink of the unknown. Above lour the walls of an impressive citadel, and below rush the waters of the Bitlis Suyu, a tributary of the Tigris. On the main street of Bitlis is the fine **Şerefiye Camii** with a pointed *türbe* (tomb or shrine) attached, built in 1528 by a local Kurdish emir. Further up the main street is the 12th-century Ulu Camii with its detached minaret. The population today is largely Kurdish, but up to the 1920s about half the inhabitants were Armenian. Bitlis is famous for its light-coloured honey and its Virginia-type tobacco.

Walk Nemrut Dağı Volcano

A most unusual outing that ventures up a volcano and then descends into the crater, this exhilarating trip offers superb scenery, as well as tremendous views over Lake Van and its ring of mountains. The total distance from Tatvan is only 20km, but because 15 of these are on a poor, unmetalled road, a full hour should be allowed each way for the trip. July and August are the best times for the ascent, as there is a high chance of snow making the track impassable at other times.

Set out from Tatvan on the Bitlis road. At the edge of town is the small harbour with the large ships that ferry train passengers across the lake to Van, where the railway track resumes. Just by the harbour a road marked by a yellow sign labelled 'Nemrut', heads off to the right round the northern shore of the lake.

After 4km on this road you come to a second yellow sign pointing to the left up a dirt road. This is the track which slowly bumps its way right up to the crater rim, at 3,050m. *Yürük* (nomad) shepherds and small children can be a bit unfriendly, and stone-throwing is a common pastime, but just ignore it and drive on.

From the rim the view is stupendous, over the bleak cone itself and down into the lush vegetation within. The track continues for 3km right down inside the crater: it last erupted in 1441, so it is relatively safe to consider it dormant now. With a 7km diameter, it is one of the largest complete craters in the world. The western half holds – some 700m below the rim – a huge lake beside which are hot springs in which you can paddle. The whole area is uninhabited but for occasional nomad camps grazing their animals on the lush vegetation. There is talk of Nemrut Dağı becoming the centre of a national park. Do not confuse this with the Nemrut Dağı on pages 230–1!

Nemrut Dağı looms large above Lake Van, itself at an altitude of roughly 1,750m

Georgian valleys

■ **Set in Turkey's extreme northeastern corner, between Erzurum and Artvin, is this pocket of stunningly beautiful mountains and valleys, still inhabited by the descendants of the Georgians......■**

Gingery Georgians
Racially quite distinct from the inhabitants of surrounding towns such as Erzurum and Kars, many Georgians still have ginger hair and freckles. They are different in manner too, being rather more dignified. In these valleys you are treated as a guest who has taken considerable trouble to come and visit the remoter parts of the country.

Armenian links
Although ethnically distinct, the Armenians and Georgians shared a similar history of invasions and counter-invasions, and through frequent inter-marriage they also became mixed to some extent. Thus the Bagratid family were rulers of both Armenian and Georgian territories; their rule was punctuated by squabbles and rivalries, generally resolved by matchmaking.

Origins of the Georgians The Georgians have had little influence on the history of Turkey. They speak a non Indo-European language which belongs, like Laz (the language spoken on the Black Sea) to the Caucasian group, and they have always had close links with the Byzantine Greeks. Byzantine emperors endowed churches here, even sending architects, masons and craftsmen to build and decorate them. The Georgians provided little architectural inspiration of their own, though they may well have been the channel through which the Byzantine influence passed into Russia. The churches all have the Armenian drum and conical dome, and the stonecarvings on the external walls, with animals and rich garlands, are

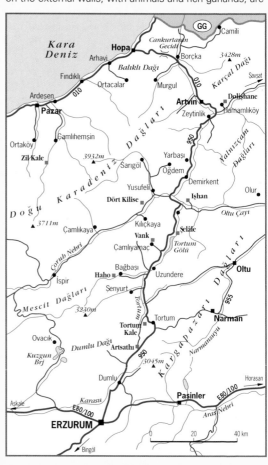

Monasteries of the Georgian valleys

Georgian valleys

reminiscent of Armenian styles. There are some 50,000 Georgians in Turkey, and the Georgian language is still spoken in the remoter valleys and mountains of the extreme northeast.

From Queen Tamara to the Ottomans In the 12th century Georgia entered a period of relative peace, and it reached a high point under the leadership of Queen Tamara, a gentle and humane leader as well as a shrewd administrator and diplomat. By the time of her death in 1212 she had extended her kingdom, with its capital at Tiflis, to include Armenians, Kipchaks, Kurds, Azerbaijanis, Muslims and Christians alike. In the 13th and 14th centuries Georgia suffered heavily from Mongol attacks under Ghenghis Khan and Tamerlane, whose armies left its towns and villages in ruins. Thus weakened, Georgia was unable to withstand the increasing power of the Ottomans, and in 1552 a detachment of Janissaries was stationed in the ancient Bagratid fortress of Ardanuç. By the 17th century most Georgians had converted to Islam, though in fact the Ottoman Empire exercised only a loose control over it, content to let its princes and barons squabble among themselves in their endless family feuding.

Georgian churches The best of the lovely Georgian churches, relics of the Christianity that died out under the Ottomans, are to be found between **Tortum** and **Artvin**. Some are still in use as village mosques and are therefore well maintained, while others are severely dilapidated.

Some 25km north of Tortum, a sign points over a bridge to **Bağbası**, the Turkish name of the village in which the 10th-century church of **Haho** lies. This interesting church, with its conical dome in the local soft yellow sandstone was originally part of a monastic complex, and has now been carefully restored by the villagers and converted to become their mosque. The walls bear highly comic reliefs of biblical scenes, such as Jonah and the Whale. Look out for the strange mythical beasts that appear in some of the scenes.

Fifteen kilometres further north along the main road, a track forks off to the left to reach the colossal monastery church of **Vank**, a derelict shell standing in the heart of the village. Inside there still remain some 11th-century frescoes showing the faces of angels and Mary and Jesus, and on the gable outside are reliefs of the archangels Michael and Gabriel. Like Haho, Vank was originally part of a 10th-century monastery.

Some 35km north of the Vank turn-off is a fork right to Olur, after which a dirt track winds up to the 11th-century bishop's church of **Işhan**. Set in the middle of the village beside some small ponds, the church sits on a terrace overlooking the mountains. The windows are richly decorated with stonecarvings, and inside there are still some murals of flying angels.

Mountain scenery
The Georgian valleys form one of the loveliest parts of Turkey, with narrow gorges running between hillsides covered in bright green deciduous forests and lush vegetation. Heavy rainfall means that the region is full of rushing rivers, poplar trees and flowery meadows. The silvery Lake Tortum (Tortum Gölü), with its sheer sides, was formed just three centuries ago by a colossal landslide that dammed the river. The Tortum waterfalls, which fall from the end of the lake are the highest in Turkey, at 48m; since 1960 they have been regulated by a new dam, so that from May through the summer months the falls stop.

219

The conical dome of the 10th-century church at Haho, now restored and converted by the villagers to become their mosque

EASTERN TURKEY

Kurdish majority
With its predominantly Kurdish population, Diyarbakır has tended to be a natural centre of Kurdish dissident groups. After the 1980 coup, thousands of dissidents were locked up in its prison, the most notorious in Turkey. More recently, some young dissidents have been turning to Sufism (mystic Islam) as a channel for their energies, much to the relief of the authorities. In the words of one Kurdish student: 'Who needs the Kurdish Workers' Party when you've got God?'

Magnificent walls
The magnificent black basalt city walls of Diyarbakır have a rampart walk, of which the best stretch is from the Urfa Gate to the Mardin Gate, where a wide grassy path allows two or three people to walk abreast. Sunset is the best time, with unforgettable views towards the Tigris Valley.

Diyarbakır viewed from the town walls

►► **Diyarbakır**   *212B1*

Positioned at the highest navigable point on the Tigris and backed by the eastern Taurus mountains, Diyarbakır dominates the expanse of the northern Mesopotamian plain. Inside its walls, the city exudes the confidence that comes from having been a key city with its own special identity for centuries, and it hums with vitality. It is divided into distinct quarters – Armenian, Christian, Kurdish and Arab – each with its own churches or mosques and community buildings, and behind the large carved wooden doors on the narrow winding streets there are hidden courtyards. Diyarbakır has more historic mosques, churches and other notable buildings than any other Turkish city except Istanbul.

Visiting the various quarters takes several hours of dusty and strenuous walking. Apart from the 5km-long walls, the monuments to look out for are the **Nebi Camii** (the Mosque of the Prophet), near the Harput Gate, with its striped minaret, built in 1524 by the White Sheep clan; the **Saray Kapı** (Palace Gate), the most beautiful of the gates and the entrance to the citadel; and the dour black basalt **Süleymaniye citadel mosque**, built by the Artukids in 1160. Do not miss, either, the **Ulu Cami** (the Great Mosque), modelled on the great Umayyad Mosque at Damascus and built by Malik Shah in 1091–2, making it the very first of the great Seljuk mosques of Anatolia. Other major monuments are the elegant **Safa Mosque**, Persian in feel with its graceful white minaret; the **Syrian Orthodox Church** set in its own lovely courtyard and still used by the 25 or so Syrian Orthodox families here; and the Armenian **Surp Giragos Kilesesi**, the only other Christian church still in use in the city.

Environs of Diyarbakır Hasankeyf► Originally founded by the Romans as a frontier outpost, this ruined capital city of the 12th-century Artukid (Kurdish) dynasty stands on a spectacular clifftop overlooking the Tigris. The bridge whose crumbling supports can still be seen in the river was another skilled Artukid construction, described by early travellers as the grandest in all Anatolia. The clifftop city, covering some 2 square kilometres, is

reached via a narrow gully behind the modern town of Hasankeyf.

Mardin►► This important Syrian Christian centre 100km southeast of Diyarbakır, covers a craggy hillside with the lovely Syrian-influenced architecture that inspired Arnold Toynbee to call it 'the most beautiful town in the world'. It faces south over the Syrian desert. Many of the decorated Arab-style buildings are now decaying, but enough remains to hint at their past splendour. The town's masterpiece is the **Sultan Isa Madrasa**, a 14th-century Artukid (Kurdish) monument, recognisable by its two white ribbed domes. A rough path leads up from it to the ruined citadel on the hill summit, inside which are the ruins of a vast palace and mosque dating from the 15th century.

Tûr Abdin►► Literally 'The Servants' Plateau', this highland region (between Mardin and Cizre, with Midyat at the centre) is the Mount Athos of the Syrian Orthodox Church. During the Middle Ages there were four bishoprics and 80 monasteries here, and the population grew prosperous through trade and farming. Tragically, these Syrian Christians, of whom there were 200,000 just 80 years ago, have now dwindled to 2,000, caught up in the crossfire of the PKK Kurdish rebels and the Turkish government forces. The Metropolitan (bishop) at Mar Gabriel is waging a one-man stand to try to keep his people together: one of the incentives he offers is free education for 40 boys a year. Only four of the monasteries are still functioning, served by a handful of monks. The two to visit today are **Deyrulzaferan** near Mardin, and **Mar Gabriel**.

Black and white
In contrast to the black Diyarbakır, Mardin is sometimes called the White City, because of the distinctive pale limestone used in its buildings. Some of the mosques in Diyarbakır also feature a black and white striped effect created by alternating layers of basalt and limestone. One theory holds that the stripes also represent the black and white totem sheep of the two Turcoman tribes, the Akkoyunlu (White Sheep) and the Karakoyunlu (Black Sheep), both of whom set up important states in this part of Turkey.

221

The minarets (below and left) both exhibit the black and white stripes typical of Diyarbakır mosques (see panel above)

The Kurds

■ **Ancient and traditional enemies of the Armenians, the Kurds are a distinct racial group indigenous to the region known as Kurdistan, which today straddles the modern borders of Turkey, Iran, Iraq, Georgia, Armenia and Syria......■**

222

Devil in a cabbage
Some 50,000 Kurds are still said to be Yazidis, or peacock-god worshippers, often referred to in the west as devil-worshippers. They worship the sun, and water is also sacred to them. Their Manichaean creed views the universe as a struggle between light and dark, good and evil, but they never refer to Satan by name. They abhor the colour blue and never eat cabbage, believing that the devil inhabits the leaves.

Minority status There are 25 million Kurds spread across these six countries, making them the world's largest stateless people. By far the greatest number are in Turkey, with Iran and Iraq having roughly similar numbers. The Kurds have always been a nomadic mountain people, and in Turkey today they are known officially as 'mountain Turks', the existence of a separate Kurdish race being studiously ignored by the authorities. Had the 1920 Treaty of Sèvres been implemented, Kurdistan would have become an autonomous state, but the Turks, rallied by Atatürk, rejected the treaty. Ironically the Kurds joined Atatürk in warding off the Greek Christians and Persians. When Atatürk declared the Turkish Republic and abandoned the sultanate for a secular state, they felt betrayed. In the Kurdish revolts that followed, in the 1920s and 1930s, hundreds of thousands of Kurds were killed or deported by the Turks. Kurdish guerrilla raids on the Turkish government security forces continue today.

Language problems The Kurdish language – Indo-European in origin, like Persian, Armenian and most western European languages – has several dialects all of which are mutually unintelligible, a fact which has not helped the Kurds in their attempts to unite: there are no fewer than seven rival Kurdish national movements. Within Turkey, the language used to be banned; Kurdish children must still go to Turkish schools and speak Turkish there with their friends, reverting to Kurdish when they are at home with their families.

A Kurdish mother and child in characteristic dress

Current aspirations Three million Kurds now live in the 'enclave' set up after the Gulf Crisis of 1991 to protect them from Saddam Hussein's forces, a tiny area in Iraq's northeastern corner dubbed Kurdistan. As you cross into it from Turkey, 'Kurdistan' is stamped into your passport by Kurdish border guards. There is an emerging government here, with a fledgling army (currently 15,000 strong; the aim is to double its size in the coming years). Power is shared by the PKK (Kurdish Workers' Party) and the KDP (Kurdish Democratic Party). A Kurdish national anthem has been chosen and is played regularly on the new Kurdish TV stations. Questioned about their aims, Kurdish spokesmen say that they want a free, democratic,

The Kurds

The Kurdish character

Although historically they have practised a policy of evasion in the face of invading armies, the Kurds have been far from unwarlike themselves, and have been ready to fight in other people's wars away from their home ground. The great Saladin, hero of the Crusades, was a Kurd, and the Kurds are naturally proud to have produced one of the greatest heroes of Islam. Ethnically distinct, the men have long, bony faces with aquiline noses, and the women are forthright and unveiled. Traditional ceremonies, such as weddings and Now Rouz (Kurdish New Year) continue to be practised, to the accompaniment of haunting Kurdish music, despite attempts to discourage them.

A Kurdish family in the doorway of their beehive hut

secular, socialist state, ideally forming a federation with Kurds in Turkey, Iraq, Iran and Syria. Since May 1993 the PKK in Turkey has stepped up its activities, directing random attacks at popular tourist sites with the specific intent of hitting Turkish tourist revenues.

Since 1984, the civil strife in southeast Turkey has cost about 10,000 lives. The Turkish authorities regard Kurdish aspirations as a threat to the unitary Turkish state, in which everyone is equal and everyone is a Turk – *Ne mutlu Türküm diyene* ('How happy is he who can say he is a Turk') was one of Atatürk's chief slogans. Kurdish nationalism is here in conflict with Turkish nationalism, and far from making concessions, the approach of Tansu Çiller, the new prime minister, to the Kurdish problem is to attempt to stamp it out and to exploit any existing divisions, setting Kurd against Kurd.

Kurdish architectural gem

Standing isolated in the midst of ploughed fields near Hasankeyf is one of the best-preserved and loveliest of all Kurdish monuments, the *türbe* (tomb) of the Ayyubid king Zeyn El-Abdin, descendant of Saladin. Built of red brick with an onion-topped dome, it is covered on the outside with exquisite turquoise glazed tiles.

Kurds remain close to their nomadic roots and so tend to furnish their houses sparsely, but no Kurdish home is without its carpet

Ishak Paşa's indulgent palace – intended as the most beautiful dwelling in the world – sits above a dusty plain close to the Iranian border

Doğubayazıt
212C2

A drab frontier town, Doğubayazıt is of interest only as a base for the ascent of Mount Ararat (see pages 228–9), or (more usually) for a visit to the ultimate 'Turkish château', the pleasure palace *extraordinaire* of Ishak Paşa, which is located 6km away.

Ishak Paşa Sarayı▶▶ Built in about 1800 by Ishak Paşa, the feudal overlord of this area which was nominally under Ottoman control, this remarkable palace dominated the lucrative silk caravan routes from its vantage point on the hillside. It is usually open daily 8–4, or later on a fine day, and the ticket office is tucked just inside the palace's vast courtyard.

The palace has a sybaritic air, and it was certainly conceived more as a pleasure dome than as a defensive castle. The largest section is given over to the harem, with its maze-like series of rooms, large blackened kitchen and dining area, bathrooms and 14 long thin harem bedrooms. The superb colonnaded feast room originally had mirrors in the blind arches, so that the harem women could partake of the feast without being seen by the pasha's guests. The *selamlik* (reception) and mosque areas are also very fine, though a little more modest. In the late 19th century, during preparations for the war against Russia, the palace was used as a barracks: the stained-glass windows, bought at great expense, all disappeared, to be replaced by sheets of newspaper; the marble pillars and alabaster carvings were chipped and hacked; and 400 soldiers slept in the bedrooms intended for the pasha's concubines.

Flooded sites
The Keban Baraji (Keban dam) was the first of a series of dams to be built on the River Euphrates, designed to bring electricity and irrigation to neglected parts of the country. With its construction, however, 50 known archaeological sites were flooded, most of them early Bronze Age settlements which might have contributed important evidence about man's first settled existence in Anatolia after he had stopped his nomadic wandering and hunting. Five foreign archaeological teams, all self-financed, excavated as many of these sites as possible before the flooding in 1974; their findings are displayed in the new museum at Elazığ, on the campus of the Euphrates University.

One of the pleasures of a stop in Elazığ is sampling the excellent local Buzbağ wine

A decorative detail from the Ishak Paşa Sarayı

▶ **Elazığ** *212A2*

A modern, unremarkable town possessed of a good hotel, Elazığ makes a comfortable place to stay on the way to points further east. Some 5km to the north, on a hill overlooking the lake, stands the old fortress city of **Harput**, now almost derelict. Just 100 years ago Harput had 800 shops, 10 mosques, 10 religious schools, 8 churches, 8 libraries, 12 *hans* (inns) and 90 baths, but its population moved down to Elazığ when the new town was built, prompted partly by earthquakes in the region. Following the yellow signs to the *kale* (castle), you pass the 12th-century Ulu Cami, with its severely leaning minaret, before reaching the castle itself, set on its rocky outcrop. It is also worth looking at the 14th-century castle of **Eski Pertek**, once the proud guardian of the Euphrates Valley, now an indignant rocky island cut off in the middle of the lake and accessible only by boat.

Erzincan *212A2*

Erzincan was rebuilt after the terrible earthquake of 1939; its very name means 'life-crusher'. The destruction wrought here was especially sad, as 19th-century Erzincan was considered to be one of the most beautiful cities in Asia, with over 79 mosques. Twenty kilometres east of Erzincan is the important Urartian site of **Altıntepe** (Golden Hill), where Turkish archaeologists have discovered a wealth of jewellery, bronze and pottery in tombs built into the hillside.

EASTERN TURKEY

Bleak enough for wolves
Set in a great bowl at an altitude of nearly 2,000m, Erzurum is Turkey's highest provincial capital, ringed by broad, eroded mountains. The landscape is harsh, and the dull grey stone of the buildings is in perfect harmony with it. In 1958, Erzurum was chosen (in preference to Van) as the site for eastern Turkey's main university. Unless they are dedicated archae-ologists or agriculturalists (the two strongest faculties at the university), teachers from Ankara and Istanbul are unwilling to come to the severe climate and limited entertainment of Erzurum. In the winter months wolves have been spotted roaming the campus.

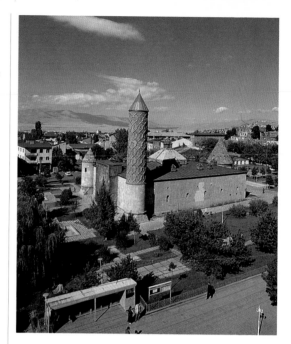

The Yakutiye Madrasa in Erzurum, built in 1310 by the Mongol rulers of Persia

A shoe shine in Erzurum

► ▬▬▬ **Erzurum** *212B2*

A god-forsaken place on its high plateau, mercilessly cold in winter, with its streets of shops and lights at night, Erzurum can still seem like a haven of civilisation and modernity in comparison with the other cities of eastern Turkey. The local speciality is *oltutaş*, or black jet, made into necklaces, worry-beads, ornaments and just about everything else. Apart from the walls of the citadel there is nothing left in Erzurum from before the Seljuk conquest in the 11th century. Severe earthquakes and years of wars have taken their toll, but there are still some fine buildings to see near the centre of town, notably the **Yakutiye Madrasa** and the **Çifte Minare** (Twin-Minaretted) **Madrasa**.

The Yakutiye, built in 1310 by the Mongol rulers of Persia, is the most attractive building in Erzurum, with pretty turquoise tiling on the minaret and traces of green and yellow in the portal. Flanked by two lions and an eagle, this portal shows a markedly Persian influence, displaying a more feminine quality than is to be found in Arab or Turkish architecture.

The Çifte Minare Madrasa is Erzurum's most famous building, built in 1253 by Sultan Alaeddin Keykubad II, grandson of the builder of the great fortress at Alanya (see page 142). Used for years as a military store, it has now been restored, though its two fluted brick minarets have far fewer turquoise tiles than that of the Yakutiye Madrasa. Behind the *madrasa* are three conical Seljuk *kumbets* or tombs, attractively carved in stone. Try to stroll as well into the old citadel area, enclosed by crum-bling walls and still with a few rusting cannons lying about. It has an unusual clock-tower, originally an 11th-century Seljuk minaret.

Kars   212C3

In wet weather – and it is frequently wet here – Kars is about the most dismal spot in eastern Turkey. *Kar* means 'snow', and Kars can get up to 13 metres of it. Today the town has little to offer besides its Russian buildings from the turn of the century and its Armenian **Church of the Apostles**, set in a scruffy clearing near the river and Ottoman bridge. Built in 932 in coarse black basalt by the Armenian Bagratids, the church is not easy on the eye. The carvings of the twelve apostles on the outside of the dome are so crude as to be faintly grotesque.

Environs of Kars Ani►► The real reason anyone comes to Kars is to visit Ani, the ruined Armenian city of a hundred gates and a thousand churches. Because of its proximity to the Armenian border, a permit is required, a formality which takes half an hour at the Kars tourist office. The military escort which used to accompany visitors has now been abandoned, and you are free to wander around the ruins of this extraordinary city at your leisure. No city in Europe in the mid 10th century could rival the size and magnificence of Ani, and in the East only Constantinople, Baghdad and Cairo could match it. In the superb architecture here you can see the inspiration for much that we now know as the Seljuk style, including the powerfully built walls and the graceful *türbe* shapes which were to become the standard form for mausoleums for centuries to come. The Armenians were celebrated stonemasons, and the quality of the workmanship that is still on view here testifies to their technical virtuosity, the best in the world at that time. The Mongol raids, a severe earthquake in 1319 and the advent of Tamerlane – the *coup de grâce* – destroyed forever this city whose population at its height was said to number 200,000, four times the current population of Kars.

Swastika origins
On the inside of the great gates of Ani are many swastikas. This motif has been used for thousands of years – as a symbol of the sun, infinity and continuing fertility – in Sumeria, China, India, Egypt, Scandinavia, Greece and the Americas. It is found in Rome's catacombs, on Inca textiles and on relics unearthed at Troy. It is also one of the sacred signs of Buddhism. The word comes from the Sanskrit *svastika*, meaning prosperity; the sign was thought to bring good luck.

Who cares about mud?
A 19th-century traveller in Kars asked an aged Turk who had just waded across the muddy street to visit his friend's house, 'Why don't you clean the street?' Looking surprised, the old man answered: 'The mud will dry up in the summer. Why worry about it now?'

The spectacular Girvelik Selalesi Falls near Erzincan (see page 225)

■ **Eastern Turkey offers a tremendous range of climbing for the mountaineer, from the near-tropical landscapes of the Pontic mountains along the Black Sea to icy peaks permanently covered in snow, such as Mount Ararat and the Hakkari range in the extreme southeast......■**

Noah's Ark
According to Armenian tradition, Mount Ararat is the centre of the universe, and the Armenians themselves came down from its slopes. It is also cited in Genesis as the final resting place of Noah's Ark after the Flood. In recent years the search for the Ark has gained momentum, with the convinced and ever-hopeful climbing the mountain from Doğubayazıt. Some claim to have found pieces of the biblical vessel.

Behind the nomad encampment rises the snowy peak of Mount Ararat, dominating the Anatolian plateau for a radius of over 50km

Volcanoes The flat countryside of the Anatolian plateau is naturally dominated by any major mountain peaks, especially volcanoes such as **Nemrut Dağı** (see page 217: not to be confused with the other Nemrut Dağı described on pages 230–1), **Erciyes Dağı** (near Kayseri, see page 184) and above all **Ararat (Büyükağri Dağı)**. At 5,165m this is Turkey's highest mountain, dominating the landscape in every direction. In summer the snow line retreats up the mountain to cover the top third, while in winter it comes down to the base, itself at 1,800m above sea level. From afar, Ararat looks deceptively easy to climb, but in practice the jagged lava fields are very tricky; climbers regularly lose their lives in attempting the ascent, often because of the changeable weather, the mountain's speciality. It was first climbed in 1829 by a Professor Parrot, and, when safe, weekly expeditions are organised by a few agencies from Doğubayazıt, usually taking three days to go up and two down. Attacks by PKK terrorists can mean that the route is closed; when open, the requisite permit must be applied for at least three months in advance or longer for Ark-hunters' expeditions (see page 265). The Turks have long been convinced that the CIA has a listening post on the summit of Ararat, and that the Ark-hunting groups are really CIA agents up to no good.

Boiling bath
In the simple hotels at Ayder, hot springs take the place of baths. Men and women have set bathing times and the scalding-hot water reaches 57°C.

Unique freedom
The beauty of climbing in these remote mountains is well summed up by the English climber, Sidney Nowill, who described it as the sensation of living 'for a time completely free of every worldly link, self-reliant and untrammelled by any human agency or service, something which is healthful and cleansing to achieve, if only once in a lifetime'.

229

The Kaçkar mountain range is becoming increasingly popular with climbers

Women from a remote Anatolian village near Mount Ararat

The Arabs traditionally believed that Ararat was the roof of the world, and the source of the two great rivers, the Tigris and the Euphrates. The Kurds, too, regard Ararat as their mountain; one of the main Kurdish rebellions in Atatürk's day actually made its headquarters on the peak.

Ala Dağları Since the loss to climbers of the Hakkari area, the Ala Dağ range, southeast of Niğde, offers the best substitute, with the great advantage of easy access. The base point is Çamardı, a small town reachable on a tarmac road, from where guides and mules can be arranged. No permits are required.

Kaçkar Dağları This range, which lies inland from the eastern end of the Black Sea between Trabzon (see page 246) and Hopa (see page 241), is becoming increasingly popular because of its accessibility and the fact that it lies outside Kurdish territory. The favourite jumping-off point is **Ayder**, reached along the attractive valleys of **Hemsin** and **Çamlihemşin**. Ayder has about half a dozen simple hotels to accommodate trekkers, one of which boldly calls itself the Hilton. From this base you can attempt anything from a one-day eight-hour trek to 3,000m, to a week's full-scale climbing. Mountain guides are available and permits are not necessary.

Antiochus, deluded king and creator of this grandiose folly

Less and less remote
Before a track was built up in it in the 1960s, the summit of Nemrut Dağı was accessible only by donkey and on foot and took two days. Now the whole way has a tarmac surface, and the ascent takes less than two hours. Snow makes the road impassable between the beginning of October and the beginning of May, however.

Bird sanctuary
Birecik, near Urfa, is one of the world's two remaining nesting places for the bald ibis, now nearly extinct. It leaves Birecik in July to fly to its winter home in Morocco. Its return in mid-February is regarded as heralding the coming of spring, and is celebrated each year by the villagers in a remarkable festival.

▶▶▶   **Nemrut Dağı**   *212A1*

Along with Cappadocia and the Sumela Monastery (see page 245), Nemrut Dağı, with its colossal stone heads on the mountain top, is one of the best-known and most visited sites east of Ankara.

Historically Nemrut Dağı is of no significance whatever, being no more than a vast funeral monument to King Antiochus, ruler of a small local dynasty who suffered delusions of grandeur. The kingdom, called Commagene, was established in the 1st century BC by Antiochus' father, Mithridates, and remained independent until AD72, when the Roman Emperor Vespasian incorporated it into the Roman province of Syria.

On the drive up from Kahta, the nearest town (there are minibuses if you do not have your own transport), you pass a fine Roman bridge. Higher up, near Eski Kahta, a fork in the track leads up to **Arsameia**, the Commagene capital, with a superb relief of Mithridates shaking hands with Hercules, a cave cistern, and the scattered column bases of ancient Arsameia on the hilltop. It also makes an excellent picnic spot away from the crowds

Continuing up to the summit (which at 2,150m is most impressive) of Nemrut Dağı, the road ends near a building offering souvenirs and simple refreshments. It is always chilly at the summit because of the altitude, and it is best to arrive there after the morning mists have cleared. A 10-minute walk up the path, past the tumulus which is the burial place of King Antiochus, brings you to the eastern terrace behind the tumulus. The deluded Antiochus claimed descent on his father's side from Darius the Great of Persia, and on his mother's from Alexander the Great, and the statues on this and the western terrace reflect this mixed Persian and Macedonian ancestry.

Antiochus himself (the one with the beard and moustachios) makes his appearance among the great kings and gods as their equal. The statues reflect the oriental and Hittite practice of enthroning images of gods on mountain tops. On the western terrace, where the five deities sit facing the sunset as opposed to the dawn, do not miss the dramatic lion relief. This is in fact a complex astronomical chart showing the conjunction of the planets Mars, Jupiter and Mercury, with stars and a crescent moon.

Environs of Nemrut Dağı Harran▶ Close to the Syrian border below Nemrut Dağı, Harran, like Urfa, is visited for its biblical associations (it is said that Abraham lived here), and also for its beehive houses, a form of architecture which has not changed since biblical times. Their extraordinary shape is dictated by the only material to hand in abundance – the mud of Mesopotamia. Near by is the vast and ruinous **Ulu Cami**, founded in the 8th century as part of the earliest university complex.

Malatya▶ A 19th-century new town, like Elazığ, Malatya is quite a centre of commerce with a fast-growing population. With its tourist-standard hotels and surprisingly sophisticated shopping, it makes a good base. Near by are the ruins of **Eski Malatya**, a Roman/Byzantine walled town, and the scant remains of **Aslantepe** (Lion Hill), the capital of a neo-Hittite kingdom (c.1000–700BC).

Şanlıurfa (Urfa)▶ Şanlı, meaning 'glorious', commemorates the fight Urfa put up against the invading French armies in 1920, but it is a town of no great beauty apart from two monuments: the 12th-century Seljuk **Ulu Cami**, modelled on the great mosque at Aleppo, and the **Pool of Abraham**, full of sacred carp. According to legend, the pool was created by God to extinguish the funeral pyre on which the angry Assyrian king Nimrod was preparing to burn Abraham.

Carried away by his delusions of grandeur, Antiochus followed the oriental and Hittite practice of enthroning images of gods on mountain tops

The Pool of Abraham at Şanlıurfa

Military escort
On the Syrian border, south of Adıyaman, is the famous site of Carchemish, capital of the most powerful of the neo-Hittite kingdoms which prospered after the collapse of the Hittite empire at Hattuşaş (c1200BC). Because of its closeness to the border a permit is needed, and a soldier escorts all visitors. Such luminaries as TE Lawrence, DG Hogarth and Gertrude Bell dug here, and some of the first clues to the identity of the Hittites were found here. Little remains on site today.

EASTERN TURKEY

A sheep market in northeastern Turkey

A Kurdish grandmother and child near Lake Van

▶ Van   212C2

One of the high points of any visit to eastern Turkey, this region was formerly one of legendary fertility. Just a century ago the lakeshore was thickly wooded – 'Van in this world, Paradise in the next', ran the old Armenian proverb. The town itself is nothing special, having none of the sophistication and hum of Diyarbakır (see pages 220–1), none of the beautiful architecture of Mardin (see pages 220–1), none of the atmosphere and fascination of Bitlis (see page 216). What it does have is proximity to Lake Van, 4km away, as well as two of the best hotels in eastern Turkey in which to base yourself for exploring the region. (See pages 234–5 for details of the lake area). Van's small museum (open 8:30–12, 1–7 except Mondays) is worth a visit for its stunning collection of Urartian artefacts.

Van Kalesi (Van Castle)▶▶ A visit to this freakish Urartian citadel, capital of the Urartian Empire for 300 years, is best made at sunset to enjoy the changing moods of the lake. Also called the Rock of Van, this narrow rock outcrop is nearly 2km long and 100m high, with sheer sides dropping to the south. Climb and follow all the little paths that weave about the citadel and you will discover the foundations of a Urartian temple, the tombs of four Urartian kings cut into huge chambers, and the crumbling Ottoman castle resting on large Urartian masonry blocks. In Ottoman times, 3,000 Janissaries were based here. Down below you will see the rubble-like mounds of Old Van, a city once enclosed by 16th-century walls and with one of the largest populations in Anatolia, two-thirds of it Armenian. Today it is a vivid example of a town which has been quite literally razed to the ground, with only the shells of a few mosques left. How and why this total destruction was wrought by the Turks after World War I remains a matter of controversy.

Environs of Van Akdamar►► See pages 234–5.

Çavuştepe► This royal Urartian citadel, 22km from Van on the Hakkari road, is the second largest after Van Kalesi. The buildings on the summit were for the royal family only, while ordinary Urartians lived on the plain below. As well as the temple buildings, palace and sacrificial altar, notice the extraordinarily advanced water system, with its series of large cisterns hollowed out of the rock for collecting the rain or snow.

Güzelsu (Hoşap Castle)►► Like a hallucination from a fairy tale, with its crenellations and battlements, Hoşap is the best-preserved Kurdish castle in Turkey. Built in 1643, when Ottoman power was slipping, by a local Kurdish despot, it lies 48km from Van on the Hakkari road, and is open daily from 8:30 to sunset. Its colossal and impressive entrance gate leads into a surprisingly open and grassy interior. The best-preserved part is the keep, at the highest point.

Hakkari► Backed by the 4,135m-high massif of Çilo Dağı, Hakkari looks from a distance almost like an Alpine ski resort in summer. Its population of 18,000 is almost entirely Kurdish: the town is highly traditional and Ramadan is strictly observed, with no alcohol being served all month. The women are veiled and wear black from head to toe. There are no monuments of interest to the tourist here; in times of less Kurdish unrest, it is the mountains and the scenery that attract visitors.

Little-known Urartians
The Urartians were distinguished builders who always chose long thin spurs for their fortress sites. Van Kalesi and Çavuştepe are the two largest of the 30 fortress cities that are scattered over eastern Turkey. The Urartians were similar in looks and language to the Hittites, and their particular speciality was metalwork, using gold, silver and bronze. Their fine work was exported westwards, and there is mounting evidence that the ancient Greeks and Etruscans copied heavily from Urartian originals.

233

Rising from the rocky plain like a mirage in the desert, Hoşap castle is the best preserved and most picturesque of all Turkey's Kurdish fortresses

[Map of Lake Van region]

Bulanık
Haçlı Gölü
Bilican Dağları
Karahasan
Sarısu
Ağrı
Görüşlü
Erciş
Deli
Akça Dağ
Muradiye
Adaksu
Süphan Dağı 4058m
Bayramlı
Ünseli
Nazik Gölü
Aydınlar
Kefkalesi
Sodalı Gölü
Göldüzü
Ermişler
Karasu
Ovakışla
Adilcevaz
Timar
Ahlat
Yolçatı
Taşmalı Geçidi
Erçek Gölü
Yeniköprü 2935m
Kasımoğlu
Erçek
Nemrut Dağı
Nemrut Gölü
Serinkum
Van Gölü
Muş
Toprakkale
Reşadiye
Tuspa
VAN
Turna Gölü
Tatvan
Küçüksu
Hosap Kulesi
Bitlis
Kocaçay
Budaklı
Altınsaç
Akdamar
Gümüşdere
Çavuştepe
Güzelsu
3076m
İbr... şabap Dağları
Dönemeç
Gürpınar
Gevaş
0 10 20 30 km

Drive Circuit of Lake Van

Covering a total distance of 332km, this day trip is one of the most memorable experiences of any visit to Turkey. It incorporates a short boat ride to an Armenian cathedral set on its own island, and visits a volcano, a Seljuk cemetery and superb fortresses, all set against the eerie beauty of Lake Van, ringed by haunting mountains. The roads are all tarmac-surfaced (if a little potholed) and traffic-free: you are quite likely to have whole sections of the lakeshore entirely to yourself. It is best to take your own provisions.

Lake Van at sunrise

Setting out from Van towards Gevaş, you come after 47km to a yellow sign to **Akdamar**, beside a small landing stage. In the morning you will find boats here waiting to ferry you the 2km across to the tiny island. There, in solitary splendour, stands the Armenian cathedral. Out of season (from October to May) you will have to hire a boat: this is perfectly straightforward but rather more expensive.

Steps climb up to the cathedral, built in 915 by King Gagik I of the independent Armenian kingdom of Vaspurakan (Armenia was the first country to adopt Christianity as its national religion, in AD303). The reliefs that cover the outside have never been restored, yet survive in remarkable condition despite the harshness of the climate. Depicting Old Testament stories, they are a masterpiece of early Armenian art. The series telling the story of Jonah and the Whale is one of the most hilarious, with a whale (the Armenians had never seen one) resembling an elongated pig with ears and teeth. Also recognisable are Abraham and Isaac, David and Goliath, and on the back wall Adam and Eve, heavily defaced.

The grassy island is a popular picnic spot for Turkish families, especially at weekends and holidays. There is also

a pebbly beach from which, in the summer months, the hardy can slip into the clear, silky waters of the lake. The alkaline sodas leave a wonderfully smooth feeling on the skin, and a level of salinity six times higher than that of the sea means that even the most leaden of swimmers can float.

Continuing the circuit westwards towards Tatvan, the road leaves the lake for a time and zigzags up a high mountain pass with beautiful bubbling streams and flower-filled meadows. From Tatvan, follow the yellow sign to **Nemrut** (see page 217), the volcano whose eruptions aeons ago formed Lake Van by creating a huge dam of lava, thereby blocking the outflow. The level now remains constant, as the melted snow that flows into it each winter evaporates during the hot summer months. The shore views here are constantly changing – sometimes treeless and gaunt, sometimes lush and almost alpine – but they are all bathed in Lake Van's strange and timeless pale blue light. The breathtaking beauty and serenity this imparts to them will long continue to haunt you.

The next stopping place is **Ahlat**, where an atmospheric Seljuk cemetery sprawls over 2 square kilometres, its lichen-covered headstones leaning at drunken angles. Also here – ripe for exploration – is a splendidly overgrown 16th-century fortress on the shore. Scattered about are distinc-

At an altitude of 1,750m, Lake Van is a high point of any trip to Turkey

tive conical *kümbets* (dome-tombs), from the 13th to 15th centuries. The Armenian stonemasons here were famous for their work, and only Kayseri (see page 161) has tombs in such number and variety.

Some 25km beyond Ahlat you reach **Adilcevaz**, with its attractive chocolate-coloured mosque on the shore. On the hill above is a fine Seljuk fortress, from which there are wonderful lake views.

On the final stretch of the circuit look out for **Arin Gölü**, a freshwater lake whose shores are alive with a noticeably rich bird population, unlike the still and silent shores of Lake Van.

Jonah and the whale at Akdamar

THE BLACK SEA

A mosque looks out over the blue waters of the Black Sea

Itineraries
One week:
Trabzon
Trabzon (Sumela)
Trabzon
Artvin
Artvin
Erzurum
Trabzon

Two weeks:
Trabzon
Trabzon (Sumela)
Trabzon
Samsun
Amasya
Boğazkale
Sivas
Erzincan (Divriği)
Erzurum
Kars
Kars
Artvin
Artvin
Rize (Çamlıhemşin)
Trabzon

Two weeks:
Trabzon
Trabzon (Sumela)
Trabzon
Artvin
Kars
Kars (Ani)
Doğubeyazıt
Van
Van
Tatvan
Ağrı
Erzurum
Artvin
Hopa
Trabzon

Far right: an elegant bridge at Çamlı-hemşin, near Rize

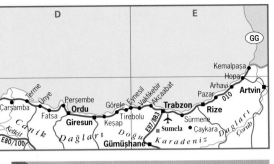

The Black Sea There are two main surprises in store for the first-time visitor to the Black Sea coast. The first is the lush green vegetation, and the second is its high concentration of buildings and population. Since the introduction of tea (see panel on page 239) the region has grown in prosperity and attracted more and more people, hence the quantity of newly built houses strung along the coast.

The best time to visit is late spring, when the blossom is out. Summer temperatures rarely exceed 28°C.

Landscape The name Black Sea is misleading, and so the green and fertile landscape here comes as a pleasant surprise. The tea plantations deck the extensive lower slopes of the Pontic mountain range, dropping down in terraces like a gently descending staircase to touch the very edge of the coast road. The mountain ranges along the coast have served to keep the region fairly isolated from the Anatolian hinterland, with the result that a host of remote valleys are still home to ethnic sub-groups such as the

THE BLACK SEA

Climatic contrast
The reason why Turks (and Arabs) call this the Black Sea and the Mediterranean the White Sea is thought to be that the sun glinting on the Mediterranean gives it a white sheen, whereas the rain of the north makes the water here seem blacker. This climatic difference is the reason why the Black Sea will never be a major tourist destination. Even in the height of summer it can rain heavily any day, and the temperature can fluctuate from a pleasant 30°C to a cool 18°C.

The Fırtına river, near Çamlıhemşin, surges down from the mountains through a beautiful but precipitous valley, in which getting from place to place and across the river requires some ingenuity

Colourful fishing boats on the coast

Laz. This also explains the strength of tradition here: Black Sea dances, for instance, have remained virtually unchanged for centuries.

Fringe history Historically the region has always lacked the dynamism of the Aegean and Mediterranean coasts, and the major events of history seem largely to have passed it by. The earliest-known settlements were founded here in the 7th and 8th centuries BC by enterprising colonists from Miletos, the greatest of the ancient Greek Ionian cities. The Milesians founded nearly 100 colonies along the shores of the Hellespont, the Sea of Marmara

Perfect for tea
The rain-saturated hillsides east of Trabzon are perfect for the cultivation of tea, and the bushes are planted up the steep hillsides to a height of 600m. Tea was introduced to the Black Sea only in the 1930s, but it remarkably quickly became the mainstay of the local economy. In 1986 the entire crop was condemned because of the nuclear disaster at Chernobyl, but even so production levels have increased to the point where some of the crop is now exported. Women dressed in colourful clothes and white headscarves do the work, clipping the bushes and collecting the tea in bags, which they empty in turn into huge baskets. You will see them carrying these baskets on their backs along the road, with only a pair of feet visible from behind.

239

and the Black Sea, including **Sinop**, **Samsun**, **Ordu**, **Giresun** and **Trabzon**. None of these ever attained much status, and the only significant kingdom to be established here was that of the Pontic kings, which sprang up after Alexander the Great's death in the 4th century BC.

Towns and sites The main resorts of the Black Sea lie within easy striking distance of Istanbul, at **Kilyos** to the west, **Şile** to the east, and **Akçakoca** and **Amasra**, though the most attractive part of the coastline begins east of Samsun. **Samsun** itself is easily the largest city, but also the least interesting. **Trabzon** and **Sinop** are the most worthwhile places to stay for a few nights. The only real tourist attraction is the **Sumela Monastery**, inland from Trabzon. The general absence of ancient ruins in this area is due partly to the fact that the Romans penetrated only to the western parts of the coast, and partly to the heavy rainfall, which has washed all but the strongest ruins away altogether.

Crossing a suspension bridge inland from Pazar, near the eastern Black Sea coast

THE BLACK SEA

Blossoming hills
West of Giresun the coast-line becomes very pretty. The towns are more resort-like, cleaner, less sprawling. The trees covering the hillside right down to the edge of the road are spectacular. They are all either hazels (fındık), providing an important Turkish export, or cherries, and in late spring the hills are smothered in blossom.

Fishy staple
Food along the Black Sea coast is generally good, far better than in eastern Turkey. The fish available vary with the season. In April there is turbot (kalkan), and from May onwards there are red mullet (barbunya), tuna (palamut) and anchovies (hamsi). Anchovies, the most abundant and the cheapest, are the staple diet of the fishing villages.

A stretch of sandy beach near Tirebolu

▶ **Amasra**   *236B2*

Founded originally by the Milesian colonists, Amasra is now an attractive resort, beautifully situated on its own wooded peninsula, with a Genoese castle on its citadel. It is a relaxing, sleepy place, divided into two sheltered bays by the peninsula. The castle is heavily fortified and the walls and gateways are still largely intact. Notice the Genoese coat-of-arms scattered about liberally on the walls. There are also two Byzantine churches in the town's maze of alleyways, one now a ruin and the other still in use as a mosque. For swimming you are best advised to go a little out of town to find the beaches to the east.

▶ **Bolu**   *236B1*

Known to the Romans as Polis, this town lies in the mountains that separate Ankara from the sea, and is the centre of the region's most popular mountain recreation area. The hills here are not as steep as further east along the Black Sea, but are heavily forested. The woodland includes many deciduous trees such as oaks, rarely seen in Turkey today, making a welcome change from the heavy and somewhat monotonous dark green of the conifers of the Pontic Alps. **Lake Abant** to the south is especially beautiful, and is full of trout for the fisherman. Skiing is to be found at **Kartalkaya**, southwest of Bolu.

▶ **Giresun**   *237D1*

A bustling town some two hours' drive from Trabzon (see page 246), Giresun is an attractive place dominated by its castle, Giresun Kalesi, which crowns the acropolis of the ancient Milesian colony of **Cerasus**. It was from here that the Roman general Lucullus, who captured the town in the Pontic Wars in 69BC, brought back the first cherry trees to Europe. The name Cerasus is the origin of the words cherry and cerise. Just offshore is a small island

Fishermen bringing in their catch: the Black Sea coast is famous for its abundant fish

with a second castle: Jason and the Argonauts are said to have put in here on their quest for the Golden Fleece, and to have been attacked by birds dropping feathered darts. Today it is called **Büyük Ada**, and is inhabited by fishermen. It can easily be visited by boat.

▶ Hopa   237E1
A small and simple town, Hopa seems like a haven of sophistication if you arrive at it after a spell in the interior of eastern Turkey. A number of charming small hotels overlook the pebbly beaches.

▶ Kastamonu   236C1
Inland from Inebolu, this sleepy town has some fine old Ottoman houses. Overlooking them is a castle built by Tamerlane, now a ruin but still with impressive walls and main gateway. Kastamonu is a good stopping place on the way to the **Ilgaz Milliparkı** (National Park), which has skiing facilities.

▶ Konuralp   236B1
The village of Konuralp, near Düzce between Bolu and Akçakoca, is interesting for its traditional wooden houses, as well as the remains of ancient **Prousias** and **Aypium**. The theatre, lying among the houses and gardens, still has most of its rows of seats. The school playground serves as an open-air museum for carved fragments and sarcophagi found in this ancient Bithynian town.

Amazonian habits
The land around the Black Sea was associated in ancient times with the Amazons, remarkably independent women who were described by Strabo as spending ten months of the year 'off by themselves, performing their individual tasks such as ploughing, planting, pasturing cattle and particularly training horses, though the bravest engage in hunting on horseback and practise warlike exercises. The right breasts of all are seared when they are infants, so that they can easily use their right hands for any purpose, and especially that of throwing the javelin... They have two months in the spring when they go up into the neighbouring mountain which separates them from the Gagarians, who also go thither to sacrifice with the Amazons and also to have intercourse with them for the sake of begetting children, doing this in secrecy and darkness, any Gagarian at random with any Amazon.' Any girls born as a result of this yearly encounter were kept by the Amazons, and any boys born were taken to the Gagarians.

241

Drive Amasra to Safranbolu

From Amasra, one of the prettier resorts on the Black Sea (see pages 240–1), you can make a half-day trip inland through pine-clad hills to the towns of Bartin and Safranbolu, famous for their profusion of splendid old Ottoman wooden houses.

Set off inland from Amasra, following signs to Ankara. The small road winds its way up the pine-forested Pontic mountains, offering splendid views over Amasra and the coast. After some 16km you reach **Bartin,** with its many timbered houses, especially round the bazaar.

Another spectacular drive through the mountains, climbing up to a pass, brings you after 81km to the spectacular town of **Safranbolu**, set in a steep-sided gorge. All around are Ottoman houses and mansions with their half-timbered gables, whitewashed walls and red-tiled roofs. Offering as it does the largest concentration of these houses anywhere in Turkey, Safranbolu is relatively well established on the tourist track, but in a pleasantly run-down sort of way.

As you stroll the narrow streets, look out for the fully restored Ottoman baths and the large, ramshackle caravanserai (called **Cincihanı**) which dominates the town centre. There are plans to turn this into a hotel. The **Arasta bazaar** has been restored and is well stocked with souvenir and antique stalls. Also restored is **Kaymakamlar Evi**, the Governors' House, open to the public as an example of a typical Ottoman mansion. Stroll up to the castle above the town for more lovely views.

The harbour at Amasra

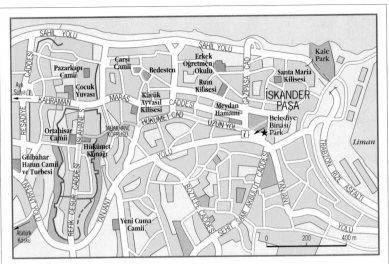

Walk **Trabzon Towers**

243

This walk takes you from Trabzon's main square and along its major shopping street to the famous old walled citadel and its churches, before climbing to the citadel summit and the remains of the romantic royal palace of Trebizond's exiled Byzantine dynasty. The total distance is about 3km one way and it takes 1¼ hours.

Head west from the main square along **Uzun Yol** (Long Street), which becomes Hükümet Caddesi. On a small side street to the right as the road begins to go downhill, you will discover Trabzon's oldest church, **St Anna** (Kücük Ayvasil Kilesesi), dating to the 7th century. It is always locked. Carry on to reach the walled citadel and **Ortahisar Camii**, built in the 10th century as the Byzantine church of Panayia Chrysocephalus (Goldentopped Virgin), so-called because of its copper dome. Now follow the long steep hill to the summit and its *kale* (castle keep). Little children will guide you through a few back gardens, from which you emerge on to a magnificent stretch of crenellated battlements, above a vertical drop of 100m or so down into the gully below. This is all that remains of the palace of the exiled Comnene emperors and their lovely princesses, and it is from this

vantage point that you can best imagine the fabled *Towers of Trebizond* (Rose Macaulay, 1956) in their 15th-century heyday. Of this spot Miss Macaulay wrote: 'All the centuries of lively Byzantine chatter, they had left whispering echoes in that place where the hot sun beat down...'

Aya Sofya has 13th-century frescoes

THE BLACK SEA

The harbour and Genoese castle at Şile

The coastline to the north of Sinop

Rize   *237E1*

The tea capital of the Black Sea, Rize is the largest town on the coast east of Trabzon. Its prosperity has been built entirely on tea, introduced to Turkey in the 1930s from Georgia (in the former Soviet Union) where it was planted at the end of the last century.

Inland some 25km west of Rize is Çaykara►, which has a remarkable old wooden roofed bridge, unique in Turkey.

The magnificent mansion of Kestel Kale► (sometimes called Memisağa Konağı) lies hidden behind a high hedge some 4km east of Surmene. Built in about 1800 by the local lord of the valley, this remarkable brick and timber building has a splendid overhanging roof that makes it look like a gigantic mushroom.

Samsun   *236C1*

Founded as ancient Amisos by the Greeks from Miletos in the 7th century BC, Samsun is today the largest and busiest port on the Black Sea, and the centre of Turkey's tobacco industry. Nothing of historical interest remains to be seen here because the Genoese, who were given trading privileges here by the Seljuks, burned the city down when it fell to the Ottomans in the 15th century.

Şile   *236A1*

Just 70km from Istanbul, Şile has a pleasant beach which becomes very crowded during holiday times. It also has a Genoese castle.

► Sinop
236C2

The only natural harbour along the Black Sea, Sinop is known to have served as the port for the Hittite capital Hattuşaş, due south from here (see pages 198–9), and in the 8th century BC was the largest of the Milesian colonies. Of its illustrious past little remains beyond the ruined Genoese castle, the 13th-century Alaeddin Mosque and the Alaiye Madrasa, now a museum. Pleasant meals can be taken at the variety of quayside fish restaurants.

►►► Sumela
237E1

The 48km excursion inland from Trabzon to the stunning mountain monastery of Sumela takes a good half day. The monastery's unforgettable setting, clinging to the sheer rock face, where it hangs as if by levitation above the heavily wooded slopes and mountain mists, makes it look more Tibetan than Turkish.

The road ends at a forest clearing with an attractive restaurant, from which a path zigzags up to the monastery. The ascent takes about 30 minutes, depending on your level of fitness, and some may perhaps feel the effects of altitude (it is 1,250m above sea level). Behind the imposing 18th-century façade only a few crumbling monks' cells remain. The original monastery was founded in the 6th century to house an icon of the Virgin painted by Saint Luke, and it was inhabited continuously thereafter until 1923, when the Greeks were expelled from the country in the 'exchange of populations' (see pages 16–17) and all the monks were forced to leave. A fire soon afterwards was responsible for much of its present ruined state.

The surviving frescoes on the inner façade and on the ceiling of the cave church are outstanding. On the façade, notice especially the top row, a fascinating series telling the story of Adam and Eve. The most striking fresco in the cave church depicts the Virgin and Child seated on a golden throne.

Best timings
If at all possible, time your arrival at Sumela for 1pm or later; before this coach tours flock here in continuous streams. Remember, too, that in wet weather the path up to the monastery gateway gets very muddy, so take suitable footwear. Do not forget your purse, either, as a fee is charged at the top. The monastery stays open until 5pm.

Inland excursions
It is worth making the detour inland from Pazar (between Rize and Hopa) to the beautiful Hemsin valleys, and to the attractive village of Çamlıhemşin with its neat wooden houses. To the south is the impressive castle of Zil Kale, perching on a heavily forested hill and with trees growing out of its turrets.

The spectacularly sited monastery at Sumela, clinging perilously to the sheer cliff face

THE BLACK SEA

▶▶   **Trabzon (Trebizond)**   *237E1*

As long as you adjust your expectations of Trabzon downwards from the fabled city you may have read about, the city does have some interesting sights to offer and can even grow on you after a few days. The **Cathedral of Haghia Sophia**, 3km west of the main square, is justly the most famous site, outshining all Trabzon's other architectural monuments; these include ten churches, a number of which were converted to mosques by the Ottomans, a convent and an Armenian monastery. All these are relics of the Comnene dynasty founded by Alexius Comnenus, 22-year-old son of the Byzantine Emperor Manuel I, who fled Constantinople just before its fall to the Fourth Crusade in 1204.

Trebizond's Greek roots went back to the 7th century BC, when it was founded by the great sea-trading Milesian colonists. It grew in prosperity through trade with Persia, with camel caravans coming from Erzurum and Tabriz laden with silk and spices. Through its role as the last flickering flame of Byzantium, a distant outpost defiant against Islam after the fall of Constantinople, Trebizond acquired a certain romantic mystique in Europe.

Aya Sofya (Cathedral of Haghia Sophia)▶▶ is best visited by car or taxi, as it is a good hour's walk from the centre. Built in the mid-13th century, in the heyday of the Comnene Empire, as a monastery church, it was converted to a mosque in 1461, after the Ottoman conquest. As was usual, the walls were whitewashed and covered with hard plaster, which inadvertently preserved them for posterity; the uncovering of the murals that lay beneath took a full six years in the 1950s. Today it is a museum (closed Mondays).

The Georgian market in Trabzon

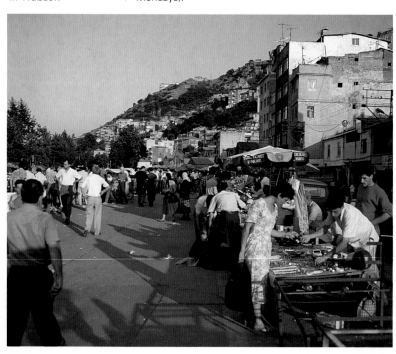

The magnificent frescoes for which the cathedral is famous adorn the walls and ceiling of the narthex (vestibule). Among the most beautiful are the Marriage Feast at Cana, the Feeding of the Five Thousand and Christ Walking on the Water, all of the late 13th century and in the Byzantine tradition, with some Cappadocian influence. They are thought to have all been the work of a single artist. On the northern façade, looking out to the Black Sea, the external porch has a heart-rending fresco depicting Job plagued by boils.

A short excursion should if possible be made to **Atatürk Köskü►**, Atatürk's summer residence, high up in heavily wooded hills 4km behind the city. An attractive white stucco villa set in beautifully manicured gardens, it serves today as a museum of Atatürk memorabilia. Atatürk himself graced it with his presence just once, for three days back in 1921.

For other Trabzon sights see page 243.

Ünye   237D1
Along the rocky shore near Ünye are caves inhabited by seals. Just east of Ünye a road leads inland to **Niksar** (source of one of Turkey's main mineral waters), and after 6km you will see the striking castle of **Çaleoğlu** set up on a volcanic hill. Inside, it still has a tunnel with 400 steps leading down to water. Ünye itself is a resort with good-quality motels and *pansiyons* along the beach.

Zonguldak   236B1
A coal-mining centre and industrial port, Zonguldak is the second largest city in the Black Sea region after Samsun, but it has nothing to offer the tourist.

Skilled manipulators
The Comnene dynasty and its capital Trebizond flourished because of Trebizond's position, the skill of its traders and a string of beautiful and marriageable princesses who helped to cement useful alliances with potentially troublesome neighbours. Though only the size of a province, it posed as an empire – Byzantium in exile. It sustained its pretentions with a court of pomp and ceremony, and acquired a reputation beyond its achievements through diplomatic manoeuvring, palace revolutions and civil wars – truly Byzantine in the popular sense of the word.

247

Although Ünye itself is not exceptional, it enjoys a lovely setting and there are delightful bays and fishing villages along the coast

FOCUS ON

The Laz

■ A seafaring race of obscure Caucasian origins, the Laz inhabit the region between Rize and Hopa. They are remote cousins of the Georgians, but with the important difference that they converted to Islam early and have remained staunch Muslims.....■

Unlazy Laz

Often wrongly defined by other Turks as anyone who lives east of Trabzon, the Laz are a hard-working people with a good deal of business acumen. Much of Turkey's shipping is owned and operated by Laz, using crews from their own villages, while the women work in the tea plantations. Because of their relative prosperity they have become the butt of Turkish humour, with many jokes referring to their supposed stupidity and slowness.

The colouring of this Laz herb seller hints at the distant relationship between the Laz and the Georgians

The Laz were loyal to the Turks in the wars against Russia, while the Christian Georgians and Armenians were viewed as suspect. Their language, too, is related to Georgian; it is still spoken in the villages, though it is not written. There are thought to be about 100,000 Laz still living in and around Pazar, Ardeşen, Fındıklı, Arhavi and Hopa, as well as some inland enclaves.

Laz business enterprises have brought them a certain affluence. They are relatively progressive in outlook and in their dress, which is colourful and fashionable. Often extrovert by nature, they traditionally enjoy dancing and playing the bagpipes. Their houses, well-made of timber and stone, and always set in gardens, are unlike others in Turkey. Never clustered together in rows and terraces, they are spread out along the tops of ridges to ensure breathing space.

The ancient Greeks described the Laz as savage tribesmen, and they have a reputation for being fiercely aggressive as enemies but generous as friends. Rather like most Turks, they are patient and good-natured until pushed beyond a certain point. 'The Laz talks with a pistol,' runs a local saying.

Istanbul's international airport

By air

Istanbul Most international flights arrive at Atatürk Airport in the suburb of Yeşilköy, 20km west of the city centre. Taxis to the centre take 30 minutes and are reasonably priced. Turkish Airlines run buses every hour to Şişhane in the centre, which are cheaper but do not stop *en route*. Onward flights to North Cyprus (Ercan) depart from the international airport, while transit flights to other cities within Turkey depart from the nearby domestic terminal, linked by a shuttle bus.

Other cities International flights also arrive at Ankara, Izmir, Antalya, Adana, Trabzon and Dalaman airports. Ankara airport (Esenboğa) lies 30km north of the centre, a half-hour taxi-ride, while Izmir airport (Adnan Menderes) is 20km south of the centre, about 45 minutes by taxi.

By sea There are three ways to arrive in Turkey by boat. Turkish Maritime Lines (TML) operate comfortable car ferries from Venice to Izmir, once a week from April to October. Daily services operate from North Cyprus all year round from Girne (Kyrenia) to Taşucu (near Adana) and Alanya, and from Mağosa (Famagusta) to Mersin. There are also ferries from the Greek islands of Lesbos, Chios, Samos, Cos, Symi and Rhodes (see pages 110–11).

By train Rail travel via Europe has been severely disrupted by the troubles in former Yugoslavia. The Istanbul Express leaves daily for Istanbul from Munich, Vienna and Athens, with connecting services from Sofia in Bulgaria. Weekly services to Istanbul leave from Moscow, Budapest and Bucharest.

By coach Regular coach services run to Turkey from Austria, France, Germany, Holland, Italy, Switzerland and Greece, and from the other direction, Iraq, Iran, Jordan, Syria, Saudi Arabia and Kuwait.

By private car No special documents are required for visits of less than three months; the car is

IÇ HATLAR, YOLCU - OTO BİLETİ

DENİZYOLLARI

№ 222472

Bu bileti alan yolcu iç sayfadaki şartları kabul etmiş olmaktadır.

simply entered on the driver's passport as imported goods. For stays of over three months you must obtain a *carnet de passage* from the **Turkish Touring and Automobile Club**, Halaskargazi Caddesi 364, Şişli, Istanbul (tel: 0212 231 4631) or from your own national car club. Ask your insurance company to provide a Green Card to extend your insurance cover to Turkey.

Customs regulations
Duty-free limits on entry are 200 cigarettes, 50 cigars, 200g of pipe tobacco, 1.5kg instant coffee, five 100cc or seven 70cc bottles of wine and/or spirits, and five bottles of perfume, 120ml maximum each. The import of all narcotics is strictly forbidden and carries stiff prison sentences. On leaving, you need to show proof of purchase for a new carpet, or a certificate from a museum directorate for an old one.

Travellers with disabilities
Istanbul international airport has adapted lifts and toilets, and the arrival hall, baggage collection point and customs are all on the ground floor, so trolleys and wheelchairs can easily be manoeuvred straight to the taxi rank. Ramps have been installed in many museums and in the state theatres, opera and concert halls. Turkish State Railways (TCDD) offer a reduction of 70 per cent for disabled travellers, and 30 per cent for those accompanying them. For more information contact: **Ortopedik Özürlüler Federasyonu**, Gürabba Huseyinama Caddesi, Bostan Sokak, Mermer Iş Hanı, Aksaray, Istanbul (tel: 0212 534 5980).

Visas
Visas (valid three months) are required by British and Irish nationals and can be bought on entry at the airport. They are valid for three months and cost £5 or its equivalent in foreign currency. Change is rarely available. Visas are not required for visitors holding Australian, Canadian, New Zealand or American passports. Other nationals should enquire at their nearest consulate or embassy.

Foreign currency
There is no limit on the amount of foreign currency that can be taken into Turkey. Keep any exchange slips, as you may be asked to show them when converting Turkish lira back into foreign currency, or to prove that souvenirs have been purchased with legally exchanged foreign currency. There is no departure tax, so change all Turkish lira back into foreign currency at the airport, where the rate is likely to be better than in your own country.

251

A ferry on the Golden Horn

When to go

Istanbul, Aegean and Mediterranean coasts The tourist season runs from 1 April to 31 October. May, June and September are the best months; July and August can be too hot for sightseeing in the midday sun. The swimming season in the Sea of Marmara and northern Aegean is from June to September, while in the southern Aegean and Mediterranean you can swim from April to November. Istanbul is at its best from April to June, and in September and October.

Central Anatolia The skiing season is from December to April, and summer visits are best from June to September.

Eastern Turkey Skiing is from November to June, and summer visits are best from June to September.

Black Sea coast June to September is the swimming season, with summer temperatures rarely exceeding 28°C. Winters are mild with high rainfall.

What to take

Loose light cotton clothing is best, with a pullover for the cooler evenings. In the Black Sea, and Central and Eastern Anatolia much warmer clothing will be needed, even in the height of summer. Comfortable shoes are essential for scrambling over rocky archaeological

Dancers at the Silifke Music and Folklore Festival

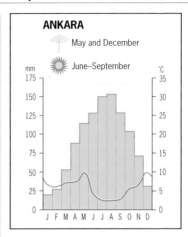

ANKARA

☂ May and December

☀ June–September

ANTALYA

☂ January and December

☀ May–September

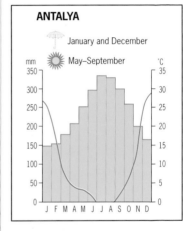

İSTANBUL

☂ November–January

☀ June–August

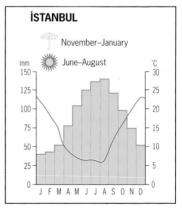

sites, and sun hats, sunglasses and high-protection factor sun cream are recommended. A headscarf is useful for women when visiting mosques, and a torch can be handy when visiting castles, caves and tunnels. If you like instant coffee for breakfast, bring your own jar and just ask for hot water, as the standard breakfast drink in non-tourist places is black tea. Colour print film is widely available, though expensive; colour transparency (slide) film is virtually unobtainable. Spare toilet rolls are always useful.

National holidays
Government offices and businesses shut on these days, but shops and tourist sites remain open.
1 January: New Year's Day
23 April: National Independence and Children's Day
19 May: Atatürk Commemoration and Youth and Sports Day
30 August: Victory Day (end of War of Independence)
29 October: Republic Day

Religious holidays
The **Feast of Ramadan** (*Şeker Bayramı*) is a three-day national holiday celebrating the end of the month of fasting. The **Feast of the Sacrifice** (*Kurban Bayramı*) is a four-day holiday commemorating Abraham's willingness to sacrifice his son Isaac. Shops (except food shops, which are open from the third day), bazaars, offices and banks are shut during these festivals, the dates for which follow the lunar calendar and therefore move back by 11 days each year. For 1995, the Feast of Ramadan ends at the end of February and the Feast of the Sacrifice begins in the second week of May. Museums and tourist sites are open as usual.

Time differences
Turkish time is GMT + 2 hours.

Australia +8, Canada –7, UK –2, Ireland –2, New Zealand +8, USA –7

Money matters
The monetary unit is the Turkish **lira** (TL). Exchange rates are published daily in the newspapers. Most banks exchange foreign currency, as do most hotels of three stars and upwards. There are also numerous exchange offices in major cities, offering better rates and open longer hours than banks. Visa cards can be used to obtain local currency from cash dispensers at **İş Bank** and **Yapı-Kredi Bank** (the latter also accepts Eurocard and MasterCard). Eurocheques and travellers' cheques can be cashed at banks and hotels. Credit cards are now widely accepted.

253

❏ **Opening times**
● **Government offices**
8:30–12:30, 1:30–5:30, closed Saturdays and Sundays
● **Banks** 8:30–12:00 or 12:30, 1:00 or 1:30–5:00, closed Saturdays and Sundays
● **Shops** 9:30–1:00, 2:00–7:00, closed Sundays
● **Grand Bazaar**, Istanbul 8:00–7:00, closed Sundays
● **Museums** 8:30–12:30, 1:30–5:30, closed Mondays
● **Archaeological sites** 8:30–dusk, daily

Information on opening times has been provided for guidance only. We have tried to ensure accuracy, but things do change and readers are advised to check locally before planning visits to avoid any possible disappointment. ❏

❏ **Statistics**
Area: 780,000 sq km
Population: 60 million, 39 per cent of whom live in the countryside.
Major cities: Istanbul 8 million, Ankara 3.5 million, Izmir 3 million, Adana 2 million, Bursa 1.5 million, Antalya 1 million. ❏

A bus – Izmir transport

Domestic air travel Turkish Airlines (THY) operates internal flights between Ankara, Istanbul, Izmir, Adana, Antalya, Dalaman, Diyarbakır, Elazığ, Erzurum, Gaziantep, Kars, Kayseri, Konya, Samsun, Şanlıurfa, Trabzon, Malatya and Van. All major cities have THY offices where tickets can be bought. Fares are good value and flights are frequent. There is a 90 per cent discount for children under two travelling on your lap, 50 per cent for children from two to twelve, and 10 per cent for a family or married couple travelling together. THY buses run from all city airports to the THY office in the city centre, and all major cities have THY offices. The main ones are in **Istanbul** (tel: 0212 574 8200/663 6300 or fax: 0212 240 2984) and **Ankara** (tel: 0312 312 4900/309 0400 or fax: 0312 312 5531).

Intercity buses Many private companies offer frequent day and night services between all Turkish cities. The buses – comfortable, air-conditioned, reliable and inexpensive – depart from the bus station (*otogar*), and seats should be booked a day or two in advance, either at the *otogar* or at a travel agent.

Train Turkish State Railways run between many major cities, offering *couchettes*, sleeping cars and restaurants, with first- and second-class seating, but trains are both more expensive and less efficient than the bus network. On the European side, trains from Edirne and Greece arrive

at **Sirkeci Station** near Eminönü Square in Istanbul, while on the Asian side trains from Ankara and all points east terminate at **Haydarpaşa Station** (20 minutes across the Bosphorus by ferry). The **Mavi Tren** (Blue Train) is a fast intercity service, leaving Haydarpaşa twice daily.

Ferries Turkish Maritime Lines (TML) operate several coastal services from Istanbul's Karaköy, Sirkeci and Eminönü, as well as car ferries from Istanbul to Izmir, Marmaris and Mersin three times a week. From May to September, TML also operate a Black

Ferries are frequent and very cheap

Sea line from Istanbul to Trabzon, departing Mondays and calling at Sinop, Samsun, Ordu and Giresun. **TML Central Office** is at Karaköy, Rıhtım Caddesi, Istanbul tel: 0212 249 9222/244 0207 or fax: 0212 251 9025. Ferries across the Bosphorus are frequent and very cheap. Main departure points are the quays beside the Galata Bridge at Eminönü and Karaköy; Beşiktaş and Kadataş on the European side; Usküdar and Kadiköy on the Asian shore.

Typical
Turkish yellow taxis

❏ The favourite means of public transport outside the cities in Turkey is the bus, remarkably efficient, punctual, comfortable and cheap. If you are travelling light and on a tight budget, the bus system is excellent. If you are travelling with children and rather more luggage, then car hire is immensely more convenient, and also enables you to drive straight to the more remote sites. Within the cities taxis are the most popular, and are very good value. ❏

Taxis and dolmuş Yellow taxis are the best way to get about in Turkish cities. They are metered, with a day tariff (one light on the meter) and a night tariff (two lights on the meter). The night tariff operates between midnight and 6am, and costs 50 per cent extra. Tips are not usual. The *dolmuş*, recognisable by its yellow band, is a shared taxi which follows specific routes. Passengers pay according to the distance travelled and may alight at any convenient place. Fares – cheaper than a taxi – are fixed by the municipality.

Trams Within Istanbul, high-speed trams run from Aksaray to Ferhat-paşa and Topkapı to Sirkeci. This line will shortly be extended to the airport. An old-fashioned tram has been reinstated along Istiklal Caddesi, between Tünel Square and Taksim.

Student and youth travel Turkish Airlines, Turkish Maritime Lines and Turkish State Railways offer reductions to holders of most internationally recognised student cards. Students are also entitled to accommodation at Turkish Youth Hostels: The main office is in Istanbul at the **Topkapı Atatürk Student Centre**, Topkapı, Londra Asfaltı, Çevizlibag Durağı (tel: 0212 582 0461).

An old-fashioned tram runs along
Istiklal Caddesi in Istanbul

255

Car rental desks, Istanbul airport

Car hire This is expensive, though better deals can frequently be had by booking in advance. Drivers must be over 21 and have a valid driving licence from their own country. Third party insurance is compulsory, and it is advisable to take out additional collision damage waiver (CDW) and personal accident insurance, which give you comprehensive cover. Cars commonly offered are Murat (a locally made Fiat) and Renault, with Suzuki Jeeps for those who want four-wheel drive. Seat belts are compulsory in front seats only, so specify if you want them in the back. It is also worth asking in advance what the rental firm undertakes to do if the car breaks down.

Car breakdown If you break down in your own car, call the **Turkish Touring and Automobile Club** (Istanbul head office tel: 0212 231 46 31). There are also numerous repair garages in towns, usually grouped together, and spare parts are readily available. Turkish mechanics are surprisingly resourceful when it comes to mending foreign makes of car.

Driving tips
Traffic regulations Traffic drives on the right in Turkey. The speed limit is 50 kph in towns, 90kph on state highways and 120kph on motorways. Traffic police frequently carry out spot checks, especially at the entry to towns, where the limit changes from 90kph to 50kph. On-the-spot fines are levied according to the level of speeding. Turkish road signs conform to international protocol and the Turkish highway code is similar to the European one. The road network is extremely good and generally well maintained. The only really busy road is the Istanbul-to-Ankara highway, which continues as the E23, the E5 and the E24 transit routes to Iran,

❏ Night-driving outside the cities can be an unnerving experience in Turkey, as oncoming vehicles frequently have no lights; their drivers switch them on at the last minute, when they are nearly on top of you, so dazzling you completely. Agricultural vehicles often drive on the road with no lights at all, and broken-down lorries often display no warning triangle. Cat's eyes are very rare, so it is important to make sure that your own lights are strong and properly adjusted to give maximum visibility. ❏

Syria and Iraq respectively. These three routes carry heavy goods vehicles and should be avoided if possible. All other roads are pleasantly clear of traffic, and driving in most parts of Turkey is a positive pleasure.

Petrol Petrol stations selling super (four-star equivalent), normal (two-star equivalent) and diesel are abundant in all western parts of the country, though less so in central and eastern regions. Unleaded petrol is found only in the biggest cities. Petrol stations on the main highways often have service stations and restaurants attached, and are open round the clock.

❏ **Road signs**
Dur: stop
Dikkat: watch out, e.g. because of road works ahead
Şehir merkezi: town centre
Yellow signs indicate archaeological sites ❏

Spot checks on speeding are common on the edge of towns; offenders are liable to on-the-spot fines

Tourist Information ▶

Avanos Kayseri ▶

◀ **Göreme 8**

◀ **Nevşehir**

The media

Turks are avid readers of the numerous Turkish newspapers, many of them printed in colour. Foreign newspapers and magazines, mainly English, American and German, are available in the big cities and tourist centres one day late. The only English language daily, the *Turkish Daily News*, is bland but informative. The *Voice of Turkey* radio, to be found on the FM waveband, broadcasts daily in English on general subjects and current events, 7:30–12:45 and 6:30–10 local time, on the following frequencies: 100.6MHz, 97.4MHz, 101.6MHz, 100.5MHz, 101.9MHz and 103MHz. For further information contact: **TRT External Services**, PO Box 333 Yenişehir, Ankara 06443 tel: 0312 431 4211 fax: 431 0222

258

❏ **Useful Telephone Numbers**

110 fire service
112 emergency ambulance services
115 international operator
118 directory enquiries
131 operator
155 intercity police
156 gendarmerie (country areas) ❏

Post Offices The main post offices (PTT) in Ankara and Istanbul are open 8–12 midnight Monday–Saturday, 9–7 Sundays, while the smaller ones throughout the country are open 8:30–12:30 and 1:30–5:30, closed Saturdays and Sundays. *Poste restante* letters should be addressed '*postrestant*' to the central post office (*Merkez Postanesi*) in the relevant town. Proof of identity is required on collection. Most post offices also offer fax and 'valuable despatch' services, and will exchange foreign currency,

A Turkish post office sign

international postal orders and travellers' cheques. An express postal service (*Acele Posta Servisi* or APS) is available for sending letters, documents and small packages abroad.

Telephones The cheapest way to telephone in Turkey is from a PTT telephone booth, though most hotels of three-star standard and above have direct-dial national and international lines from their rooms. PTT offices sell phone cards and three sizes of *jeton*, for local, intercity and international calls. Cheap rates within Turkey apply between 6pm and 8am. International

Phone cards are widely available

calls are cheap between 12 midnight and 8am and on Sundays. To call abroad from Turkey, dial 0, then dial 0 again for an international line, followed by the country code and the individual number. UK country code is 44, Ireland is 353, USA is 1, Australia is 61, Canada is 1 and New Zealand is 64.

Language guide
Pronunciation

c = j, as in cami (mosque) = **jami**
ç = ch, as in Foça = **Focha**
ğ = soft g, unpronounced, but used to extend the preceding vowel, as in dağ (mountain) = **daa**
ı (dotless i) = the initial 'a' in away, as in Topkapı = **Topkapeu**
ö = oe, as in Göreme = **Goereme**
ş = sh, as in Kuşadası = **Kushadaseu**
ü - as in French *tu*, e.g. **Ürgüp**

Numbers

1 bir	8 sekiz
2 iki	9 dokuz
3 üç	10 on
4 dört	20 yirmi
5 beş	50 elli
6 altı	100 yuz
7 yedi	1000 bin

Greetings and polite expressions

hello merhaba
goodbye (said by the person staying behind) güle güle
goodbye (said by the person leaving) allaha ısmarladık
good morning günaydın
good evening iyi akşamlar
good night iyi geceler
please lütfen
thank you mersi or teşekkür ederim
how are you? nasılsınız?
I am well thank you iyiyim, teşekkür ederim

Everyday expressions

yes evet
no hayır or yok
there is var
there is not yok
I want istiyorum
I would like coffee please kahve istiyorum, lütfen
how much is this? bu ne kadar?
expensive pahalı
cheap ucuz
money para
very beautiful çok güzel
toilet tuvalet
men's (toilet) baylar
ladies' (toilet) bayanlar

Time

today bugün
yesterday dün
tomorrow yarın
what is the time? saat kaç?

Travel

airport hava alanı
port liman
is it far? uzak mı?
where is...? ...nerede...?
bus station otogar
petrol benzin
oil (engine) yağı
tyre lastik

brakes frenler
it does not work çalışmıyor

Food

bread ekmek
water su
mineral water maden suyu
fruit juice meyva suyu
wine şarap
sweet wine tatlı şarap
dry wine sek şarap
red wine kırmızı şarap
white wine beyaz şarap
beer bira
ice buz
breakfast kahvaltı
tea çay
coffee kahve
milk süt
sugar şeker
jam reçel
cheese peynir
soup çorba
salad salata
fish balık
eggs yumurta
chips patates
ice cream dondurma

259

Crime and police

Rates of petty crimes such as theft have always been low, as in all Islamic societies, but with rising unemployment are on the increase in the cities. Pickpocketing has also become more common in the bazaar areas. Violent crime such as mugging or rape is far rarer than in western countries. In the event of a crime, report the matter to the **tourist police**, recognisable by their beige uniforms and maroon berets. They have offices in all towns throughout the country (Istanbul tel: 0212 527 4503/528 5369; Ankara tel: 0312 212 0437; Izmir tel: 0232 449 0438).

Traffic police wear navy uniforms and white caps; any traffic accident should be reported to them. **Market police,** in blue uniforms, patrol the markets and bazaars to check commercial practice. The **Jandarmas** (gendarmerie) are soldiers in green army uniform with a red armband: duties include keeping the peace, preventing smuggling and the like.

> ❏ **Emergency telephone numbers**
> ● Ambulance 112
> ● Police 155
> ● Fire 110 ❏

Crowded areas such as this in Istanbul are fertile ground for pickpockets

Embassies and consulates

Australia Ankara: Gaziosmanpaşa, Nenehatun Caddesi No 83 (tel: 0312 436 1240/43); Istanbul: Etiler, Tepecik Yolu Uzeri No 58 (tel: 0212 257 7050).

Canada Ankara: Gaziosmanpaşa, Nenehatun Caddesi No 75 (tel: 0312 436 1275/79); Istanbul: Gayrettepe, Büyükdere Caddesi No 107, Bengun Han, Kat 3 (tel: 0212 272 5174).

Republic of Ireland Istanbul (Honorary Consul), Harbiye (tel: 0212 246 6025).

United Kingdom Ankara: Çankaya, Şehit Ersan Caddesi No 46/A (tel: 0312 427 4310/15); Istanbul: Beyoğlu/Tepebaşı, Meşrutiyet Caddesi No 34 (tel: 0212 244 7540); Izmir: 1442 Sokak No 49, P.K. 300 (tel: 0232 214 1795); Antalya: Kazim Özalp Caddesi No 149/A (tel: 0242 241 1815).

United States of America Ankara: Kavaklıdere, Atatürk Bulvarı No 110 (tel: 0312 426 5470); Istanbul: Tepebaşı, Meşrutiyet Caddesi No 104/108 (tel: 0212 251 36 02); Izmir: Alsancak, Atatürk Caddesi No 92 (tel: 0232 844 9426).

Health, vaccinations and pharmacies

There are no mandatory vaccination

❏ **Preventative measures**
Drink bottled water, as the tap water, though chlorinated, can become contaminated in the water tanks. Eat raw salad not at all, or in small quantites, squeezing lots of lemon juice on it. Eat plenty of yogurt and bread, to counterbalance the olive oil in meat and vegetable dishes. Use a high-protection sun cream, and from June to August stay out of the sun from 11 until 3. ❏

requirements. Immunisation against typhoid, tetanus, polio, and hepatitis A is recommended. There is no risk of malaria in the Mediterranean coastal regions, but east of Ankara anti-malarial tablets are recommended between March and November. Avoid swimming in fresh water near the Syrian border because of bilharzia. AIDS is present in Turkey, as in all parts of the world.

For minor problems go to the pharmacy (*eczane*) and describe your symptoms. Most medicines, including antibiotics, are available over the counter. In cities there is always a 24-hour chemist; normal opening hours are 9–7 except Sundays. If necessary your hotel will call a doctor, but there will be a charge for this. In Istanbul the three best hospitals are the **Bristol Hospital** in Nişantaşı (tel: 0212 231 4050), the **International Hospital** at Yesilköy (tel: 0212 574 7802) and the **German Hospital** in Taksim (tel: 0212 251 7100). All treatment must be paid for, so make sure that your travel insurance includes medical cover.

Dangers
In the sea, watch out for the black sea urchins that lurk on rocks in shallow water. Their spines are poisonous and very painful if stepped on. On land poisonous snakes and scorpions are sometimes to be found in remote, little-trodden areas. These can easily be avoided by watching your step, and if you do chance to step on one sturdy footwear provides sufficient protection.

Seek medical attention if you are stung by the Mediterranean scorpion

261

Camping

Most campsites in Turkey have a restaurant, cooking facilities, hot showers and electricity. Some offer simple chalets for those without tents. Some of the best are operated by the **BP-Mocamp** chain. Altogether there are around 40 campsites in the Istanbul and Marmara region, 35 in the Aegean, 30 in the Mediterranean and 15 in Central Anatolia (mainly Cappadocia). East of Adana there are no campsites, and along the Black Sea coast there is none between Zonguldak and Hopa. The Turkish camping organisation is **Türkiye Kamp ve Karavan Derneği**, Nenehatun Caddesi 96, Gaziosmanpaşa, Ankara (tel: 0312 136 31 51). Caravans can be hired from **Anadolu Karavan**, Çırağan Müvezzi Caddesi 9/1, Beşiktaş, Istanbul (tel: 0212 260 1480 or fax: 0212 260 1466).

A child gives a helping hand with a heavy load

Children

Turkey is an excellent place for children, as Turks love them and are very welcoming in their shops, hotels and restaurants.

Pushchairs can be awkward, as

CONVERSION CHARTS

FROM	TO	MULTIPLY BY
Inches	Centimetres	2.54
Centimetres	Inches	0.3937
Feet	Metres	0.3048
Metres	Feet	3.2810
Yards	Metres	0.9144
Metres	Yards	1.0940
Miles	Kilometres	1.6090
Kilometres	Miles	0.6214
Acres	Hectares	0.4047
Hectares	Acres	2.4710
Gallons	Litres	4.5460
Litres	Gallons	0.2200
Ounces	Grams	28.35
Grams	Ounces	0.0353
Pounds	Grams	453.6
Grams	Pounds	0.0022
Pounds	Kilograms	0.4536
Kilograms	Pounds	2.205
Tons	Tonnes	1.0160
Tonnes	Tons	0.9842

MEN'S SUITS							
UK	36	38	40	42	44	46	48
Rest of Europe	46	48	50	52	54	56	58
US	36	38	40	42	44	46	48

DRESS SIZES						
UK	8	10	12	14	16	18
France	36	38	40	42	44	46
Italy	38	40	42	44	46	48
Rest of Europe	34	36	38	40	42	44
US	6	8	10	12	14	16

MEN'S SHIRTS						
UK	14	14.5	15	15.5	16	16.5	17
Rest of Europe	36	37	38	39/40	41	42	43
US	14	14.5	15	15.5	16	16.5	17

MEN'S SHOES						
UK	7	7.5	8.5	9.5	10.5	11
Rest of Europe	41	42	43	44	45	46
US	8	8.5	9.5	10.5	11.5	12

WOMEN'S SHOES						
UK	4.5	5	5.5	6	6.5	7
Rest of Europe	38	38	39	39	40	41
US	6	6.5	7	7.5	8	8.5

❑ Mosque playgrounds

Children love mosques. There is plenty of space in the courtyard, with the ablution fountain for chasing round; there are windows with huge sills for peeping out of and climbing on to; and, perhaps best of all, there is no pressure to be sober and pious. ❑

there are so many steps to negotiate in cities such as Istanbul, but there always seems to be an obliging Turk willing to help carry them up steps or navigate any apparent impasse.

The best stretches of coast for children, with safe sandy bays, are Alanya, Altınkum, Çeşme, Içmeler, Keimer, Ölü Deniz, Patara and Side. It might be best to avoid Kaş and Kalkan, where the beaches are generally rocky, and the Black Sea beaches near Istanbul, where there are dangerous undertows.

For babies, pharmacies stock disposable nappies for infants up to 12kg, as well as tins of babies' powdered formula milk and packets of instant baby food which only need mixing with mineral water. Baby products such as those manufactured by Johnson's are available in all pharmacies, as are Turkish equivalents of the usual children's medicines.

Electricity

Current is 220 volts throughout the country, 50 cycles, with two-pin European plugs.

Etiquette

When visiting a mosque, always remove your shoes before stepping on the carpet, leaving them outside in the rack provided. Women should wear a headscarf to cover their hair. Avoid visiting on Fridays or at prayer times; the larger city mosques close daily to non-Muslims from noon until 1pm for midday prayers in winter, 1–2pm in summer. During Ramadan, do not walk around in public in the daytime eating, smoking or drinking.

Nudity on beaches is against Turkish law. Toplessness, introduced by the Germans, is quite widespread in the Aegean and Mediterranean resorts, but always use your discretion. It is considered offensive to hug or kiss members of the opposite sex in public, and to blow your nose in public. A too-firm handshake is thought impolite.

Hitch-hiking

Hitch-hiking is not illegal but neither is it widespread – and hitch-hikers are an unusual sight. Because public transport is so cheap, most people simply use the bus.

Men washing their feet before entering a mosque in Istanbul

263

Maps
Turkish tourist offices provide a free road map which is adequate for most purposes. If you want a more detailed map, Kümmerley and Frey and Roger Lascelles both produce larger-scale maps.

Organised tours
All resorts and tourist centres have travel agencies which operate organised tours and excursions. One of the principal ones in Istanbul is **Istanbul Vision** at Cumhuriyet Caddesi No 12/C, Elmadağ (tel: 0212 241 3935, fax: 0212 241 5764), which collects clients from their hotels.

Photography
Never risk photography where a notice expressly forbids it, as this is an offence which carries a prison sentence. Higher entry charges for cameras and video cameras are often levied at tourist sites.

Places of worship
There are mosques for Muslim worship on most street corners throughout Turkey. Istanbul, with its large Christian and Jewish communities, also has the Catholic **San Antonio di Padova** on Istiklal Caddesi, Beyoğlu;

Turkish resorts now offer a wide variety of watersports

the Anglican **Christ Church (Crimean Memorial)**, Serdar Ekrem Sok. 82, Beyoğlu; and the **Neve Shalom Synagogue** on Büyük Hendek Caddesi, Şişhane.

Stamps
Stamps can be bought at all sweet/cigarette kiosks in resorts and at some souvenir shops. In cities, you can buy them from hotels or post offices.

Tipping
When a 10 or 15 per cent service charge is added to your restaurant bill, you should still leave a further 5 per

---

❏ **White-water rafting**
Though still in its infancy, this sport is now practised in Turkey, especially on the Çoruh river, between Bayburt and Artvin in eastern Turkey. Sobek Expeditions, PO Box 1089, Angels Camp, CA95222, USA (tel: 209 736 4524) offer two-week trips. ❏

cent for the waiter. In smaller restaurants, where a service charge is not automatic, leave 10 per cent. Taxi drivers do not expect tips as such, but it is normal to round the fare up. In a Turkish bath the masseurs/masseuses will be delighted with a tip of 50 per cent. Mosque attendants should be given a reasonable tip if they have opened a mosque or *medrasa* for you; shoe attendants expect small change.

Toilets
On the whole Turkish plumbing is surprisingly good. In hotels and *pansiyons* toilets are generally clean and of the conventional sitting-down variety. Toilet paper is something of a rarity in public places, as most Turks prefer to use the water pipe by the cistern. The worst public toilets are on the old ferry steamers that ply up and down the Bosphorus and to the Princes' Islands.

Watersports and sports
Watersports are on the increase on the Aegean and Mediterranean coasts, with most larger resorts such as Fethiye, Alanya, Kuşadası, Bodrum and Marmaris offering windsurfing, waterskiing, paragliding and pedaloes. Scuba diving is also popular, with professional diving centres at Fethiye and Turunç Bay running five-day courses leading to internationally recognised qualifications. There are also fully equipped marinas at Istanbul, Çanakkale, Çeşme, Sığacık, Kuşadası, Bodrum, Datça, Marmaris, Göçek, Fethiye, Kalkan, Kaş, Finike, Kemer and Antalya. For more yachting information get in touch with the **Istanbul**

Sailing Club, Fenerbahçe (tel: 0216 336 0633).

Tennis courts are available at Antalya, Bodrum, Fethiye, Gümbet, Içmeler, Kemer, Kuşadası, Ölü Deniz, Marmaris and Side. Ballooning, cycling and horseriding are alternative means of viewing the extraordinary landscapes of Cappadocia. Skiing, hitherto the exclusive preserve of Turks, is now popular with tourists, notably at Uludağ, near Bursa, Turkey's premier ski resort.

Permits for climbing Mount Ararat (if safe to do so) should be obtained three months before the ascent either from the Turkish embassy or from Trek Travel, Aydede Caddesi 10, 80090 Taksim, Istanbul (tel: 0212 254 6707; fax 253 1509).

Women travellers
As long as they are careful about body language and etiquette, women travellers should encounter few problems. You are less likely to receive unwelcome attention if you are accompanied by a man; if this is not possible, it may be best to travel with Turkish women. Too much eye contact with male strangers is to be avoided; this is frequently misread as encouragement. Images of women in western films and magazines have fostered the misapprehension that western women are 'available', so counteract this through careful dress and behaviour. In particular, women walking alone at night, or in pairs, are regarded as inviting attention. If you receive uninvited attention, the best response is to shout *ayip!* (shame on you!) loudly enough for passers-by to hear. The culprit may then be shamed into retreat.

There are Turkish Information Offices in Austria, Belgium, Denmark, Finland, France, Germany, Israel, Italy, Japan, Kuwait, the Netherlands, Spain, Sweden, Switzerland, the United Kingdom and the USA.

United Kingdom 170–3 Piccadilly, London W1V 9DD (tel: 0171 734 8681/734 8682 fax: 0171 491 0773)
USA 821, United Nations Plaza , New York, NY 10017 (tel: (212) 687 2194/5/6; fax: (212) 599 7568)
1717 Massachusetts Avenue NW Suite 306 Washington DC 20036 (tel: (202) 429 98 44; fax (202) 429 5649)

Within Turkey each town has its own tourist office, open the same hours as government offices (see pages 252–3 for details). The airports at Istanbul, Ankara, Izmir, Adana, Trabzon and Dalaman also house tourist offices.

Istanbul Central Office, Beyoğlu Mesrutiyet Caddesi No 57/5 tel: 0212 245 6875/243 3472; fax: 252 4346
  Entrance to the Hilton Hotel, Harbiye (tel: 0212 233 0592)
  Karaköy Maritime Station (tel: 0212 249 5776)
  Sultanahmet Square (tel: 0212 518 1802)
Izmir Büyük Efes Hotel (tel: 0232 489 9278)
  Alsancak Harbour (tel: 0232 422 1022)
Ankara Central Office, Gazi Mustafa Kemal Bulvarı No 121, Tandoğan (tel: 0312 488 7007)

Adana Central Office, Atatürk Caddesi, No 13 (tel: 0322 359 1994)
Antalya Central Office, Selçuk Mah, Mermerli Sokak, Ahiyusuf Cami Yanı, Kaleiçi (tel: 0242 472 0541; fax: 472 6298)
Bodrum Bariş Meydanı (tel: 0252 316 1091)
Bursa Central Office, Fevzi Çakmak Caddesi, Fomara Han Kat 6 (tel: 0224 254 2274/253 0411)
Diyarbakır Central Office, Kültür Sarayı, Kat 6 (tel: 0412 212 7840)
Konya Central Office, Mevlana Caddesi No 21 (tel: 0332 351 1074; fax: 350 6461)
Marmaris Iskele Meydanı No 2 (tel: 0252 412 1035)
Side Side Yolu Uzeri (tel: 0242 753 1265; fax: 753 2657)
Trabzon Central Office, Vilayet Binası Kat 4 (tel: 0462 232 5833)
Ürgüp Park Içi (tel: 0384 341 4059)
Van Cumhuriyet Caddesi No 19 (tel: 0432 216 3675)

Ballooning in the Göreme Valley, Cappadocia

HOTELS AND RESTAURANTS

HOTELS AND RESTAURANTS

ACCOMMODATION

Accommodation in Turkey covers the full range, from five star Hiltons and Sheratons in the big cities right through to simple family *pansiyons* in the towns and villages. Even in these, a private shower and toilet in each room is the norm. Most visitors find standards surprisingly high, and service is always helpful and friendly. In the following listings accom-modation is grouped in three price categories: £££ is expensive, at $100–175 for a double room with breakfast; ££ is moderate at $60–100; and £ is cheap, at $30–60. If no telephone number is given, there is none.

ISTANBUL
Grand Hotels
These are Istanbul's top luxury hotels, spread about the city.

Çırağan Palace Hotel Kempinski (£££) Çırağan (tel: 0212 258 3377; fax: 259 6686). An elaborately restored Ottoman palace in a superb setting on the lower Bosphorus, offering 294 spacious rooms, gourmet cuisine in its many restaurants and a fabulous outdoor swimming-pool on the edge of the Bosphorus. This is probably Istanbul's top hotel.

Conrad Istanbul (£££) Beşiktaş (tel: 0212 227 3000; fax: 259 6667). Stylish new hotel run by Hilton Hotels, set up on a hill in the commercial quarter with wonderful views of the Bosphorus and the Yıldız Gardens. Inside, there's a health club and swimming-pool; outside there's another pool and floodlit tennis. Excellent inter-national cuisine. There is a total of 627 rooms.

Swissôtel The Bosphorus (£££) Maçka (tel: 0212 259 0101 fax: 259 0105). Set on the hill above Dolmabahçe Palace, this splendid new hotel offers 600 rooms with fine views, several restau-rants and bars, indoor and outdoor pools, shopping arcade and fitness club, tennis and Turkish bath.

The older grand hotels, such as the Hilton, Sheraton, Mövenpick and Divan, are streets behind the above three as far as both glamour and comfort are concerned.

Stamboul: the Old City
These hotels are all within walking distance of the main tourist sites, and many are in renovated Ottoman houses.

Ayasofya Pansiyonlar (££) Sultanahmet (tel: 0212 513 3660; fax: 513 3669). Charming group of brightly painted old wooden houses, furnished in Ottoman style, between the Topkapı and Aya Sofya. Restaurants, cafés, bars and a Turkish bath. 57 rooms.

Citadel Hotel (££) Kennedy Caddesi 32 (tel: 0212 516 2313; fax: 516 1384). On the coast road overlooking the Sea of Marmara, below Aya Sofya, this excellent hotel offers 31 rooms with traditional atmosphere, superb Turkish cuisine in indoor and outdoor settings, the latter incorporating parts of the original city wall.

Halı (£) Klodfarer Caddesi 20, Çemberlitaş (tel: 0212 516 2170; fax: 516 2172). Set close by the Covered Bazaar, this beautifully restored old building offers 35 rooms all with en-suite facilities.

Hippodrome (£) Mımar Mehmetağa Cad. 17 (tel: 0212 517 6889; fax: 516 0268). Attractive 17-room Ottoman house with a pleasant terrace, close to the Blue Mosque. No restaurant.

Ibrahim Paşa (£) Terzihane Sok. 5 (tel: 0212 518 0394; fax: 518 4457). Small 19-room hotel in a renovated house with a pretty terrace, tucked away in a corner of the Hippodrome close to the Blue Mosque. The hotel runs to a café but no restaurant.

Kalyon (£££) Sarayburnu (tel: 0212 517 4400; fax: 638 1111). Recently refurbished 1960s motel on the coast road below the Blue Mosque, overlooking the Sea of Marmara. 110 rooms, pleasant sea view, terrace and international cuisine.

Kariye (££) Edirnekapı (tel: 0212 534 8414; fax: 521 6631). This attractive 22-room hotel, in a converted Ottoman house, is in a quiet location just inside the city walls, beside the Kariye Museum and a taxi ride from the Aya Sofya area. The hotel also has an excellent restaurant set in a peaceful garden.

Küçük Ayasofya (££) Şehit Mehmetpaşa Sokak 25, Sultanahmet (tel: 0212 516 1988; fax: 516 8356). Located lower on the hill from the Blue Mosque near the Sokullu Mehmet Paşa mosque, this rebuilt Ottoman house has 14 rooms, all with bath and simple decor.

Merit Antique (£££) Laleli (tel: 0212 513 9300; fax: 512 6390). Formerly known as the Ramada, this is the only five-star hotel in the old city. The building is a restored turn-of-the-century apartment block close to the Grand Bazaar, offering 275 rooms, an indoor heated pool, health club and excellent Turkish and Chinese cuisine.

Pierre Loti Hotel (££) Çemberltaş (tel: 0212 518 5700; fax: 516 1886). A small three-star hotel with 36 rooms offering good value close to the Grand Bazaar. Attractive terrace garden fronting the main road. The hotel also has a pleasant restaurant.

Poem (££) Akbıyık Caddesi, Terbıyık Sokak 12, Sultanahmet (tel: 0212 517 6836; fax: 529 3807). A pretty restored Ottoman wooden house with just 8 rooms, some with sea views. Within walking distance of all the main sights in the old city.

President (£££) Beyazıt (tel: 0212 516 6980; fax: 516 6999). A four-star hotel close to the Covered Bazaar with 204 rooms and a popular English-style pub.

Sokullu Paşa (££) Şehit Mehmetpaşa Sokak 5/7, Sultanahmet (tel: 0212 518 1790; fax: 518 1793). An elegant 18th-century mansion with 37 rooms located below the Blue Mosque. The garden has a fountain; the restaurant is in a Byzantine wine cellar, and there is also an original Turkish bath.

Sümengen (££) Mimar Mehmetağa Caddesi, Amiral Tafdil Sokak 21, Sultanahmet (tel: 0212 517 6875; fax: 516 8282). Close to the Blue Mosque with good views to the rear over the Sea of Marmara, this elegant 19th-century house has 30 rooms with en-suite facilities.

Turcoman Hotel (£) Asmali Çeşme Sokak 2 (tel: 0212 516 2956; fax: 516 2957). Next to the Museum of Turkish and Islamic Art (Ibrahim Pasa Sarayı), this 12-room hotel has good breakfast-time views over the Hippodrome.

Turkuaz Mansion Hotel (££) Kumkapı (tel: 0212 518 1897; fax: 517 3380). A very attractive 1870s pink and grey mansion, offering 14 rooms, garden, terrace bar and Turkish bath. Five minutes' walk from the Blue Mosque area.

Yeşil Ev (£££) Sultanahmet (tel: 0212 517 6785; fax: 517 6780). In a marvellous location between the Blue Mosque and Aya Sofya, this 20-room hotel in a restored Ottoman house offers a large rear garden with outdoor restaurant and fountain. The most popular (and the most expensive) of the renovated Ottoman hotels.

Beyoğlu and the Bosphorus

These hotels are located either in the European business quarter, a 15-minute taxi ride away from the old city, or on the Bosphorus itself.

Bebek Hotel (££) Bebek (tel: 0212 263 3000; fax: 263 2636). The hotel enjoys the perfect waterside location and stylish terrace bar, but rather like a sleepy guesthouse.

Büyük Londra Hotel (£) Tepebaşı (tel: 0212 245 0671; fax: 249 1025). An 1850s building with a beautiful façade and an air of faded grandeur. Some of its 54 rooms have fine views of the Golden Horn. Close to (but much better value than) the famous Pera Palace.

Büyük Tarabya (£££) Tarabya (tel: 0212 262 1000; fax: 262 2260). Hideous 1960s carbuncle, once Istanbul's grandest hotel, this 261-room hotel offers good Bosphorus views well away from the city centre. It is much used by businessmen.

Elan (£) Meşrutiyet Caddesi 213, Tepebaşı (tel: 0212 252 5449; fax: 249 9326). 42-roomed comfortable hotel near the American and British Consulates, with views of the Golden Horn. Air conditioning.

Fuat Paşa Hotel (££) Büyükdere (tel: 0212 242 9860; fax: 242 9589). A pretty house on the Bosphorus front at Büyükdere, 30 minutes by taxi from the old city. It offers 51 rooms, indoor and outdoor restaurants and a Turkish bath.

Golden Age I (£££) Topçu Caddesi 22, Taksim (tel: 0212 254 4906; fax: 255 1368). 112 rooms in the heart of the Taksim/ Elmadağ district, modern and fully equipped. Health centre with jaccuzi.

Hidiv Kasrı (££) Çubuklu (tel: 0212 331 2651; fax: 322 3434). Set on the Asian shore overlooking the Bosphorus, this former Khedive's palace sits in splendid isolation, 12 km outside the city centre, in its own rose garden and woodland. It offers 14 rooms with sumptuous art nouveau decor, and a charming restaurant.

Pera Palace (£££) Tepebaşı (tel: 0212 251 4560; fax: 251 4089). The famously grand turn-of-the-century terminus for the Orient Express is now overpriced and overrated, and offers 139 rooms with period furniture, an elegant *patisserie* and bar.

Sed Hotel (££) Kabataş (tel: 0212 252 2710; fax: 252 4274). A 50-room hotel in the quiet backstreets within walking distance of the Dolmabahçe Palace. Immaculately furnished with marble floors and elegant pillars, giving it a boutique feel. The buffet restaurant is good value.

HOTELS AND RESTAURANTS

Vardar Palace Hotel (££)
Sıraselviler Caffesi 54–6,
Taksim (tel: 0212 152 2896;
fax: 152 1527). Built a
century ago in the
Levantine-Seljuk style, this
refurbished 40-roomed
hotel is close to Taksim
Square. Modern, functional
decoration.

ISTANBUL ENVIRONS
Bursa

Çelik Palace (£££) Çekirge
(tel: 0224 233 3800; fax: 236
1910). A sumptuous 173-
room hotel, the best in
Bursa, with its own hot
thermal springs, indoor
pool, two Turkish baths and
shopping centre.

Termal Hotel Gönlüferah (££)
Çekirge (tel: 0224 233 9210;
fax: 233 9218). A 62-room
modern three-star hotel
offering Turkish thermal bath
and good restaurant.

Büyükada

Splendid Palas Hotel (££)
Büyükada (tel: 0216 382
6950; fax: 382 6775). Less
than 100m from the ferry
terminus pier, this 74-room
run-down but very
atmospheric wooden turn-
of-the-century mansion sits
right on the waterfront, with
a terrace offering superb
views over the other
islands. Its twin domes
conceal water tanks,
essential on an island with
no springs or streams.

Çanakkale

Tusan Hotel (££) Güzelyalı
(tel: 0286 232 8210). In a
wonderful woodland setting
with a private beach, 14km
outside Çanakkale, this 64-
room hotel offers
watersports and indoor and
outdoor restaurants.

Anzac Hotel (£) Saat Kulesi
Meydanı (tel: 0286 217 7777;
fax: 217 2018). A simple 27-
room hotel in the city centre
with pleasant roof bar and
restaurant.

Edirne

**Rüstempaşa Caravanserai
Hotel** (££) İki Kapili Han
Caddesi 57 (tel: 0284 225
2195; fax: 212 0462). A
converted Ottoman
caravanserai in the centre of
Edirne.

THE AEGEAN
Altınkum

Göçtur Hotel (££). A
modern hotel 2km from the
resort centre, 40m from the
famous sandy beach, with a
pleasant swimming pool,
terrace and Turkish bath.

Ayvalık

Chalet Chopin Pension (££)
Altınoluk (tel: 0266 396
1044; fax: 396 0697). Set on
the Bay of Edremit, well
placed for visiting Troy and
Pergamum, this extra-
ordinary old millhouse sits
up on a hillside overlooking
the sea. It has only four
rooms, traditionally
decorated, but its well-
known restaurant seats 150
people. It also has a pool.

Cunda Hotel (££). (tel: 0266
327 1598; fax: 327 1943).
Newly opened, this small
hotel stands right on the
sandy beach of Alibey
Island, connected to Ayvalık
by a narrow spit and small
bridge. The owner has his
own jetty and boat for
exploring the islands in the
bay. Simple, good value
restaurant.

Behramkale

Assos Behram Hotel (£)
İskele (tel: 0286 721 7016;
fax: 721 7044). Attractive 20-
room stone-built hotel right
on the harbourfront, with
watersports and indoor and
outdoor restaurant.

Assos Eden Beach (££)
Kadirga Koyu (tel: 0286 752
7039; fax: 757 2054). A 68-
room hotel right on the
beach, with watersports and
children's playground,
restaurant and cafeteria.

Bodrum

**Eldorador TMT Holiday
Village** (££) (tel: 0252 316
1232; fax: 316 2647). A well-
designed holiday complex
with 239 rooms and 32
villas on its private beach
1.5km from Bodrum centre,
offering two pools, watersports and good children's
facilities.

Manastir Hotel (££)
Kumbahçe (tel: 0252 316
2854; fax: 316 2772). Built
on the site of an old
monastery on the hillside
overlooking the harbour
and castle, with two
restaurants, a pool with
children's section, a fitness
centre and sauna.

Mandarin Pension (£)
Gümüşlük. Set in mandarin
groves 20km west of
Bodrum, just 50m from the
sea, this *pansiyon* has 20
village-style rooms. A
simple beach bar offers
light snacks and the
renowned Gümüşlük fish
restaurants are a short stroll
away.

Myndos Hotel (££) (tel: 0252
316 3080; fax: 316 5252).
This 72-room hotel 1.5km
from the centre of Bodrum
is attractively arranged
round a pool with children's
section. There are both
indoor and outdoor
restaurants and tennis is
available.

Secil Hotel (£) Türkbükü. In
a fishing village a 30-minute
drive from Bodrum, this 20-
room family-run hotel offers
a large swimming pool and
a peaceful setting. The
beach is two minutes away.
There is a restaurant and
also a bar.

Çeşme

Marinisa Hotel (£). Set on
one of Çeşme's most beau-
tiful sandy bays, 1.5km from
the resort centre, this simple hotel offers homely
accommodation, a pool,
restaurant and bar.

ACCOMMODATION

Dalyan

Göl Hotel (£). Two minutes from Dalyan marina, this pretty lakeside hotel with basic accommodation has a pool, restaurant and bar. The famous Istuzu beach is 35 minutes away by water taxi.

Sultan Palace (££). Some 10 minutes upriver from Dalyan, this exceptional and traditional Turkish hotel is totally isolated on its hillside, set in gardens by a large pool. It offers good food and the famous turtle beach is 40 minutes away by courtesy water taxi.

Efes – see Kuşadası

Foça

Club Méditerranée Foça Holiday Village (£££) (tel: 0232 812 1607; fax: 812 2175). A 376-room complex with superb watersports facilities, scuba diving, pool and Turkish bath.

Villa Dedem (£) Sahil Caddesi 66 (tel:0232 812 1700; fax: 812 1700). A 20-room hotel on the seafront with a restaurant on its top floor.

Izmir

Balçova Thermal Hotel (££) (tel: 0232 259 0102; fax: 259 0829). This 196-room hotel 5km outside Izmir has two thermal swimming pools and a fully equipped medical rehabilitation centre for rheumatic disorders.

Büyük Efes Hotel (£££) (tel: 0232 484 4300; fax: 441 5695). This luxury hotel, Izmir's best, stands in the city centre in its own gardens, with two outdoor pools and one indoor, no fewer than five restaurants and a fitness centre.

Kaya Hotel (£) Çankaya (tel: 0232 483 9771; fax:483 9773). A modest 55-room hotel in the city centre, with restaurant and lobby bar.

Kuşadası

Club Kervanseray (££) (tel: 0256 614 4115; fax:614 2423). A converted Ottoman caravansarai right in the centre of Kusadası, with 40 rooms decorated tradition-ally and set around the lush central courtyard where the restaurant is situated. Attractive, but inclined to be noisy in season.

Kısmet Hotel (££) (tel: 0256 614 2005; fax:614 4914). Standing on its own small peninsula some 2km from the town, this exclusive hotel set in sub-tropical gardens offers excellent international cuisine. Many heads of state have stayed here, attracted by its secluded position.

Nero Hotel (£) Güzelçamlı koyu (tel: 0256 646 1795; fax: 646 1794). A well-designed 53-room hotel with two restaurants and a pool with children's section and attractive poolside terrace.

Marmaris

Doğan Hotel (£). Set on the Bay of Orhaniye, on the west coast of the Bozburun peninsula, this secluded family-run hotel sits right on the beach with pretty gardens, attractive restaurant and Turkish bar. Many boat trips are available for those keen to explore the neighbouring coastline.

Gökçe Hotel (£). Lying off the beaten track on its own farmland this family-run hotel is a five-minute walk from Turunç and its beach. It has an excellent restaurant and a pool.

Grand Azur and **Laguna Azur** (£££) (tel: 0252 412 8201; fax: 412 3530 and tel: 0252 455 3710; fax: 455 3622). The Grand Azur is the most prestigious hotel in Marmaris, overlooking a marina and beautiful sandy beach, with lush tropical gardens and a host of restaurants, bars and shops. The Laguna Azur, on a quiet beach with palm-trees in Içmeler, is its much smaller sister hotel, with just 64 rooms decorated in art deco style.

Muğla

Petek Hotel (££) (tel: 0252 214 1897). Muğla's best hotel offering a comfortable overnight stop in the centre of town for touring travellers who do not wish to drive down the peninsulas of Bodrum or Marmaris.

Pamukkale

271

Club Polat's Hotel (£££) (tel: 0258 271 4111; fax: 271 4092). A 225-room hotel set in the village of Karahayıt below Pamukkale, with thermal and semi-Olympic pools, indoor and outdoor restaurants, and a tennis court.

Koçak (££) (tel: 0258 272 2099; fax: 272 2112). A 94-room hotel set up on the plateau, with a fine swimming-pool with children's section, an attractive garden and both indoor and outdoor restaurants.

Turizm (£). Set right beside the Roman Baths Museum and the public baths, this 16-room hotel offers the most unusual courtyard pool, once the sacred pool of the Roman baths, full of fluted Classical columns and capitals.

Pergamum

Berksoy Hotel (££) (tel: 0232 633 2595; fax: 633 5346). A pleasant 57-room hotel 1.5km from the centre of town, offering one indoor and two outdoor restaurants, a swimming-pool and children's pool and playground.

HOTELS AND RESTAURANTS

Tusan Motel (£) (tel: 0232 633 1173; fax: 633 1938). A 42-room hotel 8km from the archaeological site, at the junction with the main Çanakkale-Izmir road, with a small but amusing Roman spa pool for wallowing. Simple restaurant.

THE MEDITERRANEAN
Adana

Büyük Surmeli Hotel (£££) Özler Caddesi (tel: 0322 352 3600; fax: 352 1945). Probably the best hotel in Adana, 1km from the city centre, with a total of 166 rooms, a pool, nightclub and casino.

Raşit Ener Motel (£) Yüregir (tel: 0322 321 2758; fax: 321 2775). A fairly modest motel running to only 16 rooms, offering a simple restaurant, pool with children's section and playground, as well as a campsite and caravan park.

Alanya

Blue Sky Hotel (£) (tel: 0242 513 3364; fax: 512 5402). A pleasant 54-room hotel in the town centre, with a good-sized pool and children's playground. Basic restaurant.

Club Alantur (£££) (tel: 0242 518 1740; fax: 518 1756). Excellent for sports enthusiasts, this hotel, set on the beach 5km outside Alanya, offers one indoor and three outdoor pools, a gym, four tennis courts, mini-golf and a very wide range of watersports, including scuba diving. It has a total of 365 rooms and 12 flats, with four restaurants.

Melody Banana Hotel (£) Keykubat Caddesi (tel: 0242 513 3424; fax: 513 8837). A simple, centrally placed hotel with 38 rooms, with access to all the sporting facilities of the adjacent Banana Hotel.

Anamur

Hermes Hotel (££) (tel: 0324 814 3950; fax: 814 3995). A 70-room hotel on the beach, with a pool and children's section, windsurfing and two restaurants.

Antakya

Büyük Antakya Hotel (£££) Ataürk Caddesi (tel: 0326 213 5860; fax: 213 5869). Antakya's best hotel, a modern block in the city centre with 72 rooms, nightclub, casino and indoor and outdoor restaurants. No pool.

Antalya

Argos Hotel (££) Kaleiçi (tel: 0242 247 2012; fax: 241 7557). A very attractively converted Ottoman house in the old quarter above the marina, with 15 rooms, pool, live music and restaurant.

Lara Hotel (££) Lara Yolu (tel: 0242 323 1460; fax: 323 1449). Set right on the cliff 8km outside Antalya on the Lara road, and with an attractive pool terrace. There are two restaurants, and watersports from the beach below.

Marina (££) Kaleiçi (tel: 0242 247 5490; fax: 241 1765). Set in private gardens of date palms and banana trees, this luxurious small hotel was winner of the Best Hotel in Turkey award in 1992. Very comfortable spacious rooms on split level, and a restaurant with an excellent menu.

Tütav Türkevleri Hotels (££) Kaleiçi (tel: 0242 248 6591; fax: 241 9419). Standing 300m from the old harbour within the walls of the old fort, this group of converted Ottoman wooden houses offers 20 rooms, baby-sitting, a pool, indoor and outdoor restaurants, a sauna and a choice of three cafeterias.

Villa Perla (£) Kaleiçi (tel: 0242 248 9793; fax: 241 2917). Charming family-run hotel in a converted Ottoman house, with 16 rooms, private courtyard garden for outdoor eating and small pool.

Eğridir

Eğridir Hotel (££) (tel: 0246 311 4992; fax: 311 4219). Modern 51-room hotel in the centre of town, with balconies for breakfast overlooking the lake. Restaurant terrace, but no pool.

Fethiye

Anıl Pension (£) Çalıs Yolu (tel: 0252 613 1192; fax: 613 1711). Modest 17-room *pansiyon* near Çaliş beach, 5km from Fethiye centre, with a small pool and restaurant offering occasional Turkish shows.

Kemal Hotel (£) Geziyolu (tel: 0252 614 5009; fax: 614 5009). Set at the quieter end of the waterfront in Fethiye, by the fishing boats, this simple modern hotel offers 21 rooms, a roof bar and indoor and outdoor restaurants. No pool.

Letoonia Holiday Village (££) (tel: 0252 614 4966; fax: 614 4422). Set on its own peninsula 4km from the centre of Fethiye, this 680-room, 110-villa complex is considered one of the loveliest holiday villages in the area, offering three sandy beaches, two swimming-pools, three restaurants, three snack bars and the full range of watersports, including scuba diving.

Finike

Anadolu Hotel (£) (tel: 0242 855 3804; fax: 855 3805). A pleasant 25-room hotel 2km from the centre, set back from the beach and coast road. Breakfast and simple meals are served on the roof terrace.

Kalkan

Dionysia Diva Hotel (£) Cumhuriyet Caddesi (tel: 0242 844 3681; fax: 844 3139). Two attractive small hotels, both with stunning sea views and excellent roof terraces for bars and breakfast. Kalkan centre is just a five-minute walk away.
Kalamar Hotel (£) (tel: 0242 844 3190; fax: 844 3194). A 68-room hotel with pool and a long stone-paved waterfront with ladders for sea swimming. Kalkan is 1.5km away.
Patara Prince Hotel (££) PK 10 (tel: 0242 844 3920; fax: 844 3930). Immaculately designed hotel of 54 rooms standing within the Club Patara, an ambitious re-creation of a Roman town, complete with triumphal arch, forum and fountains. There is a magnificent balustraded terrace with large pool. Excellent cuisine in four restaurants. A free water taxi takes you across to Kalkan marina 10 minutes away.
Pension Patara (£) Close to the town's shingle beach and tea garden, this pretty *pansiyon* has 10 rooms overlooking the harbour, and an attractive roof terrace on which breakfast is served by the family.
Pirat Hotel (££) (tel: 0242 844 3178; fax: 844 3183). A popular 128-room hotel overlooking the marina, with friendly staff all in nautical uniform. Excellent cuisine and pool with children's section. Reckoned to be the best hotel in town.

Kaş

Aqua-Park Hotel (£££) (tel: 042 836 1901; fax: 836

1906). This luxurious and exclusive complex of villas and chalet-style rooms spread over the Kaş peninsula is very well equipped for watersports, with scuba diving, three swimming pools and two water chutes. It has 116 rooms and 24 apartments, and offers a free bus link to Kaş town centre, 5km away.
Club Antiphellos (££) Çukurbağ Peninsula (tel: 0242 836 2651; fax: 836 2654). An attractive hotel with 16 rooms and a pretty pool and terrace, set on an isolated peninsula with access to a rocky beach. It offers watersports and a volleyball court, and has indoor and outdoor restaurants.
Me & Di Hotel (££). (tel: 0242 836 1914; fax: 836 1426). Set up on a hillside above the Kaş–Kalkan road, this exclusive 17-room hotel offers excellent, friendly service, a lovely pool in a private courtyard, villa-style rooms, each with its own terrace, pretty gardens and good restaurant.
Melisa Pension (£). Family *pansiyon* in a quiet street near Kaş harbour, with 16 good-sized rooms and breakfast on the rooftop terrace. No pool or restaurant.

Kemer

Antalya Renaissance (£££) (tel: 0242 824 8431; fax: 824 8430). Modern five-star hotel in a delightful setting in the resort of Beldibi, between Kemer and Antalya. Its excellent range of watersports from a private beach, large outdoor and indoor pools, tennis courts, fitness centre, Turkish bath and sauna and range of restaurants and shops make it virtually a self-contained resort in itself.

Beltaş Hotel (££) Beldibi (tel: 0242 824 8192; fax: 824 8344). Well-designed 75-room hotel set in lush gardens with private beach, watersports, pool with children's section, playground and tennis court. Indoor and outdoor restaurants.
Princess Orange (£) Tekirova (tel: 0242 821 4059; fax: 821 4069). Pretty 48-room hotel set round a pool in Tekirova centre, with a cafeteria and outdoor restaurant.

Kızkalesi

Club Hotel Barbarossa (££) (tel: 0324 523 2364; fax: 523 2090). Comfortable, pleasantly designed hotel with 103 rooms on a private beach 23km from Silifke, with views across to Kızkalesi. Good pool, watersports, disco, indoor and outdoor restaurants.

Mersin

Mersin Hilton (£££) A. Menderes Bulvarı (tel: 0324 326 5000; fax: 74 326 5050). Modern five-star block 3km from the city centre, with 188 rooms, pool, health bar, tennis courts, gym, disco, casino and two restaurants.

Ölü Deniz

Meri Motel (££) (tel: 0252 616 6060; fax: 616 6456). The best-placed hotel in Ölü Deniz, right on the lagoon, with a private beach ensuring total tranquillity, and 75 rooms climbing up a steep hillside. Not suitable for the elderly or tiny children, the Meri offers a lovely terrace restaurant with live music, windsurfing and playground. No pool.

Patara

Xanthos Hotel (££). Set in beautiful sprawling gardens arranged around a large pool, this attractive hotel has 16 rooms, a lovely terrace and bar area, and a tennis court. Simple restaurant.

Side

Turquoise Hotel (£££) (tel: 0242 756 9330; fax: 756 9345). Five-star luxury complex set 3km from the resort centre, in a peaceful beach and forest setting. Huge pool, gym, watersports, tennis courts, children's pool and crèche.
Pamphylia Hotel (££). Standing right on the beach on the southern side of the peninsula, a short walk from the old town centre, this traditional hotel offers an attractive terrace restaurant overlooking the sea, and pretty wooden balconies.
Sevil Pension (£). Friendly family-run *pansiyon* a short walk from the old centre and the main beach. Breakfast only in the courtyard gardens. No pool.

Silifke

Altınorfoz Hotel (££) Susanoğlu (tel: 0324 722 4211; fax: 722 4215). Four-star beach complex, 17km from Silifke, with watersports, pool with children's section, Turkish bath, nightclub and casino, indoor and outdoor restaurants.

Montana Hotel (££) A 90-room hotel in a spectacular forest setting, 2km from the lagoon and 3km from the beach, offering two splendid pools linked by a cascade, extensive gardens, pool snack bar and restaurant.

CAPPADOCIA
Avanos

Altınyazı (££) Zelve-Göreme road (tel: 0384 511 2010; fax: 511 4960). Plush four-star hotel with 84 elegant and traditionally decorated

rooms. Turkish bath, disco, restaurant and babysitting. No pool.

Göreme

Ataman Hotel (££) (tel: 0384 271 2310; fax: 271 2313). Traditional stone-built house in the town centre, renovated to a high standard and offering 33 rooms, three indoor restaurants and one terrace restaurant, indoor and outdoor pools, Turkish bath, gym, disco and tennis.

Kayseri

Hattat Hotel (£) Osman Kavuncu Caddesi (tel: 0352 231 9331; fax: 232 6503). Simple and modern 72-room hotel in the city centre with a roof restaurant.

Ortahisar

Burcu Hotel (££) (tel: 0384 343 3200; fax: 343 3500). A converted caravanserai surrounded by 49 rooms with indoor and outdoor restaurants.

Üçhisar

Kaya Club Méditerranée Hotel (££) (tel: 0384 219 2007; fax: 219 2363). Spectacular 70-room hotel set up on the rock with superb views and pool terrace, restaurant, night-club and children's pool.

Ürgüp

Alfina Hotel (£) Istiklal Caddesi (tel: 0384 341 4822; fax: 341 2424). Imaginative design cut into the rock in terraces, with 32 rooms (each with terrace), disco, indoor and outdoor restaurant and occasional Turkish show.
Esbelli House (££). Exclusive 6-room hotel in a converted fortified caravan-serai. Original rooms cut out of the rock, simply furnished in traditional style. Breakfast only.

Perissia Hotel (££) Kayseri Caddesi (tel: 0384 341 2930; fax: 341 4524). Modern four-star hotel with 230 rooms, large pool with children's section, three indoor and one outdoor restaurants, disco, nightclub and tennis courts.

CENTRAL ANATOLIA
Amasya

Ilk House (££). Set right in the centre of Amasya in a 200-year-old Ottoman house with authentic decor, complete with dowry chests and carved wood ceilings. Basement dining room and courtyard garden for breakfast. Views across the river.

Boğazkale

Hitit Motel (£) Sungurlu (tel: 0364 311 1042). Unpretentious overnight stop. Buses touring the Hittite sites often stop for meals in its excellent quick restaurant.

Ankara

Bulvar Palas Hotel (££) Atatürk Bulvarı (tel: 0312 417 5020; fax: 425 2971). Centrally located 142-room hotel with a children's playground, babysitting, and four indoor and one outdoor restaurant. No pool.
Hitit Hotel (£) Ulus (tel: 312 310 8617). Modest older hotel below the citadel, on the hill leading up to the museum, with simple rooms and a restaurant.
Sheraton Ankara Hotel and Towers (£££) Kavaklıdere (tel: 0312 468 5454; fax: 467 1136). Ankara's best hotel, in the city centre, with 311 rooms, pool, health centre and jacuzzi, three indoor and one outdoor restaurant.

Konya

Başak Palas (£) Hükümet Meydanı (tel: 0332 351 1338;

fax: 351 1339). Basic hotel in the city centre with 39 rooms, breakfast hall and snack bar only.

Dergah Hotel (££) Mevlana Caddesi (tel: 0332 351 1197; fax: 351 0116). Central 82-room hotel with restaurant, bar and sauna.

Huma Hotel (££) Alaaddin Bulvarı (tel: 0332 350 6389; fax: 551 0244). Centrally located traditional-style building with 30 rooms, restaurant and disco.

Kütahya

Erbaylar Hotel (££) Afyon Caddesi (tel: 0274 223 6960; fax: 216 1046). A 42-room modern hotel with restaurant and bar.

Tokat

Büyük Tokat Hotel (££) (tel: 0356 214 5426; fax: 214 3175). A 60-room four-star hotel in a central location, offering a swimming pool, sports facilities, restaurant and bar. Quite a surprise to find a place like this in a place like Tokat.

EASTERN TURKEY
Artvin

Karahan Hotel (£) tel: 0466 212 2800; fax: 212 2420). A 57-room hotel offering neat rooms and a good restaurant with fine views from its terrace.

Diyarbakır

Demir Hotel (££) Izzet Pasa Caddesi (tel: 0412 221 2315; fax: 222 4300). The best hotel in Diyarbakır, offering a pool and 58 rooms with a good restaurant and bar.

Kervansaray Hotel (££) (tel: 0412 223 5019). Renovated 17th-century Deliller Hanı, with courtyard garden and restaurant.

Doğubeyazıt

Isfahan Hotel (£) (tel: 0472 215 5139; fax: 215 2044). Simple 42-room hotel in the

town centre with a surprisingly good restaurant.

Elazığ

Büyük Elazığ Hotel (£) (tel: 0424 212 2001; fax: 238 1899). Modern 100-room hotel in the centre, used by business people, with a functional restaurant and bar. Nothing better in town.

Erzurum

Büyük Erzurum Hotel (££) (tel: 0442 218 6528; fax: 212 2898). A centrally located 50-room modern hotel with balconies, with a Turkish bath, restaurant and bar.

Oral Hotel (££) (tel: 0442 218 9740; fax: 218 9749). A 90-room modern hotel in the centre; busy dining-room and bar used by tours.

Kars

Anihan Motel (££) (tel: 0474 223 7404). New motel on the outskirts of town with 96 rooms, restaurant and bar; the only decent accommodation anywhere in the area.

Malatya

Büyük Malatya Hotel (£) Yeni Cami Karşişi (tel: 0422 321 400; fax: 321 5367). Simple 52-room hotel offering bed and breakfast only.

Mardin

Denktaş Turistik Tesisleri (££) Derik (tel: 0482 212 1508). A 44-room hotel with a swimming-pool, restaurant and bar; probably the best place to stay in the area.

Nezirhan Hotel (££) Nusaybin (tel: 0482 415 1425; fax: 415 1199). An unlikely place in the middle of nowhere on the transit route to Iraq, with 68 rooms, a swimming-pool, nightclub and disco, and three indoor and two outdoor restaurants.

Nemrut Dağı

Bozdğan Hotel (££) Adıyaman (tel: 0416 216 3999; fax: 216 3630). Modern 74-room hotel in the centre of Adıyaman, with a pool and children's section, restaurant and two bars.

Zeus Motel (£) (tel: 0416 715 2428). Motel in a superb location right up by the summit of Nemrut Dağı, offering simple rooms and a basic restaurant.

Şanlıurfa

Harran Hotel (££) Atatürk Bulvarı (tel: 0414 313 4743; fax: 313 4918). A modern faceless building in the city centre with 63 rooms, the best in Urfa, with indoor and outdoor restaurants, pool and Turkish bath.

Van

Akdamar Hotel (££) (tel: 0432 216 8100; fax: 212 0868). Older 69-room hotel with an attractive top-floor restaurant and good service.

Büyük Urartu (££) Cumhuriyet Caddesi (tel: 0432 212 0660; fax: 212 1610). The newest hotel in Van, three-star, 75 rooms, two restaurants, two bars and a disco.

THE BLACK SEA
Bolu

Abant Palace Hotel (£££) (tel: 0374 224 5012; fax: 224 5011). Set on the shores of Lake Abant and much used by Ankara residents at weekends, this five-star hotel offers 171 rooms, with an indoor pool, restaurant with lake view, nightclub, disco, seven bars, tennis and children's playground.

Düzce

Çobantur Hotel (££) (tel: 0374 514 1132). A comfortable 43-room hotel with restaurant and bar.

HOTELS AND RESTAURANTS

Kilyos

Kilyos Kale Hotel (£) Kale Caddesi (tel: 0212 201 1818; fax: 201 1823). Hotel with 36 rooms and pretty terrace restaurant; clifftop location.

Ordu

Belde Hotel (££) (tel: 0452 214 3987; fax: 214 9398). Fine hotel on its own spit of land 1km outside Ordu, with a large pool, Turkish bath, sauna, gym, nightclub, disco, and indoor and outdoor restaurants.

Safranbolu

Havuzlu Konak (££) (tel: 0372 725 2883; fax: 712 3824). Immaculately restored Ottoman mansion in the city centre, offering 11 rooms with two indoor and one outdoor restaurant.

Samsun

Yafeya Hotel (££) Cumhuriyet Meydanı (tel: 0362 435 1131; fax: 435 1135). A 96-room modern hotel in the city centre with two restaurants and a café.

Şile

Değirmen Hotel (£) Plaj Yolu (tel: 0216 711 5048; fax: 711 5248). Beach hotel 60 km from Istanbul in the resort centre, with 76 rooms, disco, restaurant and a jazz bar.

Sinop

Belediye Yuvam Tesisleri (££) (tel: 0368 261 2532). Simple beach hotel with a bar and restaurant.

Trabzon

Özgür Hotel (£) Atatürk Alanı (tel: 0462 321 1319; fax: 321 3952). Simple 45-room hotel in the city centre with a restaurant and bar.

Usta Hotel (££) Iskele Caddesi (tel: 0462 321 2195; fax: 322 3793). Central 76-room hotel with a restaurant and bar. Trabzon's best.

RESTAURANTS

ISTANBUL

Grand hotels

All the grand hotels have superb if very expensive restaurants offering a range of international and Turkish cuisine. Those worth singling out are the **Çırağan Restaurant** for seafood, the **Divan** for outstanding Turkish and international cuisine, the **Dynasty** in the Merit Antique for Chinese food, **Miyako** in the Swissôtel for Japanese food and **Monteverdi** in the Conrad for classy Italian food.

The Old City

Asitane (££) Kariye Hotel, Edirnekapı (tel: 0212 534 8414). Unusual Ottoman cuisine beautifully presented in a tranquil courtyard garden accompanied by classical Turkish music.

Borsa (££) Sirkeci, opposite the railway station (tel: 0212 511 8079). Rated now as the best Turkish restaurant in Istanbul, though it is nothing to look at from the outside. Offers many rare Turkish dishes. Open lunchtime only. Very popular with business people.

Darüzziyafe (££) in the Süleymaniye mosque complex (tel: 0212 511 8414). Located in the courtyard of the original *imaret* (soup kitchen), this unusual restaurant serves authentic Ottoman cuisine. No alcohol. Popular with tour groups.

Hamdi Et Lokantası (£) Kalçın Sokak, Eminönü (tel: 0212 528 0390). Unpretentious lunchtime-only restaurant for simple grilled meat dishes. No alcohol is served. Closed Sundays.

Havuzlu Lokanta (££) Grand Bazaar (tel: 0212 527 3346). The smartest place in the bazaar, a safe bet for a lunch or coffee break. Simple Turkish food.

Hünkar (££) Perçin Sokak, Fatih (tel: 0212 5237561). Friendly place serving an excellent selection of classic Turkish dishes. No credit cards.

Kathisma (£) Yeni Akbıyık Caddesi, Sultanahmet (tel: 0212 518 9710). Old-fashioned decor and Turkish and international cuisine, with tables on three floors and a terrace.

Konyalı (££) Topkapı Palace (tel: 0212 513 9697). In the fourth court of the Topkapı itself, with good Turkish food and excellent views over the Bosphorus. Arrive early for lunch to beat the tour groups.

Küçük Hudadad (£) Kömür Bekir Sokak, Eminönü. Traditional tradesmen's *lokanta* since 1944, in the historic Şapçı Han opposite Yeni Cami. No alcohol served. Excellent soups and stews.

Pandeli (££) Spice Bazaar, Eminönü (tel: 0212 527 3909). Splendid traditional restaurant above the entrance to the Spice Bazaar, decorated from floor to ceiling in Turkish tiles. Excellent Turkish cuisine. Lunch only, closed Sundays.

Rami (££) Utangaç Sokak, Sultanahmet (tel: 0212 517 6593). Next to the Blue Mosque in a restored Ottoman building, with good Turkish cuisine, candlelight and classical music.

Sarnıç (£££) Soğukçeşme Sokak, Sultanahmet (tel: 0212 512 4291). A converted Roman cistern, between the Topkapı and Aya Sofya, remarkable for its architecture rather than the

Turkish food. Closed Mondays.

Sedir (££) Telliodalar Sokak, Kumkapı (tel: 0212 517 0264). Good seafood restaurant in this quarter bursting with fish restaurants.

Subası (£) Nuruosmaniye Caddesi, Cağaloğlu. Simple *lokanta* near the Nuruosmaniye gate of the Grand Bazaar. Only 10 tables, and delicious home-cooked Turkish food.

Sultanahmet Köftecisi (£) Divanyolu Caddesi, Sultanahmet (tel: 0212 526 2782). On the corner of Aya Sofya square near the Yerebatan Saray, famous for its meatballs and always busy. No alcohol. Also does takeaways.

Sultan Pub (££) Divanyolu Caddesi, Sultanahmet (tel: 0212 526 6347). One of the classier places around Aya Sofya offering European and Turkish food.

Ümit Restaurant (£) Nuruosmaniye (tel: 0212 512 9094). Lunchtime only *lokanta* beside the Grand Bazaar, set in the cellar of an antique inn. Clean and attractive; serves traditional Turkish food. No credit cards.

Yeşil Ev (£££) Sultanahmet (tel: 0212 517 6786). Well-located between Aya Sofya and the Blue Mosque, in a lovely courtyard setting away from the bustle of the streets. Good quality European and Turkish food, though rather overpriced.

Beyoğlu and the Bosphorus

Ali Baba (££) Kireçburnu Caddesi, Kireçburnu (tel: 0212 262 0889). Simple *lokanta* serving good fish and *meze* in a garden beside the Bosphorus. Popular for Sunday lunch.

Anadolu Kavagı (£). This northernmost village on the Asian side of the Bosphorus is full of simple and colourful fish *lokantas* .

Asır (££) Beyoğlu next to the police station (tel: 0212 250 0557). Popular Greek restaurant with excellent selection of *meze* and fish. Very smoky.

Baca (£££) Emirğan Yolu, Boyacıköy (tel: 0212 277 0808). Fashionable restaurant offering international cuisine, live music, disco and a terrace with a spectacular view of the Fatih Sultan Mehmet bridge. Reached up a long steep flight of steps.

Borsa (££) Halaskargazi Caddesi, Şair Nigar Sokak 90/1, Osmanbey (tel: 0212 232 4200). Opposite the Sirkeci railway station, this pleasant and popular restaurant is open 11.00am to 11.00pm and offers many rare classical Turkish dishes.

Cafe de Paris (££) Min Kemal Öke Caddesi 19/1, Nişantaşı (tel:0212 225 0700). A Parisian-style cafe with a set menu of steak, chips and salad. Generally crowded. Closed Sunday lunch.

Cafe de Pera (££) Fuat Uzkınay Sokak 17/2, Beyoğlu (tel: 0212 249 9598). Open 11.30am to midnight, the crepes here are very good. Popular eating place after the cinema.

Çamlıca Café (££) Şefa Tepesi, Çamlıca (tel: 0216 329 8191). Restored Ottoman pavilions set on Istanbul's highest hill with superb skyline views. Typical Turkish dishes and classical Turkish music.

Çiçek Pasajı (£) Istiklal Caddesi, Beyoğlu. Collection of small restaurants serving *meze* and meat dishes in the old flower market. Noisy and atmospheric. No credit cards.

Çiftnal (££) Yenimahalle, Ihlamur Yolu 6, Beşiktaş (tel: 0212 261 3129). In a 19th century police station, this restaurant offers grilled Turkish dishes and is open from noon to midnight.

Deniz Park Gazinosu (££) Daire Sokak 9, Yeniköy (tel: 0212 262 0415). With a wonderful terace offering Bosphorus views, this long-established fish restaurant is owned by a Greek family.

Ece (£££) Kamacı Sokak 10, Arnavutköy (tel: 0212 265 9600). Open 6.00pm till dawn, this old Greek house offers meze on the ground floor, a pop music bar on the first floor, and an excellent à la carte restaurant on the top floor.

Façyo (££) Kireçburnu Caddesi, Tarabya (tel: 0212 262 0024). Best fish restaurant in Tarabya, the Bosphorus suburb famous for its nightlife and seaside restaurants.

Four Seasons (££) Istiklal Caddesi, Tûnel (tel: 0212 245 8941). Handy for the consulates and the cinemas, this smallish restaurant has a civilised European atmosphere and good food.

Galata Tower (£££) Kuledibi (tel: 0212 245 1160). Indifferent food accompanied by Turkish music and belly-dancing, but superb location and views. Must book.

Hacıbaba (££) Istiklal Caddesi, Beyoğlu (tel: 0212 244 1886). *Lokanta* offering Turkish food with a balcony overlooking the courtyard of a Greek church.

Han (£££) Rumeli Hisarı (tel: 0212 265 2968). Good fish restaurant with a terrace overlooking the Bosphorus.

Hidiv Kasrı (the Khedive's Summer Palace) (££) Çubuklu (tel: 0216 331 2651). Splendid restored palace in art deco style overlooking the Bosphorus from the Asian side. Turkish cuisine with live music.

Huzur (Arabin Yeri) (££) Üsküdar (tel: 0216 333 3157). Long-established unpretentious fish restaurant with amazing sunset views of the Asian side of the Istanbul skyline.

Kadife Chalet (££) Kadife Sokak 29, Bahariye, Kadıköy (tel: 0212 437 8596). Open 10.00am till 10.00pm this pretty restaurant with period decor is set in an Ottoman house and offers Ottoman and international dishes.

Kamil (£) Gümüşsuyu Yolu 9/1, Beykoz (tel: 0212 331 0594). Good small fish restaurant on the Asian side of the Bosphorus, with interesting meze and unusual atmosphere.

Kız Kulesi Deniz Restaurant (££) Salacak Sakil Yolu, Üsküdar (tel: 0212 341 0403). Excellent views towards the old city from Üsküdar across the Bosphorus, with delicious seafood.

Körfez (£££) Kanlıca (tel: 0216 413 4314). Very smart fish restaurant on the Bosphorus, reached by the restaurant's private boat from Rumeli Hisarı.

Liman Lokantası (££) Karaköy (tel: 0212 244 1033). Located above the Turkish Maritime Lines' waiting room, this old classic has good views and excellent food. Lunch only, Monday to Friday.

Rejans (££) Beyoğlu (tel: 0212 244 1610). Opposite San Antonio's church, Istanbul's classic Russian restaurant, now a bit shabby.

Süreyya (£££) Istinye Caddesi, Istinye (tel: 0212 277 5886). One of Istanbul's gastronomic landmarks, serving superb Russian, Turkish and European

cuisine. Must book. Closed Sundays.

Ziya (£££) Ortaköy (tel: 0212 261 6005). Under the Boshporus Bridge, offers Turkish and international cuisine with a fabulous view and tables outdoors in the summer.

Istanbul environs
Bursa

Hünkar Doner Kebab House. (£) The best of the well-located clutch of restaurants looking out over the quiet cobbled square of the Yeşil Cami.

Büyükada

Büyükada (£). A simple café on the summit of the hill by the Monastery of Saint George, offering a lunch of cheese, olives and red wine. A long steep path leads up to it from the middle of town.

Many fish restaurants line the promenade, with simple kebab houses in the little town square.

Edirne

Balta Restaurant (££) (tel: 0284 225 5210). The best restaurant in town, in the Balta Hotel.

THE AEGEAN
Afrodisias

Near the village of Dandalaz, 3km before the site, is a cluster of riverside restaurants offering fresh trout.

Ayvalık

The best restaurants in this region are on Ali Bey island just opposite Ayvalık, notably **Artur Restaurant** (££) (tel: 0266 327 1014) and **Günay Restaurant** (££) (tel: 663 71048). On the road west of Ayvalık, beyond Çanlık, the **Şeytan Sofrası (Devil's Dining Table) Restaurant** (£) has unremarkable food but a

spectacular setting overlooking the Gulf of Edremit. Further afield, near Altınoluk on the north of the Gulf of Edremit, the remarkable **Chalet Chopin** (Değirmen) (££) (tel: 0266 396 1313; fax: 396 1370) offers delicious Turkish food with live music in a beautiful garden.

Behramkale

There are several good fish restaurants on the harbour front.

Bodrum

No one could ever try all the restaurants in Bodrum – they are everywhere and ever-changing. Among those to look out for are the **Han Restaurant** (££) on Kale Caddesi (tel: 0252 316 1615), in a converted 18th-century caravanserai with dancing and live music in the central courtyard, and the **Mausolus Restaurant** (££) in Neyzen Tevfik Caddesi (tel: 316 4176).

Çeşme

Körfez Restaurant (£) Yalı Caddesi (tel: 0232 712 6718). A good simple restaurant in the centre.

Sahil Restaurant (££) Cumhuriyet Meydanı (tel: 0232 712 6646). The best of the town's fish restaurants.

Dalyan

Freshwater fish is the speciality here, and there are many restaurants along the riverbank in town, of which you could try **Beyazgül** (££), **Denizatı** (£) and **Begonvil** (££).

Efes (Ephesus)

Bahçesaray Restaurant (£) is an attractive restaurant at Meryemana Kavsağı (tel: 0232 892 3486).

Efes Restaurant (££) (tel: 0232 892 2291). Very - conveniently located at the ruins, offering a fair range of adequate if unexciting food.

Foça

Well-known for its fish restaurants along the harbour front, of which the **Ali Baba** (££), the **Bedesten** (£) and the **Palmiye** (££) should be tried first.

Izmir

Altınkapı Restoran (££) 1444 Sokak, Alsancak (tel: 0232 422 2648). Good food, popular in 'arty' circles.
1888 Restaurant (£££) Cumhuriyet Bulvarı, Alsancak (tel: 0232 421 6690). Delicious Mediterranean specialities, notably some fine Jewish dishes. Live music at weekends.
Deniz Restoran (££) Atatürk Caddesi, Kordon (tel: 0232 422 0601). One of the best seafront restaurants, with imaginative *meze* and unbeatable squid.
Kemal'in Yeri (££) 1453 Sokak, Alsancak (tel: 0232 422 3190). A wonderful fish restaurant with friendly service.
Liman Restoran (££) Atatürk Caddesi, Kordon (tel: 0232 422 1876). Good seafood restaurant on the waterfront.
Mask (£££) 1453 Sokak, Alsancak (tel: 0232 463 0425). An expensive restaurant with elegant decor, dancing and international cuisine.
Palet Restoran (£££) Atatürk Caddesi, Kordon (tel: 0232 425 0440). Expensive, floating, fish restaurant.
Park Restoran (£££) Kültürpark İçi (tel: 0232 489 3590). Another plush, expensive restaurant, this one, however, is floating. It offers good international cuisine with French leanings.
Vejetaryen Lokantası (£)

1375 Sokak, Alsancak (tel: 0232 421 7558). Pleasant vegetarian restaurant.

Kuşadası

A colossal range and selection of restaurants is available here. Look out in particular for **Ada Restaurant** (££) in a fine setting on Güverçin island, **Ali Baba** (££) in the market, **Golden Bird** (££) by the yacht marina, and **Turban Marina** (££) in the market by the yacht marina.

Marmaris

An enormous selection and price range is available in this popular tourist destination. The best settings are along the promenade, especially at dusk. Among the best are **Bamboo Restaurant** (£) at İçmeler, **Han Restaurant** (£) in front of Pension Dede in Turunç Bay, **Ayyıldız** (££) in the old market area, **Bigma** (££) on the waterfront, **Green House** (££) in the backstreet of Hacı Mustafa Sokak, and **Kervansaray** (££) in Yunus Nadi Caddesi.

Pamukkale

There is not a huge amount to choose between the many restaurants on offer here: location is probably the deciding factor. The **Kervansaray Hotel** (££) offers good food from its rooftop restaurant, and the Gürsöy and Mustafa restaurants are also worth a try.

Pergamum

Asklepieion Restaurant (£) Izmir Caddesi 54 (tel: 0232 633 1050) is the best in the town of Bergama.
Berksoy Restaurant (££) Izmir Yolu (tel: 0232 633 2595). Good food from the restaurant of th hotel of the same name.

THE MEDITERRANEAN
Adana

Ağacpınar Tesisleri (£) Ceyhan-Adana Eski Karayolu 10km. Ağacpınar Koyu (tel: 0322 321 9166). Good restaurant outside town on the Ceyhan road.
Gözde Restaurant (££) Çifte Minare Camii Yanı (tel: 0322 453 5501). Pleasant food by the Çifte Minare mosque.

Alanya

From the huge range and selection all along the main road and the seafront, the **Canus** (£), the **Halimağa Konağı** (££), the **Mola** (£) and the **Yakamoz** (££) are among the best.

Antakya

Didem Turistik Tesisleri (£) Reyhanli Yolu Uzeri (tel: 0326 212 1928). A good range of Turkish dishes is on offer here.
Saray Restaurant (££) Atatürk Bulvarı 57 (tel: 0326 617 1383). The best place in the city centre, with Turkish specialities.

Antalya

The best restaurants with the most enjoyable ambience tend to be found in the old quarter round the renovated marina area. Among the most notable are **A La Turca** (££), **Hisar** (££), **Kral Sofrası** (£), **Orkinos** (£) and **Yat Restaurant** (££). In addition **La Trattoria** (££) at Fevzi Gakmak Caddesi 3/C (tel: 0242 243 3931), run by a Turkish man and his English wife, serves very good European food in a bistro setting.

Burdur

Akçeşme Dinlenme Tesisleri – Salda Gölü (£) (tel: 0248 631 3488). On the Burdur–Denizli road by Lake Salda, 4km from Yeşilova. Good for lunch.

HOTELS AND RESTAURANTS

Eğridir

Eğridir Restaurant (£) Cami Mh. (tel: 0246 311 6333) and **Liman Restaurant** (£) Cumhuriyet Caddesi (tel: 0246 312 3441), both these restaurants offer good lake fish and *meze*.

Fethiye

Among the wide choice of restaurant along the harbour promenade, the best are reckoned to be **Rafet** (tel: 0252 614 1106) and the **Çın Restaurant** in the Likya Hotel (tel: 0252 611 2233).

Finike

Petek Restaurant (£) in the village centre serves surprisingly good traditional Turkish cuisine.

Kale

Güneyhan Restaurant (£) Saint Nicolas Kilisesi Yani (tel: 0242 871 3810). Well placed beside Saint Nicholas' church.

Kalkan

Kalkan is renowned for its excellent cuisine, probably because a number of the hotel and restaurant owners are originally from Istanbul: it is claimed that it is difficult to get a bad meal here. Among the best restaurants are the **Korsan** (££), the **Han** (££), the **Kalkan Han** (££) and the **Lipsos** ££).

Kaş

Mercan Restaurant (££) Çarşı İçi, Liman Başı (tel: 0242 836 1209). Good Turkish food in the town centre.
Merkez Restaurant (££) Cumhuriyet Meydanı 18 (tel: 0242 836 1629). Consistently high-standard Turkish cuisine.

Kemer

Most of the best of the many restaurants here are situated round the yachting marina, notably the **Arsemia** (££), the **Ayısığı Tesisleri** (£), the **Duppont** (££), the **Miço** (£) and the **Yörük Parkı Restaurant** (££).

Kizkalesi

Most of the best restaurants in this and the Silifke area are in Narlıkuyu, the village by the caves known as Cennet Cehennem (Heaven and Hell). Look out in particular for the **Deniz** (£), the **Çınaraltı** (££), and the **Lagos** (£).

Mersin

Ali Baba 1 Restaurant (££) Uluçarşı Otopark Girişi Karşisi (tel: 0324 223 3088). A convenient place to eat after shopping, located by the main car park entrance.
Ali Baba-Kordon Restaurant (££) The best place to eat in Mersin, near the Hilton Hotel.

Ölü Deniz

Beyaz Yunus Restaurant (££) (tel: 0252 616 6036). The best of the restaurants on the lagoon and beach.

Side

Toros Restaurant (££) Liman Caddesi (tel: 0242 753 2005). Good Turkish food in front of the old harbour.

CAPPADOCIA

Avanos

The best of the many restaurants along the riverbank are the **Altınocak** (££), the **Tuvanna** (££), the **Yonca** (£) and the **Motif** (££).

Göreme

The best restaurants to try here are the **Konak Türk Evi** (££), in a splendid converted Ottoman mansion, the **Ali Baba** (££), built in traditional style, and also the **Kösem** (£) opposite the museum in the town centre.

Kaymaklı

Erciyes Restaurant (£) is a new restaurant beside the underground city, offering simple Turkish food.

Kayseri

The town offers a handful of acceptable restaurants: the **Beyaz Saray** (££), the **Ekol Turistik Tesisleri** (£) in Tuna Caddesi and the **Yıldız** (££) in Kumarlı Mevkii are perhaps the best.

Ortahisar

Kaya Restaurant (££) Ulus Meydanı (tel: 0384 343 3100) Traditional Turkish cuisine.

Üçhisar

Bindallı Restaurant (££) (tel: 0382 219 2187). The restaurant is hollowed out of the tufa rock, and the crockery is traditional Cappadocian pottery.

Ürgüp

There are several good restaurants here, all offering traditional Turkish and Cappadocian specialities. Try the **Şömine** (£), a well-established, bustling place with good pot kebabs, the **Han Çırağan** (££) and the **Hanedan** (££).

CENTRAL ANATOLIA
Afyonkarahisar

Ikbal Turistik Tesisleri (£) Akören Köyü, Sincanlı (tel: 0272 213 1399).

Ankara

Chez Le Belge (££) Gölbaşı (tel: 4841478). At Gölbaşı, 20km south of the city, specialising in fresh crayfish.
Iskele (££) Tuna Caddesi, Kızılay (tel: 0312 433 3813). The freshest fish in Ankara.
Kale Restaurant (Boğacızade Konağı) (£££) (tel: 0312 310 2525). This restaurant, in a delightfully converted Ottoman house

near the museum in the old quarter, serves Turkish cuisine to the accompaniment of classical Turkish music and a fabulous view over the city from the terrace.
La Bohème (££) Gaziosmanpaşa (tel: 436 3101). French cuisine, Ankara-style.
Mangal 2 (££) Çankaya (tel: 0312 440 0959). Turkish cuisine in a restored Ankara house.
Merkez Lokantası (££) Çiftlik Caddesi (tel: 0312 213 1750). Specialises in roast lamb, stuffed lamb and lamb kebabs.
Poupée Dönen (£££) Atakule (tel: 0312 440 7412). Fabulous views from the top of Atakule Tower and international cuisine.
Rıhtım (££) Kavaklıdere (tel: 0312 427 2432). Good range of Turkish cuisine. Popular meeting place for the young.
Yunus's (£££) Çankaya (tel: 0312 438 5856). Italian and Turkish cuisine, a special vegetarian menu and live music.

Konya
The best of the not very impressive collection of Konya restaurants are the Damla (£) in Hükümet Alanı, the Metin (£) in Cumhuriyet Alanı and the **Hanedan** (£) in Mevlana Caddesi. The **Mevlana Restaurant** (£) by the Ince Minare Museum is also a reasonable bet.
Sivas
The **Şadırvan Restaurant** (££) in the town centre offers surprisingly classy Turkish cuisine.

EASTERN TURKEY
Diyarbakır
Food in Diyarbakır is good, always fresh, and the local speciality is lamb. The best of the restaurants in town are the **Hacı Baba** (£), the

Sinan (£), the **Beş Kardeş** (£) and the restaurants of the Demir and Büyük hotels.

Dogubeyazit
The restaurant of the Isfehan Hotel (££) offers the best food in town.

Erzurum
The **Güzelyurt** (££) and the **Tufan** (££), both on Cumhuriyet Caddesi in the city centre, offer the highest standard here.

Gaziantep
In this town noted for its good food with strong Arab influence, the best restaurant is the **Kervansaray**, Kervanbey Passage, on Hurriyet Caddesi, with a pleasant outdoor terrace.

Malatya
The **Melita Restaurant** (££) is the best here. Round the corner from the Sinan Hotel, with a regular business clientele, it serves Turkish specialities, beautifully presented, with everything swathed in rose petals.

Mardin
The restaurants here are worth trying for their excellent *meze*, heavily Arab-influenced, with humus and tahine among their specialities. Try **Cumhuriyet Lokantası** (£) and **Kafkaş Lokantası** (£).

Nemrut Dağı
The further up the mountain you go, the worse and more expensive the food gets, so the best bet is the hotel restaurants in Kahta, where the turnover is highest. None is especially recommended

Şanlıurfa
The best food is in the restaurants of the **Harran** and **Turban** hotels.

Van
The restaurants of the **Akdamar** and the **Büyük Urartu** hotels are the safest choice, though it is worth trying the **Kösk Restaurant** (£) near the museum in case they have the local *otlu peynir*, or herb cheese.

THE BLACK SEA
Bolu
Restaurants worth trying here include the **Filiz** (£), the **Idris** (£) and the **Ulusoy** (£).

Fatsa
Dolunay Restaurant (££) is part of the motel of the same name, which stands in an attractive position on its own spit of land. It also has its own private beach.

281

Giresun
The three restaurants to sample here are the **Kale** (£), the **Kerasus** (££) and the **Mehmet Effendi** (££).

Ordu
Try some of the good fish restaurants on the seafront, such as the **Midi** (££), the **Gülistan** (££), and the **Sahil Balık** (££).

Perşembe
The best place to eat here is the **Vona Restaurant**, part of the Vona Hotel.

Samsun
Nothing very exciting here, but you can try the **Çanlı Balık** (Kücük Ev) (££) and the **Altınbalık** (£) for fish.

Trabzon
The best restaurant on the coast is the **Kösk Restaurant** (££) in Akçaabat (tel: 0462 228 3223); the best in town is the **Trabzon** (£) on the main square opposite the Özgür hotel, with a very pleasant ambience and fresh fish specialities; it serves alcohol.

Chronology

7500BC First Stone Age settlements in existence at Çatalhüyük – the earliest known urban society, with religious shrines and frescoes.
1900–1300BC The Hittite Empire, with Hattuşaş (Boğazkale) as its capital, and roughly contemporary with ancient Egypt and Babylon, thrives as a mountain culture with storm and weather gods.
1259BC The Treaty of Kadesh between the Hittites and the Egyptians – the earliest recorded peace treaty.
1250BC The Trojan War between the Greeks and the Trojans, culminating after ten years' fighting in the famous ploy of the Trojan horse and the subsequent Fall of Troy (Truva), at the time the foremost trading city of the northwest Aegean.
1200–700BC The migration of Greeks to Aegean coastal regions. The kingdoms of Phrygia, Ionia, Lycia, Lydia, Caria and Pamphylia grow up in the western Aegean and Mediterranean regions. The Urartian civilisation flourishes in eastern Anatolia.
700BC The birth of Homer in Smyrna (Izmir) coincides with the beginnings of Hellenistic culture in Aegean Turkey.
546BC Cyrus the Great of Persia invades. Anatolia is under Persian rule, with local Persian governors (known as *satraps*) ruling areas.
334BC Alexander the Great conquers Anatolia, freeing it from the Persians. Hellenistic culture takes hold.
130BC Anatolia becomes the Roman province of Asia with its capital at Ephesus (Efes); a long period of peace and prosperity.
40BC Antony and Cleopatra marry at Antioch (Antakya).
AD47–57 St Paul's missionary journeys; the first Christian community at Antioch.
AD313 Christianity is accepted as the official religion by the Roman Emperor, Constantine the Great.
330 Byzantium is renamed Constantinople by Emperor Constantine and becomes the new capital of Byzantine Empire, the eastern half of the Roman Empire; Rome remains the capital of the western part.
527–65 The reign of Justinian and the height of Byzantine power; an enormous building programme goes on throughout the Byzantine empire.
636–718 Muslim Arabs (in the Holy War of their young faith, Islam) defeat Byzantines and besiege Constantinople.
1054 The schism between the Greek and the Roman churches.
1071–1243 Seljuk Turks from Central Asia conquer Anatolia; Konya becomes their capital. They establish the Sultantate of Rum, convert the population to Islam and establish Turkish as the dominant language of Anatolia.
1096–1204 The Crusades; Latin armies enter Anatolia for the first time. Constantinople is sacked in the Fourth Crusade of 1204. The Byzantine Empire is effectively dismembered.
1288 The birth of the Ottoman Empire, founded by the Muslim Osmanli (Ottoman) tribe from eastern Anatolia; its capital is Bursa.
1453 Sultan Mehmet II conquers Constantinople and renames it Istanbul as the new capital of the Ottoman Empire. Ayasofya in Istanbul, like many other churches throughout Turkey, is converted to a mosque.
1520–66 The reign of Süleyman the Magnificent and the Golden Age of the Ottoman Empire, which extended from the Danube to Aden and Eritrea, and from the Euphrates and the Crimea to Algiers. The Ottomans are the leading world power.
1682–1725 The reign of Peter the Great in Russia begins a new phase of Russo-Turkish rivalry.
1717–30 The 'Tulip Period', so-called because of Sultan Ahmet III's obsession with tulips, a century after Germany, France and Holland had been seized by a passion for these Turkish bulbs.
1839–76 The 'Tanzimat Period',

a programme of reforms in the Ottoman Empire.

1854   The Crimean War; Ottomans are supported by the British and French against the common enemy, Russia.

1895–6   The Armenian massacres, in which some 150,000 Armenians die.

1909   Abdul Hamid, the last Ottoman sultan, is deposed by the revolutionary group known as the Young Turks.

1914   Turkey enters World War I as an ally of Germany.

1915   The Gallipoli Campaign. Allied landings on Turkish soil are repulsed.

1918   The end of World War I; the Allies propose the division of the Ottoman Empire.

1919   Atatürk leads Turkish resistance in the fight for national sovereignty. The War of Independence, against both the Greeks and the British, begins.

1923   The Turkish state is proclaimed, with Atatürk as president. Minority populations are exchanged between Greece and Turkey in order to prevent future outbreaks of inter-communal conflict Half a million Greek-speaking Muslims are sent from Greece to Turkey, and 1.3 million Turkish-speaking Christians from Turkey to Greece. Reforms to modernise and secularise the state are set in motion: the Islamic faith is disestablished; the Arabic script is replaced by the Latin alphabet; the Turkish language is revived; women's veils and the fez are banned.

1938   Atatürk dies unexpectedly at the age of 57.

1939–45   Turkey decides to remain neutral throughout World War II.

1946   Turkey becomes a charter member of the United Nations.

1950   The first free nationwide elections, in which Adnan Menderes is elected prime minister, are held. A massive national debt builds up following many highly ambitious building programmes.

1952   Turkey joins NATO in a new, pro-Western stance.

1960   An almost bloodless military coup is then followed by successive inefficient governments.

1964   Though geographically 97 per cent in Asia, Turkey becomes an associate member of the EEC (European Economic Community). The emigration of 'guest-workers' to Germany begins.

1974   Turkey intervenes in (or invades, depending upon your point of view) Cyprus to protect the Turkish Cypriot community, seizing the northern third of the island. It is condemned by the international community, notably the EEC, but the island still remains divided, the border patrolled by soldiers from the United Nations.

1980   Another bloodless military coup under General Kenan Evren is followed by three years of military rule.

1983   Turkey again returns to civilian rule with Türgüt Özal elected prime minister, moving to the presidency in 1984, the first civilian president of Turkey for 30 years.

1985–90   Disputes with Greece over Cyprus and over Aegean territorial waters damage Turkey's continuing attempts to join the EEC, as does its human rights record in handling the Kurdish insurrection in the southeast.

1991–3   Süleyman Demirel is elected prime minister, forming a coalition government. He forms the post of Minister for Human Rights and promises a thorough review of policy towards the Kurdish uprising. Stringent economic reforms are introduced to combat levels of inflation of between 70 and 125 per cent.

1993–4   President Türgüt Özal dies. Veteran politician Süleyman Demirel becomes his successor and Tansu Çiller becomes, in turn, Turkey's first woman prime minister. Turkey accepts IMF (International Monetary Fund) economic reforms. Kurdish rebels carry out attacks on a few tourist sites in an attempt to discourage tourists. During the campaign of violence a British tourist dies after a bomb explodes on the beach at Fethiye.

Index

INDEX

INDEX

INDEX

INDEX

Picture credits

The Automobile Association would like to thank the following photographers, libraries and associations for their assistance in the preparation of this book.

M. ALEXANDER 229a Kaçkar Mountains, 246 Trabzon market
J. ALLAN CASH PHOTOLIBRARY 45 Galata bridge, 219 Haho church, 220 Diyarbakır, 221 Kasim Padishah mosque, 229b women and Mount Ararat
D. DARKE 128 Gerga, 160 inland Lycia, 161 Lycian walk, 235b Jonah and the whale, Akdamar
MARY EVANS PICTURE LIBRARY 34b capture of Constantinople, 35b siege of Istanbul, 40a revolution, Istanbul, 40b Yildiz-Kiosk 1909, 41a Greco–Turkish war, 43a Greek retreat, 74a Turkish bath, 75 Turkish bath, 144c Alexander the Great
THE RONALD GRANT ARCHIVE 121a The Herd, 121b Hope
ROBERT HARDING PICTURE LIBRARY 24a Whirling Dervishes, 60c flute player, 252 dancers
THE MANSELL COLLECTION 35a capture of Constantinople, 38b Suleyman II, 41b Abdul Hamid II
S. MORRIS 147a amphitheatre at Aspendos, 147b ruined city of Perge
NATURE PHOTOGRAPHERS LTD 154a large whip snake(P R Sterry), 154b Cistus albidus (B Burbidge), 155a loggerhead turtle (J Sutherland), 155b short-toed eagle(K Carlson), 261 scorpion (B Burbidge)
PICTURES COLOUR LIBRARY 51a Istanbul, 54b prayer chain, 78b Dolmabahçe Palace
REX FEATURES LTD 44b Türgüt Özal
SPECTRUM COLOUR LIBRARY 23a girls in traditional costume, 25a festival, Ephesus, 25b traditional costume, 29b Buyuk Mabet of Hittite Capital, 38a, 39a, 39b Ottoman costumes, 82 Bursa, 140b nomads, 149a Lake Egridir, 176b statue, 'old man in shoe', 177 Tokalı Kilise, Goreme, 243 narthex, Trabzon, 245 Sumela monastery
ZEFA PICTURE LIBRARY (UK) LTD Cover Nemrut Daği, 11 Antalya, 24b Antalya dancers, 228b Mount Ararat

The remaining photographs are held in the Automobile Association's own photo library (AA PHOTO LIBRARY) and were taken by Paul Kenward with the exception of pages 5b, 6a, 13a, 28b, 29a, 31a, 32a, 33, 50, 61a, 72, 73a, 74b, 79, 87, 88, 89b, 95, 96b, 97b, 98a, 104a, 104b, 113b, 115a, 116, 117, 118, 132, 133b, 136, 137a, 143a, 143c, 145, 152, 156b, 170/1, 176a, 179, 183a, 183b, 189, 191a, 193b, 196a, 249, 255a which were taken by Dario Mitideri, and the black flap and pages 2, 6b, 9b, 13b, 14a, 14b, 16b, 32b, 42a, 44a, 48a, 48b, 49, 51b, 52, 53, 54a, 54c, 56, 57a, 57b, 58a, 58b, 59, 60a, 60b, 61b, 61c, 62a, 62b, 64a, 64b, 65a, 65b, 66, 67, 69, 70, 71a, 71b, 73b, 76, 77a, 78a, 81a, 81b, 83b, 85a, 89a, 90a, 90b, 91a, 91b, 92a, 93a, 94b, 94c, 96a, 99a, 99b, 185a, 185b, 185c, 200a, 200b, 201a, 251, 260, 263 which were taken by Antony Souter.

Acknowledgements

The Automobile Association would also like to thank Zeynep Strömfelt and the Anglo–Turkish Society for their help in the production of this guide.

Contributors

Series advisor: Christopher Catling   **Designer**: Tony Truscott
Joint series editor: Susi Bailey   **Indexer**: Marie Lorimer
Copy editor: Barbara Mellor   **Verifier**: Mary Berkmen